Tools For Citizenship & Life:

Using the ITI Lifelong Guidelines & LIFESKILLS in Your Classroom
Second Edition

by Sue Pearson

Illustrated by Gwendolyn Pribble • Contributing Editor, Karen D. Olsen

Tools for Citizenship and Life:
Using the ITI Lifelong Guidelines and LIFESKILLS in Your Classroom
Second Edition

by Sue Pearson and
Karen D. Olsen, Contributing Editor

© 2000 Susan J. Kovalik
Printed in the United States of America
ISBN 1-878631-60-8

Graphics: Gwendolyn Pribble
Cover Design: Marni Erwin
Layout Design: Kristina Roe
Copy Editor: Kathleen Wolgemuth

Published by: Susan Kovalik & Associates, Inc.
Distributed by: Books For Educators, Inc.
17051 SE 272nd Street, Suite 18
Kent, Washington 98042
Phone: 888/777-9827
Fax: 253/630-7215
www.books4educ.com

Dedication

This book is dedicated to Nicky,

my canine companion,

who drags me away from the computer to play ball

and to Ms. Kitty,

my feline friend,

who is always watching my mouse.

Table of Contents

Acknowledgements

Ever since I chose education as a profession, teaching has been my vocation, my avocation, and my vacation! Along the way, many people have made a difference in my life. To each of them, I write the words to an old Shirley Temple song.

> How do I thank you?
> Where do I start?
> The words are somewhere
> Within my heart.

First, to Susan Kovalik for planting the seeds of ITI within me, nurturing the sprout that peeked through, supporting the roots that dug in, and harvesting the crop when it was ready.

Second, to my husband, Roy, and our children, Jenny and Mike, for all of their support and encouragement. I also appreciate their use of the LIFESKILLS with me—especially Patience, Caring, and Flexibility.

Third, to my friends, Cheryl Canfield, Helen Chajka, and Lesley Hughes, who accompanied me on the ITI journey and made me realize that being part of a "great group" does happen.

Fourth, to Karen Olsen, I extend great appreciation for her unlimited time as she taught me how to write something other than poetry and, in the process, became a good friend and contributing editor.

And finally, to my last class, my "combo kids," an exceptional community of fourth and fifth grade students, who became my teachers and welcomed me, a learner, into their hearts. As these children mastered the Lifelong Guidelines and LIFESKILLS, they taught me how truly powerful these tools for life can be.

Foreword

The Lifelong Guidelines and LIFESKILLS evolved over many years with input from a variety of people. Jeanne Gibbs, author of *TRIBES: A New Way of Learning and Being Together*, first introduced me to "Active Listening" and "No Put-Downs" in 1978 when I was working with gifted students. These two guidelines served as the basis of interaction in our ITI classrooms until 1985 when Robert Ellingsen, an associate, suggested adding three more: Truth, Trust, and Personal Best. We soon discovered that Personal Best needed defining, thus were born the LIFESKILLS.

At the time we were developing the LIFESKILLS, Dorothy Rich had just published her book for parents, *MegaSkills: How Families Can Help Children to Succeed in School and Beyond.* As we worked with these ten "MegaSkills," we recognized the power of identifying specific behaviors for each skill and we began to draft our own list. It took more than a year for the associates and me to agree on what defines Personal Best, what we called attributes of people you respect and admire. The definition continues to grow. We used the term LIFESKILLS to reflect their power in everyday life. We decided to call our foundational behaviors—Trustworthiness, Truthfulness, Active Listening, No Put-Downs, and Personal Best—the Lifelong Guidelines.

The everyday application of the Lifelong Guidelines and LIFESKILLS schoolwide creates a powerful bodybrain-compatible learning environment. In addition to building a sense of community that both students and teachers look forward to each day, achievement scores surge upward.

When an entire school operates from a common basis of personal interaction, and all adults are consistent with it, students can direct all of their energy and attention to learning. Thus, for full effectiveness, the Lifelong Guidelines and LIFESKILLS must start in the faculty room. For example, what does Trustworthiness look like, sound like, and feel like and what behaviors would you no longer see, hear, or feel if everyone interacted with each other within these parameters?

Of all the components of the ITI model, the Lifelong Guidelines and LIFESKILLS cause the earliest and most obvious changes in student and adult behavior. In many ways, these changes energize the rest of ITI implementation.

To the coaches for the MCSIP Program (Mid-California Science Improvement Program which used the ITI model), to Judy Eacker, Russ Eacker, Robert Ellingsen, Jo Gusman, Patty Harrington, Sally Johnson, Martha Kaufeldt, Kari Kling, Ventura Lopez, Jane McGeehan, Jacque Melin, Pattie Mills, Karen Olsen, Sue Pearson, Barbara Pedersen, Gwen Pribble, Joy Raboli, Ann Ross, Jean Spanko, Dean Tannewitz, Sr. Patt Walsh, and to all the ITI teachers throughout the world who are using the Lifelong Guidelines and LIFESKILLS daily to improve the way we interact with each other and students, thank you one and all.

Susan Kovalik
Creator of the ITI model

Introduction

WHO SHOULD READ THIS BOOK?

Who should read this book? Anyone who is working with children. Teachers, parents, counselors, social workers, administrators. Anyone who has children in their lives and wishes that they could help them grow in character and personal values; anyone who wants to help ensure that they become successful human beings personally, socially, economically; anyone who believes that preparing children to become citizens who contribute to society is an important goal.

This book offers a ready-to-use program for character development and classroom management. It describes guidelines for both adults and students to live by, now and in the future; it also describes how to teach, reinforce, and practice these guidelines. The ideas are easy to implement and they're powerful tools for building a community in which academic learning flourishes and discipline problems fade away.

INSTRUCTION MANUAL

Are you one of those learners who, when trying to put something together, always reads the directions first, even before you take anything out of the box? Or are you like my family, first dumping the contents of the box on the ground, then looking for logical connections and only reading the directions when all else fails? Whatever your approach, compare this book to a carpenter's toolbox filled with a variety of tools. Use whichever ones will support your job of constructing knowledge and building character.

How to Use This Book

Read Chapters 1-3 first, then continue in any order you choose. If you want to look ahead to the LIFESKILL "Sense of Humor" before reading about "Caring," jump to that part. Let the needs of your students and school community determine where you start and where you go. Whatever your course, you'll find many practical ideas used by ITI teachers throughout the country. Keep track of which inquiries develop the mental programs your students need. Keep a record of any changes you make for your class and add projects that you and your students create learning to incorporate these tools into everyday living.

Browse First

By glancing through each section, you'll notice the same pattern of presentation for every Lifelong Guideline and LIFESKILL topic. This is, by design, intended to make the book "user-friendly." These headings include:

- The name of the Lifelong Guideline or LIFESKILL

- An appropriate quotation

- A definition from *Webster's Ninth New Collegiate Dictionary*

- The ITI, "kid friendly" definition

- What is _____? (a discussion of what that Lifelong Guideline or LIFESKILL is)

- Why practice _____? (a discussion of why that Lifelong Guideline or LIFESKILL is important in life)

- How do you practice _____?

- What does _____ look like in real life?

- How does _____ look in school? (for staff and students)

- Inquiries to develop _____ (opportunities to practice the Lifelong Guideline or LIFESKILL)

- Signs of success (for staff and students)

- Literature links to _____ (student and teacher resources)

- Sample letter to family (support for parents, guardians, family members)

While most of these are self-explanatory, some short descriptions might enhance and expand your vision of the best way to use this book.

INQUIRIES (OPPORTUNITIES TO PRACTICE)

In the ITI model, inquiries provide opportunities to practice a skill or concept in real-world situations until it is captured in long-term memory. They are the link between what students are to learn from the curriculum and how they will apply the information and skills. Inquiries empower students to develop mental programs for applying, in real-world situations, the concepts, skills, and significant information they're learning. Inquiries give power to any curriculum because they ensure adequate time to develop the mental programs needed for long-term retention and for transferring what is being learned to new situations in the real world. Since each of the Lifelong Guidelines is a "big idea," children need time, individually and in groups, to explore understanding of each concept.

You will notice that there are no grade levels listed for any of the inquiries. You know your students better than I do. As you read each inquiry, ask yourself, "How could I adapt this for my students in our setting? What small changes will make it more age-appropriate for my group?" Or, "This is somewhat like something I once did. By making some adjustments, I can link it to a LIFESKILL."

I hope that these inquiries will be models when you write inquiries of your own that extend your students' learning. After using some of these suggested activities, try adapting others. Determine if the inquiries or activities will be done by the entire class, the learning club (small group), partners, or an individual then write them up accordingly. The following "ABC" format from the ITI model will help you to adapt and write inquiries:

- **A**lways begin with a verb that will suggest to the children what action they should take to complete the inquiry.

- **B**e specific about the task the children are to complete. Is this an individual, partner, or group inquiry? Are there specific directions about the site to be visited or materials to be used? How will the information be shared? How can I use this to assess a child's (children's) knowledge and skill?

- **C**onnect to the key point (the statement of what students are to learn). Remember, inquiries are not just fun, isolated activities; they are the practice necessary to "hard-wire" a particular concept or skill into long-term memory.

For more information about how to write inquiries, see the ITI book appropriate for your grade level. For elementary grades, *ITI: The Model* or *Kid's Eye View of Science;* for middle school, *The Way We Were . . . The Way We CAN Be: A Vision for the Middle School Through Integrated Thematic Instruction;* for high school, *Synergy: Transformation of America's High Schools Through Using Integrated Thematic Instruction.*

PROCEDURES

Procedures help you plan ahead for social interactions. Think of answers to the following questions. Will students do the work individually, in small groups, or as a whole class? What time frame will work best? Where can they work around the room? Procedures, an important classroom leadership strategy in the ITI model, describe in advance the personal and social behaviors necessary to make a routine activity successful. Examples include entering and leaving the room, what students should do when they've finished an assignment, and going to and coming from assemblies.

By writing procedures for such common activities on chart paper and/or in the group information binder, the students can refer to them whenever necessary. Procedures help prevent confusion and misbehavior, eliminate the need for stating expectations over and over, and save you time by avoiding the need to answer the same questions again and again. Guest teachers (an ITI term for substitute teachers) find procedures helpful too.

Assessment

What kinds of assessment do you plan to use? The ITI model applies the 3C's of assessment to inquiries:

- **Is it complete?** Was the assignment completed as stated in the inquiry? Is it ready to be handed in? Does it meet the specifications described in the inquiry? Does it reflect real-world standards for work performed in the workplace while remaining age-appropriate? Does it reflect pride in workmanship and personal best?

- **Is it correct?** Is the information correct? Have students used a variety of resources, including current sources?

- **Is it comprehensive?** Has the student addressed the topic as thoroughly as possible yet still remaining age-appropriate? Are all sides of an issue covered? Do resources back up the information or is the work based only on personal opinion? Does the student demonstrate an understanding of the content, e.g., can he/she explain it to another?

How will you celebrate your accomplishments within the class? With another class? With the entire school? In the community?

Signs of Success

While this section includes my own descriptors of success, you and your students should brainstorm and list your own age-appropriate descriptors. One of the most effective ways is for the class to determine what each of the Lifelong Guidelines and LIFESKILLS looks like, sounds like, and feels like and to describe non-examples—what it does *not* look like, sound like, and feel like. The contrasts help define what's desirable; the more positive behaviors he/she identifies, the more patterns he/she will have as models for behavior in various situations and settings. The descriptors then become "real," personal, and appropriate for you and your family.

Literature Link (Student and Teacher Resources)

Literature is a wonderful way to introduce and reinforce the Lifelong Guidelines and LIFESKILLS to students. First, the characters in literature provide a third-person focus; no one student's habits or characteristics are being singled out or attacked as needing improvement or adjustment. Second, many teachers read to their students daily; if you select the book with the Lifelong Guidelines and LIFESKILLS in mind, you do not have to carve out any time from an already overstuffed day. Just look at old favorites with new eyes or choose a book from our lists. Lifelong Guidelines and LIFESKILLS can be easily woven into an already existing experience. Third, children love to hear and tell stories and to share interpretations and ideas. What better venue to present positive qualities than through the attributes exhibited by fictional characters and real people?

The book lists in each section are divided into four categories: primary grades, intermediate grades, middleschool/high school, and teacher resources. Most of these are broad enough to be used with other age levels, especially if you have a favorite book from another section or if the content connects to students' studies. Whatever titles you choose, always pre-read each book for any objectionable content or words before reading aloud to the group. Also, if each child is to have his/her own copy, verify that they are all the same edition as the one you previewed.

I hope by now that your brain is in "fast forward" thinking of ways to use the literature link with your students.

FAMILY LETTER (SUPPORT FOR THE HOME CONNECTION)

The connection between home and school is vital since family and teachers share the same goal, to educate the child by preparing him or her for real life. Therefore, it is important to teach families about the Lifelong Guidelines and LIFESKILLS and to include them in the development, implementation, and maintenance stages. While sending a family letter is optional, I've included a sample letter for each guideline and LIFESKILL for your use. Or, you may adapt it or have your students write their own letters that explain each Lifelong Guideline or LIFESKILL as you introduce them.

Chapter 1

Behavior and Social Guidelines for School Communities

Today, more than ever, schools are trying a variety of "discipline" strategies to improve the behavior and social interactions of their students. Some methods, such as assertive discipline, zero-tolerance punishment systems, or rewards for certain behaviors or grades, seem to work for a short while but then the old behaviors return, often with a vengeance. In hindsight, perhaps these methods focus too much on control for the moment rather than on providing tools for living life. It may also be that our country has become "acultural," lacking a set of guidelines for behavior, and so locked into materialistic values that children are either receiving the wrong messages about values, character, and attitudes or, worse, no messages at all.

The purpose of this book is to provide a set of guidelines central to the core of a democratic society and central to creating a learning environment that enhances students' capacity to learn. These guidelines are the Lifelong Guidelines and LIFESKILLS.

ORIGINS

The Lifelong Guidelines and LIFESKILLS are part of Susan Kovalik's ITI model (Integrated Thematic Instruction), a highly effective curriculum development and instructional strategies approach that is rooted in current brain research about how the human brain learns. This "brain biology" guides the teacher's decision making when selecting the most effective teaching strategies and curricular approaches for students. (For information about the ITI model, contact Susan Kovalik & Associates*; to order the ITI book for your grade level, contact Books for Educators.**)

Applying Brain Biology

Current brain research is clear: emotions play a critical role in learning—and nonlearning. According to Dr. Robert Sylwester of the University of Oregon, "...Emotion drives attention and attention drives learning and memory."*** Therefore, teacher-student and student-student interactions must be structured with tremendous care—especially when dealing with behavior issues and their underlying character traits, values, and attitudes.

---

*   Susan Kovalik & Associates, Inc. can be reached at www.kovalik.com or 253/631-4400.
**   Books for Educators, Inc. can be reached at 888/777-9827 or www.books4educ.com
*** See *A Celebration of Neurons* by Dr. Robert Sylwester, ASCD Publications, Alexandria, VA, p. 86.

The quality and nature of the relationships between the teacher and his/her students and among students are vital factors for structuring success or failure in the classroom. The behavior guidelines of the ITI learning environment, Lifelong Guidelines and LIFESKILLS, are consistent with brain research and are based upon a common sense respect for self and others.

The Lifelong Guidelines and LIFESKILLS are literally the social outcomes we set for our students and for our fellow educators. They provide common boundaries and expectations for one's behavior and performance. When consistently followed, these principles ensure that each student's attitude and emotional state are ready for optimum learning.

Not only are these guidelines important in the educational world but they are also critical to leading a productive and successful life in the world beyond school with family, friends, neighbors, employers, and co-workers. These are basic codes for living in a trusting environment, one in which each person has the opportunity to develop and to flourish as an individual and as a contributing member of the larger community.

The Nine Bodybrain-Compatible Elements

The Kovalik ITI model uses nine elements to translate brain research into classroom and school life. When used together, these elements provide a bodybrain-compatible learning environment that helps students build an inner sense of discipline and control in the classroom and for the rest of their lives. Such inner discipline and control is fundamental for three reasons:

- From the teacher's point of view, it is the starting point and a necessary step to success in using the ITI model to significantly improve student learning

- For students, it creates an environment in which academic learning can and does flourish

- For all of us, it gives rise to an environment that creates productive, participating future citizens. It models a sense of community that welcomes one and all, where diversity is respected, and where the common good is each person's goal

Step One

The first element that translates brain biology into action is Absence of Threat/Nurturing Reflective Thinking. This element builds the foundation for all else that occurs. As described in *ITI Classroom Stages of Implementation** this first step uses the Lifelong Guidelines and LIFESKILLS to build a community of learners. The Lifelong Guidelines and LIFESKILLS are a set of standards for behavior by students, staff, and parents. They set the expectations and tone for all interactions that occur every school day—adult-adult, student-adult, and student-student. The Lifelong Guidelines and LIFESKILLS provide a common code of decency, propriety, and etiquette for all.

---

* See *ITI Classroom Stages of Implementation* by Karen D. Olsen and Susan Kovalik. This document describes curriculum, instruction, expectations, and indicators for five stages of implementing in the classroom. For a schoolwide perspective, see *ITI Schoolwide Stage of Implementation* also by Olsen and Kovalik.

THE FIVE LIFELONG GUIDELINES

The principles for living are:

LIFELONG GUIDELINES

TRUSTWORTHINESS: To act in a manner that makes one worthy of trust and confidence

TRUTHFULNESS: To act with personal responsibility and mental accountability

ACTIVE LISTENING: To listen attentively and with intention to understand

NO PUT-DOWNS: To never use words, actions, and/or body language that degrade, humiliate, or dishonor others

PERSONAL BEST: To do one's best given the circumstances and available resources

Just imagine what a better place the world would be if every person would practice and live by these Lifelong Guidelines! It would be so easy if we could be like Jack in the Beanstalk and give each child five magic pills every morning—one for each Lifelong Guideline—and then watch the character traits grow. However, there is no magic ingredient here—just consistency and perseverance.

THE LIFESKILLS

The LIFESKILLS, listed on the next page define the Lifelong Guideline of Personal Best. They do not stand alone. According to Susan Kovalik, the purpose of the LIFESKILLS is to "guide students, individually and in groups, to an understanding of the personal and social behaviors that will enable them to do their personal best and thus enhance the likelihood that they will succeed in attaining their goals."

DO THEY LOOK FAMILIAR?

As you read through the Lifelong Guidelines and LIFESKILLS, you may think, "These are the things my mom and dad were always reminding me of when I was growing up," or "I'm doing some of this in my classroom already. The students definitely need to learn these skills for success in life. I just never realized how important it is to focus on them daily and in-depth."

The Lifelong Guidelines and LIFESKILLS are also the answer to the question, "Who are the heroes in your life and what are the qualities about them that you admire?" Today, more than ever, students need heroes that demonstrate the qualities necessary for living a full and successful life, personally and as a contributing citizen.

LIFESKILLS

CARING: To feel and show concern for others

COMMON SENSE: To use good judgment

COOPERATION: To work together toward a common goal or purpose

COURAGE: To act according to one's beliefs despite fear of adverse consequences

CURIOSITY: A desire to investigate and seek understanding of one's world

EFFORT: To do your best

FLEXIBILITY: To be willing to alter plans when necessary

FRIENDSHIP: To make and keep a friend through mutual trust and caring

INITIATIVE: To do something, of one's own free will, because it needs to be done

INTEGRITY: To act according to a sense of what's right and wrong

ORGANIZATION: To plan, arrange, and implement in an orderly way; to keep things orderly and ready to use

PATIENCE: To wait calmly for someone or something

PERSEVERANCE: To keep at it

PRIDE: Satisfaction from doing one's personal best

PROBLEM SOLVING: To create solutions to difficult situations and everyday problems

RESOURCEFULNESS: To respond to challenges and opportunities in innovative and creative ways

RESPONSIBILITY: To respond when appropriate; to be accountable for one's actions

SENSE OF HUMOR: To laugh and be playful without harming others

Getting Started

Chapter 2

Lifelong Guidelines

TRUSTWORTHINESS

TRUTHFULNESS

ACTIVE LISTENING

NO PUT-DOWNS

PERSONAL BEST

There are innumerable ways to begin using the Lifelong Guidelines and LIFESKILLS. Advice from those who have gone before you: Plan thoroughly before you begin, set and keep to an organized schedule when you do begin, and be willing to suspend any sense of disbelief in the power that the Lifelong Guidelines and LIFESKILLS can have in your life and in that of your students. Your most rewarding and satisfying years of teaching are just around the corner!

Consider the following planning steps:

- Take time to reflect; do a self-evaluation

- Determine if you will be implementing the Lifelong Guidelines and LIFESKILLS as part of a team at your school or solo in your own classroom

- Start with the Lifelong Guidelines; begin the first day of school

- Create a schedule for the first four to five weeks; know what you want to do each day

- Use real-world happenings to capture the "teachable moment"

TAKE TIME TO REFLECT

Before you begin, take time to assess your own personal understanding of the Lifelong Guidelines and LIFESKILLS. Which ones are strengths for you? Are some "just okay?" Are some not as strong as they need to be? Remember, these behavior guidelines are something you must live and model, not just "teach" about.

The Importance of Self-Evaluation

Evaluate yourself in relation to each of the Lifelong Guidelines and the LIFESKILLS. Where do your strengths lie? Which skills need work? If you're like the author of this book, some of the Lifelong Guidelines and LIFESKILLS made me squirm. Organization? I had to jump up from the computer and start organizing and cleaning my house. You can't just talk about the Lifelong Guidelines and LIFESKILLS, you have to do them! (See the discussion about modeling in Chapter 3.)

Bring It Home

The classroom is your living room and students need to feel welcome. As you reflect on your own use of the Lifelong Guidelines and LIFESKILLS as a teacher, it often helps to picture how you would want your own children, nieces and nephews, or grandchildren treated; then, commit yourself to treating other people's children that same way. The quality and nature of the connections between the teacher and his/her students, and among students, are the basis for all else in the classroom, especially academic learning. You need to model the behaviors you would show to honored guests visiting your home and business—behaviors that exemplify truthfulness, trustworthiness, active listening, no put-downs, and personal best.

TEAM MEMBER OR SOLO IMPLEMENTOR?

Before you begin planning, determine whether you'll be implementing the Lifelong Guidelines and LIFESKILLS as a team member or as the only teacher on campus.

ITI schools that use the Lifelong Guidelines and LIFESKILLS begin implementing them in a variety of ways. Some just dive right in! The staff agrees that these behaviors will help expedite the learning process by providing absence of threat for the students and nurturing reflective thinking. The school wants such social and behavioral guidelines, they want them now, and they also want them schoolwide.

Other sites reach schoolwide consensus more slowly, first initiating schoolwide discussions and then providing ITI training (e.g., the Lifelong Guidelines and LIFESKILLS Power Pack) and opportunities for the staff to practice and learn strategies.

In other schools, teams of teachers begin using Lifelong Guidelines and LIFESKILLS in their classrooms, using the resources of the team for support and maintaining an ongoing dialogue with other colleagues about the progress of their students.

Clearly implementation moves more quickly and with less effort if others at your school have adopted the Lifelong Guidelines and LIFESKILLS as their model for interacting with students. But never overlook the power of one—a single teacher leading the way.

Whatever your situation, you can start now. Start in your own classroom and let the Lifelong Guidelines and LIFESKILLS grow from there. They have a way of taking on a life of their own as students, parents, and other staff embrace their use.

Starting with a Splash: Whole School Implementation

The most effective approach for implementation is schoolwide—commitment by all, including custodial workers, food services staff, and bus drivers, to implement the Lifelong Guidelines and LIFESKILLS with consistency. This sets clear expectations and consistent boundaries for how all are to perform and what behaviors all are to expect from others. When an entire school chooses to use Lifelong Guidelines and LIFESKILLS, the results are astounding! When everyone applies them everywhere and consistently, the message is clear: This is what is expected here, this is "the way we do things here." "The way you join this club/our learning community is to abide by these agreements." You're creating the culture and climate for learning.

Imagine how affirming it is for a visitor to enter an ITI school and see the Lifelong Guidelines posted throughout the building, especially in common areas, such as the cafeteria, gym, auditorium, hallways, buses, playground, music room, computer lab, and, yes, the teachers' lounge.

The Advantages of Implementing Schoolwide. There are many advantages from implementing the Lifelong Guidelines and LIFESKILLS on a schoolwide basis. First, there is a common focus or belief system that has been chosen as the necessary building block for developing school community. Second, continuity is apparent from class to class; everyone is hearing, understanding, and using the same terms and practicing the same actions. Third, change comes more rapidly because the Lifelong Guidelines and LIFESKILLS are in use consistently and throughout the day. Last, the "spill-over" factor is high: The students will take the desired behaviors into other areas of their lives outside school, for example at home and in group situations such as neighborhood play, sports, scouts, and so forth. With everyone involved at the same time, there is an opportunity to build common understandings and buy-in very quickly.

Team Implementation

Implementation by a small group (grade level or team) is somewhat harder because there may not be universal support or even an understanding of the importance of using the Lifelong Guidelines and LIFESKILLS as community-building strategies by those outside the team. In addition, lack of consistency—between the classroom and other locations within the school—makes the process slower. Mixed messages always interfere with the learning process, especially for students having behavior problems.

Implementing as a team or solo, rather than schoolwide, requires more time and support for students and makes adult interactions (team members with other staff) more frustrating.

Solo Implementation

If you are doing this alone, you will have to work hard to create an alternative culture on campus, one which your students will see as viable and valuable.

The process of implementation at the classroom level is, however, the same whether implementing solo, as a team, or schoolwide. In general: Start the first day of school, work intensively during the first four to five weeks, and reinforce daily thereafter.

Before school starts, identify specific, age-appropriate ways to present the Lifelong Guidelines for your students. Right now you may be thinking, "How do I get started?" "How can I grab the students' attention?"

START WITH THE LIFELONG GUIDELINES THE FIRST DAY OF SCHOOL

What usually works best is to introduce all five Lifelong Guidelines at once as a collection of behaviors to enhance learning and being together for everyone. Then, go back and teach each Lifelong Guideline in-depth using the instructional strategies described in Chapters 3 and 4 and, of course, keeping C.U.E.* (creative, useful, and catching their emotions) in mind.

However, before the first day of school, make sure you have created an environment that supports the Lifelong Guidelines and LIFESKILLS in your classroom and that you communicate to parents what you are doing.

Enhancing the Physical Environment

The physical environment speaks a continuous message to students. So, design it with care. Choose a focal point in the classroom/school to display the Lifelong Guidelines for immediate reference. The back of the room, for instance, is not a handy place. Until everyone is totally familiar and comfortable with the Lifelong Guidelines, daily visual reminders will help in recognizing and identifying expectations. With the terms and definitions posted, it's easier to remember to use target talk (see page 3.2) as a reinforcement strategy. Some teachers also prepare copies of the Lifelong Guidelines (and later, the LIFESKILLS) for every student to place in his/her binder or notebook. Providing copies for parents helps to provide a basis for common vocabulary between the home and school and allows for reinforcement and connections outside of the school day.

Parent Involvement

Parents want to know what is happening in the classroom. The Lifelong Guidelines and LIFESKILLS provide an excellent opportunity to share and make real-life connections with your students' families. Whether you're part of a schoolwide effort or working alone in your classroom, it's important to keep parents informed of the behaviors that are expected in class.

A newsletter is one vehicle for building understanding of the guidelines. First, send a general introduction to all the Lifelong Guidelines and LIFESKILLS (see the sample letters at the end of this chapter). In future issues, offer more information about the specific activities students will be doing.

For parents who want to reinforce the Lifelong Guidelines and LIFESKILLS at home, recommend the parent version of this book: *Family Tools for Teaching Character and Values: Using the ITI Lifelong Guidelines and LIFESKILLS in Your Home* by Sue Pearson and Karen D. Olsen.**

---

* C.U.E. is an acronym in the ITI model to remind teachers of the power of emotions as gatekeeper to learning and performance.

** Available through Books for Educators.

CREATE A SCHEDULE

Good teaching is not an accident. You must have a month-long plan that tells you what to do from day to day. The following plans are recommended by numerous ITI practitioners and associates of Susan Kovalik & Associates. Adopt or adapt to fit the needs of your students.

Plan #1: One a Week

The "one a week" plan is a popular one with ITI teachers. Its strength is that it allows you to focus in depth on one Lifelong Guideline (and later on, one LIFESKILL) at a time. This is particularly important with younger students.

- Week One—Trustworthiness

- Week Two—Truthfulness

- Week Three—Active Listening

- Week Four—No Put-Downs

- Week Five—Personal Best

The outline below offers suggestions for teaching and providing practice for the Lifelong Guideline each day during each of the five weeks. For example, for the first week focusing on the Lifelong Guideline of Trustworthiness:

- Monday—definition of Trustworthiness illustrated through literature and song

- Tuesday—video segment showing both use and non-use of Trustworthiness plus discussion and role playing

- Wednesday—song, T-chart, and literature illustrating Trustworthiness

- Thursday—role playing and literature illustrating Trustworthiness

- Friday—song, role playing, and journal writing illustrating Trustworthiness

For the second week focusing on the Lifelong Guideline of Truthfulness, you could use the same combination of teaching strategies as shown above or change them as you see fit. Likewise, for the third, fourth, and fifth weeks focus on the remaining Lifelong Guidelines of Active Listening, No Put-Downs, and Personal Best. Follow the suggestions or feel free to change them according to your intuition.

For descriptions of each of the above teaching strategies, such as how to use literature, songs, role-playing, and so forth, see Chapters 3 and 4.

Plan #2: One a Day and Repeat

The "one a day and repeat" plan is also workable. Designed by Joy Raboli, its strength is that it allows students to see where they are going by the end of the first week. This is useful for older students from upper elementary through high school. You decide based on your own students' needs, learning patterns, and temperament.

Under this plan, set aside a small portion of each day to develop a deeper understanding of the Lifelong Guidelines. The time of day isn't important, although most teachers prefer to have a set schedule so they are sure to teach them each day. This plan focuses on a particular Lifelong Guideline each day of the week and repeats the week throughout the month.

- Monday—Trustworthiness
- Tuesday—Truthfulness
- Wednesday—Active Listening
- Thursday—No Put-Downs
- Friday—Personal Best

For example:

LIFELONG GUIDELINES				
TRUSTWORTHINESS TRUTHFULNESS ACTIVE LISTENING NO PUT-DOWNS PERSONAL BEST				
Mon	**Tue**	**Wed**	**Thu**	**Fri**
DAY ONE TRUSTWORTHINESS	DAY TWO TRUTHFULNESS	DAY THREE ACTIVE LISTENING	DAY FOUR NO PUT-DOWNS	DAY FIVE PERSONAL BEST
ONE — **TRUSTWORTHINESS** Define~Story~Discuss	**TRUTHFULNESS** Define~Story~Discuss	**ACTIVE LISTENING** Define~Story~Discuss	**NO PUT-DOWNS** Define~Story~Discuss	**PERSONAL BEST** Define~Story~Discuss
TWO — **TRUSTWORTHINESS** Video~Tally~Graph	**TRUTHFULNESS** Video~Tally~Graph	**ACTIVE LISTENING** Video~Tally~Graph	**NO PUT-DOWNS** Video~Tally~Graph	**PERSONAL BEST** Video~Tally~Graph
THREE — **TRUSTWORTHINESS** T-chart~Role Play~Real Life	**TRUTHFULNESS** T-chart~Role Play~Real Life	**ACTIVE LISTENING** T-chart~Role Play~Real Life	**NO PUT-DOWNS** T-chart~Role Play~Real Life	**PERSONAL BEST** T-chart~Role Play~Real Life
FOUR — **TRUSTWORTHINESS** Creative Writing~Journal	**TRUTHFULNESS** Creative Writing~Journal	**ACTIVE LISTENING** Creative Writing~Journal	**NO PUT-DOWNS** Creative Writing~Journal	**PERSONAL BEST** Creative Writing~Journal
The Bears on Hemlock Mountain, The Velveteen Rabbit, The Secret Garden	*Berenstein Bears Tell the Truth, Sam, Bangs and Moonshine, Pinocchio*	*3 Little Pigs-Wolf's Point of View, Charlotte's Web, Horton Hears a Who*	*Ugly Duckling, Ira Sleeps Over, Crow Boy, Whipping Boy, Charlie Brown books*	*Amazing Grace, Stone Fox, The Giving Tree, The Three Little Pigs, Brave Irene*

(WEEK labels: ONE, TWO, THREE, FOUR — leftmost column)

Plan #3: Your Choice

A few teachers have asked why they even have to have a plan for introducing and teaching the Lifelong Guidelines and LIFESKILLS. They have felt that it should just be taught naturally, whenever the circumstances are appropriate. We, too, believe in teaching them in the most natural way possible during the "teachable moment." But, we also know that current curricular demands have a way of pushing the best of intentions aside. The result, all too often, is that focus is lost and so are the lessons to be learned.

Are these the only lessons that teach about the Lifelong Guidelines? No. There are many more. The purpose of this book is to offer some beginning points. Go back to your own roots and experiences for "hooks" that will help you make the Lifelong Guidelines and LIFESKILLS memorable and part of the fabric of classroom life.

WHEN TO TEACH THE LIFESKILLS

Remember that the LIFESKILLS are *not* separate from the Lifelong Guidelines; they *define* the Lifelong Guideline of Personal Best. Begin teaching the LIFESKILLS only when you are ready to teach the Lifelong Guideline of Personal Best.

To teach the LIFESKILLS, use the same approaches that worked well for you when teaching the Lifelong Guidelines:

- Create and maintain a schedule for at least two weeks ahead; know what you want to do each day

- Use real-world happenings and capture the "teachable moment"

- Make your "lessons" memorable

Remember that developing habits of mind and heart take time. Master the instructional strategies described in Chapters 3 and 4 so they are readily available for daily use. Above all, have fun with your students. Learning values and appropriate behaviors may be serious business but it need not be grim! Enjoy watching your students (and yourself!) grow.

USE REAL-WORLD HAPPENINGS TO CAPTURE THE "TEACHABLE MOMENT"

The real power in teaching the Lifelong Guidelines and LIFESKILLS comes from making them part of daily living. This means using real-world happenings to capture the teachable moment rather than depending on an occasional, carefully prepared or canned lesson.

For a discussion of daily teaching strategies that will allow you to capture the "teachable moment," see Chapter 3.

The "curriculum content" of the teachable moment lies right at your finger tips—your own experiences with school as a child and your students' current and past experiences with school. For older students, include current events from community, nation, and world.

Teacher's Childhood Experiences at School

Since students love hearing stories of their teacher's experiences, begin by telling about your own learning experiences in school. When did you feel safe enough in school to take a risk? What things happened that kept you from being the best student you could be? What mistakes do you still regret? What were your most embarrassing moments? Use your LIFESKILL of Sense of Humor. Avoid becoming preachy. Let children know that our lives are a work in progress and that the Lifelong Guidelines and LIFESKILLS are lifelong pursuits.

For more extended or formal lessons, invite students to share examples of situations when they have felt safe and comfortable enough for learning to take place. Ask for examples of behaviors that prohibit or limit learning for them. Provide time for small groups to create a mindmap or other visual organizer detailing conditions that promote learning for everyone. Then present the Lifelong Guidelines (or later, the LIFESKILLS) and suggest that the learning clubs organize their responses to match up with a Lifelong Guideline/LIFESKILL. For example, if one learning club's mindmap has, "It helps us when people listen to our ideas," this would support the Lifelong Guideline of Active Listening. Another group may have, "When people speak respectfully to us, we can concentrate on learning," and might decide that this links to the Lifelong Guideline of No Put-Downs. After all of the positive learning behaviors have been categorized, agree that these guidelines will be part of classroom life.

Students' Experiences at School

From a student perspective, a school day is full of experiences—good and bad. Use these events and interactions at school as gist for discussing the Lifelong Guidelines and LIFESKILLS. During community circle or class meetings, invite the students to share some of the problems they have experienced during school in previous years (and this year) that kept them from concentrating on learning, e.g., fights on the playground, name calling, use of put-downs, a bully who frightened them, and friends telling lies.

Current Events

For older students, a discussion of current issues in the news can lead into the Lifelong Guidelines and LIFESKILLS. Pose pertinent questions to promote analysis of what Lifelong Guidelines or LIFESKILLS helped the people to problem solve or accomplish what they did. And what Lifelong Guidelines and LIFESKILLS didn't the people use that got them into the predicament described in the news articles. What characteristics in people do the students admire?

Which lead to conflict or problems? Which help solve problems? Follow up with a general introduction to all of the guidelines as examples of the positive behaviors that provide a safe learning environment.

Current events of interest to students can also be the focus for more formal, extended lessons about the Lifelong Guidelines and LIFESKILLS.

Communicating with Parents

Whichever schedule you adopt/adapt, be sure you communicate to parents what you are doing, how, when, and why. The following letters can help open a teacher-parent dialogue about first the Lifelong Guidelines and then later the LIFESKILLS.

Date _____

Dear Family,

Who doesn't want to have a sense of community whether it be in the neighborhood, an organization, a church, or workplace? Community is that sense of belonging one feels when many hearts and minds come together to work toward a common goal and live by a common set of behavioral standards.

In our classroom, we will follow the Lifelong Guidelines of:

- TRUSTWORTHINESS

- TRUTHFULNESS

- ACTIVE LISTENING

- NO PUT-DOWNS

- PERSONAL BEST

These five Lifelong Guidelines provide consistent parameters and expectations of conduct in our mini-community—what behaviors to expect from ourselves and others. They are the social outcomes we set for the community. They also ensure that all students are in an environment that encourages exploring, discovering, and learning.

These behaviors contribute to a sense of workability in life, not only in our classroom now, but also as an adult.

Sometime during the sixth century b.c., Lao-Tzu (a name meaning "old sage") wrote:

"The journey of a thousand miles begins with one step."

As we venture into learning and living each guideline, I invite you to join us on our journey and provide an important supportive role in the development of our classroom community. We will keep you up-to-date with our progress through letters, newsletters and projects.

Sincerely,

_____

Your child's teacher

Date _____

Dear Family,

Our class has been working hard to learn to live by the Lifelong Guidelines in our classroom community. Our efforts will continue throughout the year as we attach new meanings and deeper understandings of their application. At this time, we are ready to progress from group standards and expectations, the Lifelong Guidelines, to those that are more individual, the LIFESKILLS.

The fifth Lifelong Guideline, "PERSONAL BEST," is defined by 18 LIFESKILLS:

CARING	FLEXIBILITY	PERSEVERANCE
COMMON SENSE	FRIENDSHIP	PRIDE
COOPERATION	INITIATIVE	PROBLEM SOLVING
COURAGE	INTEGRITY	RESOURCEFULNESS
CURIOSITY	ORGANIZATION	RESPONSIBILITY
EFFORT	PATIENCE	SENSE OF HUMOR

Just as we carefully orchestrated the presentation and teaching of the Lifelong Guidelines, we will also introduce the LIFESKILLS with care in our community, one at a time. This will assure that all students arrive at common understandings of the meanings of each and how to practice them.

Margaret Mead, famous anthropologist, provides an inspiring quote to spark our journey:

"Never doubt that a small group of thoughtful,
committed people can change the world.
Indeed, it is the only thing that ever has."

Once again, we invite you to learn with us as we venture forth in creating our classroom community.

Sincerely,

_____

Your child's teacher

Instructional Strategies Needed Every Day

Character, values, and attitudes—and their related behaviors—are engrained as habits of mind. To add to them, change them, or extinguish them requires daily practice and lots of it. To provide such opportunities requires capturing the "teachable moments" that occur through each and every day in addition to presenting specifically planned lessons.

There are several important tools or teaching strategies that should be used daily. None requires special training, just practice; you have already used some of them intuitively. The powerful on-going teaching strategies that allow you to capture the teachable moment are:

- Modeling
- Target talk
- Processing the process
- Literature
- Songs
- Journal writing
- Written procedures
- Clear criteria to clarify expectations

Take time to master each of these teaching strategies so that they are readily available at a moment's notice.

For strategies to introduce and reteach a Lifelong Guideline or LIFESKILL, see Chapter 4.

MODELING

The single most powerful strategy for teaching the Lifelong Guidelines and LIFESKILLS is modeling. As you have already discovered, "Do what I do" is always more powerful than "Do what I say."

As we all know, however, consistent modeling of our values and beliefs is more easily said than done. Be prepared for some self-evaluation. Be willing to reflect on your own conduct and to be open to fine tuning any "less than perfect" manners, attitudes, and conduct. Muster the courage to make appropriate changes as needed. Model for your students how to make changes in long-standing patterns of behavior. Remember, modeling isn't about being perfect, it's about showing others how to be the best human being possible—imperfect perhaps but always improving and always willing to make amends for mistakes.

Do As I Do

As a teacher, you are one of the most powerful role models in the lives of your students. They study us carefully, whether they appear to or not. They watch to see if we are offering up only "token" lessons about the Lifelong Guidelines and LIFESKILLS or if we truly believe that they are important social and behavioral guidelines for all to follow—at home and elsewhere. Take time to visualize exactly the kind of person you want to be and what you want mirrored in your students' behaviors. Then, define and write down strategies that will achieve these personal goals. Remember, you're on stage and actions always speak louder than words.

Learn to "walk your talk." Also learn how to discuss with your students those times when you or they fall short.

TARGET TALK

The second most powerful strategy for teaching students the Lifelong Guidelines and LIFESKILLS is to acknowledge their use moment by moment, taking advantage of the "teachable moment"—when the demonstration of, or need for, the appropriate behaviors occurs naturally. Target talk* provides an opportunity for your students to understand what the Lifelong Guidelines and LIFESKILLS look like, sound like, and feel like, and do *not* look, sound, or feel like, in varying situations. Common language, pictures, and actions begin to emerge as students experience supportive responses to their use of the Lifelong Guidelines and LIFESKILLS. You'll be surprised how quickly your students will make target talk comments about the behavior of others . . . and you. Be prepared!

The Goal of Target Talk

As Pat Belvel points out, misbehavior is a teaching opportunity. It is a symptom that students do not know enough of the appropriate behaviors and/or know too many of the wrong behaviors. She developed "target talk" as a teaching tool to provide clear pictures of expected behaviors. As adapted for use in the ITI model, it is the most powerful tool you possess for teaching students the Lifelong Guidelines and LIFESKILLS.

Additional pictures of what the Lifelong Guidelines and LIFESKILLS do and don't look like, sound like, and feel like are essential because each Lifelong Guideline is conceptually rich and its application to real life always complex. Mastering the Lifelong Guidelines and LIFESKILLS is a lifelong pursuit. Be patient. For example, the attributes of truthfulness are not only complex but often subtle and frequently circumstance-dependent. To illustrate this point, a group of

---

* Adapted from Pat Belvel's classroom management work, Training and Consulting Institute, Inc., San Jose, California. http://www.trngedu.com/

teachers attending a class at the University of California, Davis, took on the challenge to define the Lifelong Guidelines of Truthfulness. Their definition appears in Chapter 6, page 1.

If we were honest with ourselves, we have to admit that, even as adults, we also experience difficulty applying this Lifelong Guideline in our lives. Students need lots of opportunities for guided practice and heaps of patience—many subtleties come with maturity. Learning to apply the Lifelong Guidelines and LIFESKILLS is a lifetime endeavor, a work in progress. Have patience, knowing that social and self-awareness are developmental in students, but continue the dialogue on a daily basis.

How to Use Target Talk

Target talk is simple to use but you may need to leave behind a habit of providing rewards for behavior and overusing/misusing "I statements." Statements such as, "I like the way [John] is using his time while he waits for . . . ," are bondage statements that may control behavior for the moment but keep the focus on pleasing others rather than on students developing their own sense of what's right or wrong, appropriate or inappropriate. Target talk helps students develop responsibility for their behavior.

Target Talk in Three Steps. The three steps of target talk should be short and to the point. For example:

- First, use the student's name. "Mike, . . ."

- Second, label the Lifelong Guideline/LIFESKILL that the student is using. "Mike, you are using the Lifelong Guideline of Active Listening. . ."

- Third, identify the action. "Mike, you are using the Lifelong Guideline of Active Listening when you face the speaker, look interested, and are able to tell in your own words what the speaker meant."

Verbal feedback is quick and easy using these three steps.

Many teachers like to provide students with short, written messages and also encourage comments from other students. These are important because they provide a long-lasting communication, one that can be referred to again and again by the student. An easy device for capturing written comments from all students is the Acknowledgement Box.

Acknowledgement Box. Comments for the Acknowledgment Box should be brief, nonjudgmental, and follow the three-step format described above: "I want to acknowledge Jack for using the Lifelong Guideline of No Put-Downs when he gave me useful feedback about grammar and spelling on my thank-you letter to the Governor." Whenever you have a spare moment during the day, such as when getting ready to make a transition to a new activity, simply pull three or four acknowledgements from the box and read them aloud to the class. Students are always eager to hear positive things others have to say about them.

Remember, the purpose of the giving and receiving acknowledgements* is to get your students to reflect on their behavior and build their own internal dialogue about it. They will soon begin to "feel" the acknowledgement inside because they said so; the student's own perspective then becomes the motivator and guide for behavior. This decreases the power of peer pressure later on.

Avoid Value Judgment. Target talk is best done without value judgment. As the Sergeant in the TV series *Dragnet* would say, "Just the facts, ma'am." The facts are: *who*, *what* Lifelong Guideline or LIFESKILL was demonstrated, and *how* it was used. Such clear statements provide immediate feedback about use of the desired behaviors. Students see the Lifelong Guidelines and LIFESKILLS in action and make their own judgments about how useful they are. This independent valuing process is critical to building the character traits, values, and attitudes—and their related behaviors—that will last a lifetime.

Using Target Talk to Correct Misbehavior

Target talk is a very powerful—and easy to use—teaching tool for dealing with misbehavior. First ask "What happened here?" Then, "What Lifelong Guidelines and/or LIFESKILLS didn't you use?" Lastly, "What Lifelong Guidelines and/or LIFESKILLS could you have used to have avoided this happening?" Remember to stay neutral in tone. This is the teaching phase of correcting misbehavior. And always make sure students understand how their misbehavior made the other person feel. Strengthening students' awareness of how their behavior affects others is a critical step in the process to assist them in internalizing the Lifelong Guidelines and LIFESKILLS.

The consequences phase—sometimes referred to as the punishment—should always be in proportion to the gravity of the act. If the student has been rude or unfair, ask how he/she could "clean it up" or make amends with the wounded party.

If the consequences are grave, such as hitting someone, damaging their property, playing with matches, additional consequences are appropriate. Ask the student what consequences/punishment would help him/her to remember not to do such things again. Often students are harder on themselves than adults would be.

If such conversations between you and a student fail to curb the behavior, add an audience—the student injured plus whoever else was present; if necessary, add learning-club members or the entire class. However, do so only after you have created a sense of community in the classroom and with that student as a full member. In our experience, the only students that continue to misbehave are those who feel no connection to others and therefore feel they have nothing to lose by misbehaving. Students want to belong, they want to matter, they want to be loved and respected. When they are included, when they belong, they value what their peers think.

---

* Acknowledgements differ from compliments in subtle but powerful ways. Compliments arise from the speaker having applied his/her criteria for what's good or commendable. Acknowledgements are a way of applying generally accepted criteria, such as the Lifelong Guidelines and LIFESKILLS. The goal is to redirect students from relying on external standards to internal ones.

PROCESSING THE PROCESS

"Processing the process" is a term coined by Jeanne Gibbs in *TRIBES: A Way of Learning and Being Together*. It is a simple but powerful instructional strategy that asks students to analyze not what they just did but how they did it. In other words, how did the process of working together go? Did it help them or hinder them in getting the task done? What could they have done differently? Or, in the case of working with the Lifelong Guidelines and LIFESKILLS, how well did they use the LIFESKILLS of Organization and Effort? What would they do differently next time? What did they learn about working together or about themselves? Are they improving in their use of the LIFESKILL of Initiative? And so on. The teacher, sometimes with input from students, asks questions appropriate to the moment.

This same idea is also very useful before an activity. For example, "What Lifelong Guidelines and/or LIFESKILLS will you need to do well at this task? If you used them, what would it look like, sound like, and feel like; what would they not look, sound, and feel like? What do you personally need to do and not do to use those Lifelong Guidelines and/or LIFESKILLS?"

LITERATURE

There is nothing better than a great story to pique students' interest and curiosity and, in the process, to teach a meaningful lesson. For your daily focus or story time with students, select a story rich with examples of the Lifelong Guideline or LIFESKILL you are currently focusing on or that addresses an important incident/situation from the day. Which stories offer strong examples of Trustworthiness? Truthfulness? Active Listening? Integrity? Which teach the destructiveness of Put-Downs? Which support development of Personal Best or Resourcefulness? There are stories that immediately come to mind because they teach about all of the Lifelong Guidelines and many of the LIFESKILLS. For example, *Charlotte's Web* by E. B. White, *Stone Fox* by John Reynolds Gardiner, *Shiloh* by Phyllis Reynolds Naylor, *My Side of the Mountain* by Jean Craighead George, and *Red Fern* by Wilson Rawls. The strong characterizations created by the various authors grab youth (and often adults) emotionally.

At the end of the story (or chapter in the case of a longer story), discuss the use and/or non-use of the Lifelong Guidelines and LIFESKILLS. Invite your students to make connections between situations and actions of the characters and the Lifelong Guideline and LIFESKILL that you want to focus on. Provide time for them to locate and share situations in the book when the characters were using that Lifelong Guideline or LIFESKILL. Conversely, ask for examples when the characters were not using them or even deliberately ignoring them. Are students able to identify the consequences? It is always easier for students to see the consequences of the behavior of others than their own. Then, ask students to transfer both types of examples from the book into their own real-life experiences. You'll discover that such discussions strengthen relationships and help to keep the lines of communication open.

Recommended Literature

The books recommended for each Lifelong Guideline and LIFESKILL at the end of the chapter provide a beginning point. Use your personal experiences and judgment to determine which stories are appropriate for your own students, both in content and age appropriateness.

These lists, called "Literature Links," are divided into primary and intermediate grades. Following the lists of books for students are resources for teachers. The material ranges from philosophical to "how-to." Some are serious while others offer a "lighter touch." Pick and choose according to your interests and needs.

Pre-Reading Student Books Is Important

There are several important reasons for pre-reading a story before you read it aloud to your students. First, you will want to determine if the story content and language are consistent with what you want your students to experience. Such previews allow you to sidestep objectionable language or skip parts that students might find upsetting. Also determine if the content and language are appropriate for your students. While our lists are "clumped" by primary, intermediate grade levels, middle school, and high school, we all understand that students grow and mature at different rates. In addition, consider your students' life experiences before suggesting, or helping to choose, a book.

Second, check for any vocabulary or content that you or parents may find objectionable. Pre-read any book that you plan to share with your students just so there will be no hidden surprises! I have this experience to share: I once pre-read a book that I was going to use with my fourth graders and decided that the language was acceptable and created no problems. I promptly bought additional copies for a class set. Imagine my surprise later in the year as I began reading Chapter 8 from the class set and found the word "bastard"! I inwardly choked, quickly altered the syllable break to "ba-stard" and slapped a heavy accent on the last syllable. When I checked later, the original copy I had was indeed okay; the newer copies for the class set came from a different publisher and with a different attitude. To this day, I don't believe any of the students caught on *but* it does show that different versions of a book may exist. Therefore, while I have read most of the books suggested here, there might be slightly different versions lurking in bookstores and libraries around the country. Always pre-read.

A third reason for pre-reading is to familiarize yourself with the story and to look for comfortable "discussion" spots. Looking ahead helps you to find those places in the plot that would most effectively highlight the importance of the Lifelong Guidelines and LIFESKILLS and connect to your students' experiences. It also allows you to add a bit of drama to your reading.

For a discussion about how to use literature to introduce or reteach a Lifelong Guideline or LIFESKILL, see Chapter 4.

SONGS

Songs are a wonderful teaching device. They combine the power of memorable melody and the rhyme of poetry. Both significantly increase the likelihood that what is learned will be stored in long-term memory. Best of all, singing is fun and something that all can do; musical talent and training are not required. Also, rather than giving your students a stern lecture about behavior, try breaking into a song. What a delight!

Resources available to help you launch your musical career together include *Spread Your Wings: The Lifelong Guidelines* by Jeff Pedersen (available in video, CD, and audio cassette) and *LIFESKILLS* by Russ and Judy Eacker (CD or audio cassette; songbook is also available).* Or, log on to *http://www.scottsdale.org/schools/elem/DesertCanyon/iti.htm*, internet home of Jean Spanko, a gifted ITI teacher using the ITI model with middle school students. The lyrics, written to favorite oldies, are delightful and very singable. Students will pick up the melody and lyrics in a flash. Samples of Jean's work include the following:

Pride, Great Pride

(to the tune of *Ain't She Sweet?*)

Pride, great pride
Feel it way down deep inside.
When you just can't rest
Until you do your best,
Feel that PRIDE.

Mastery,
Just remember "CCC"
When it's correct, complete,
And comprehensive
How proud you'll be.

When you've got pride
You'll aim much higher.
That little spark
Becomes a fire.

Pride, great pride
Feel it way down deep inside.
When you just can't rest
Until you do your best,
Feel that pride!

Resourcefulness

(to the tune of *This Old Man*)

When you face problems tough,
Resourcefulness will be enough
Look around for answers,
Change your point of view.
Great ideas will come to you.

Keep your mind focused well;
Stay away from folks that tell you
That "This won't work,
we tried it once before."
Show those people out the door.

If you fail, don't give in
Try your first ideas again.
The solution may be
Just a step away.
Be resourceful every day.

When you're stumped, you can ask
Trusted friends to share your task.
They can listen well
And dream along with you...
Give a different point of view.

Think in ways new and strange.
There's a world that you can change.
Be resourceful and you'll
See the answer clear.
All the world will stand and cheer.

* Both are available from Books for Educators, Inc.—888/777-9827; email: books4@oz.net; www.books4educ.com

Once you have started using songs as a teaching device, encourage students to develop lyrics to their favorite tunes. Students delight in writing such songs. Plus, it extends and deepens their ownership of each Lifelong Guideline and LIFESKILL. Also, writing lyrics is a painless invitation to writing and reading.

Journal Writing

Journal writing is an excellent device to help students process what *they* are learning or thinking about a topic. With no one looking over their shoulder or judging their words, they can be reflective about what they truly think and feel. Since writing is thinking on paper, the very act of writing requires students to sort through their thoughts, reflect on feelings, and organize ideas.

Journal writing is a useful medium in many ways since it provides opportunities for students to reflect, respond, react, and reply to a wide variety of ideas, comments, and stories. It is a powerful instructional tool. Use it daily to offer for students chances to revist, review, and renew previous beliefs and thoughts and to compare them to new ones. It is particularly useful in providing adequate time to reflect about their experiences relating to the Lifelong Guidelines and LIFESKILLS.

Note: A journal differs from a diary which primarily records what occurs from day to day.

WRITTEN PROCEDURES

Perhaps the most common cause of "misbehavior" is lack of agreement about what behaviors are expected. The teacher expects "x" and that's news to the student! The result is lots of frustration for both teacher and students.

Written procedures are an important classroom leadership strategy in the ITI model. They help you plan ahead for frequently occurring events (entering and leaving the room, what students should do when they've finished an assignment), social interactions (greeting others politely and cheerfully, going to and coming from assemblies, birthday parties, classroom celebrations), and tasks (doing homework, cleaning up after learning-club projects). By describing what social and personal behaviors are expected, procedures allow students to be successful.

Think of answers to the following questions. What do students need to know and be able to do in order to do what's appropriate? How are they expected to behave? What are they expected to bring/have?

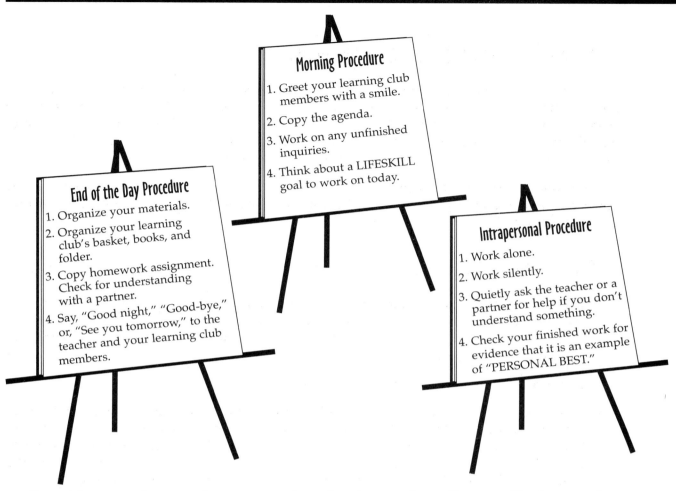

By writing procedures on chart paper and posting them on the wall or on a flip chart, students can refer to them whenever necessary. After their introduction and initial practice, some teachers create a "Procedures Binder" for each learning club. This allows for quick referral as needed while avoiding clutter. Procedures help prevent confusion and misbehavior and also eliminate the need for stating expectations over and over again. As a bonus, guest teachers (substitute teachers) find such procedures extremely helpful as well.

CLEAR EXPECTATIONS

It's difficult to do our personal best and meet other's expectations of us if the criteria for the task are not clear. Often, what is perceived as misbehavior is merely the result of not knowing what is expected, in behavior and/or performance. Written procedures describe expectations for personal and social behaviors but criteria for performing tasks or jobs are also needed. In the real world, such criteria are often called specifications. Call them what you wish, they are critical.

"Is It Done?" How to Avoid the Arguments

A common source of argument is whether or not a task was done according to expectations, whether written or not, of the person who assigned the job to be done—whether written or not. "I'm finished!" says the student. "No you're not," says the teacher. The problem: Uncommunicated or misunderstood criteria for completion. Students ought not to have to ask, "Teacher, is this right?" The criteria should be clear so that students can assess their own performance.

What kinds of assessment do you plan to use? Decide in advance so that you can communicate a clear picture to students before they begin. Your ultimate goal is criteria that meet real-world standards for acceptability and excellence.

The 3C's of Assessment. The ITI model applies the 3C's of assessment to inquiries/activities/tasks:

- **Is it complete?** Was the job completed as stated in the directions or inquiry? Does it meet the specifications described in the inquiry? Does it reflect real-world standards for work performed in the workplace while remaining age-appropriate? Does it reflect pride in workmanship and personal best?

- **Is it correct?** Is the information/action correct?

- **Is it comprehensive?** Has the student addressed the task as thoroughly as possible given his/her capabilities at this age? Did the student just follow the specific directions given to him/ her or did he/she handle closely related tasks that, if left undone, would adversely affect the outcome of the assigned job? For example, if asked to clean the sink in the classroom, did the student also wipe up the paste dripped on the nearby countertop?

Keep in mind that criteria should "grow" as the student's capabilities grow. What was personal best at six years of age is unacceptable at age nine.

Chapter 4

Strategies for Introducing and Reteaching

In addition to the instructional strategies that should be used daily, as described in Chapter 3, there are numerous strategies that are especially powerful when introducing or reteaching a Lifelong Guideline or LIFESKILL. They may be used as often as you wish but usually not every day. They include:

- Video clips
- Literature
- T-Charts
- Discussion
- Role playing
- Social/Political action
- Celebrations

Video Clips

Good videos, like good literature, are a terrific teaching resource. But not the entire movie; students typically spend more time than they should watching movies and TV. Think video segments. Even movies that may seem objectionable in their entirety have short segments with powerful messages for students (and adults). Usually a 5-8 minute clip is sufficient. Whether it models the values and behaviors you are trying to teach or whether it shows a lack of such values and behaviors, both are needed to help students get a clear picture of what they are targeting. To really know what something is, we must also know what it isn't. This is particularly important when applying values and morals to everyday life. For example, when is telling the truth being rude and uncaring? When does being trustworthy become being taken advantage of? When does doing your personal best become dangerous to your health?

Video clips are often a good lead-in to be followed by T-Charts and discussion. Charlie Brown movies, for example, contain wonderful examples of put-downs usually understandable by all ages, even five year olds. After my class learned the basics of "No Put-Downs," I had my students watch a section of the Charlie Brown videos. I asked the students to keep a tally of the number of put-downs they heard during a brief segment and then relate them to real-life situations, behaviors, and personal experiences. Students were appalled by the number of nasty comments offered in the guise of humor. The "humor" didn't seem so funny anymore.

The video, *Harriet the Spy* by Louise Fitzhugh, has a wonderful storyline that focuses on the Lifelong Guideline of Trustworthiness, or lack of it. Seeing a video scene with "new eyes" is a beginning step in seeing classroom and home behaviors before us.

To extend the video experiences, prepare follow-up topics for practicing problem solving related to current issues such as name calling, disparaging remarks about physical attributes, or references to family circumstances.

One last reminder, make sure that the video clip you select is age-appropriate, i.e., understandable by students in the age range of your class.

Literature

Ways to use literature when teaching the Lifelong Guidelines and LIFESKILLS on a daily basis is discussed in Chapter 3. With a bit more planning and focus, literature can and should be used to introduce a Lifelong Guideline or LIFESKILL. And, later, if needed, to reteach it in a focused, concerted way.

There are innumerable ways to use literature to introduce or reinforce a Lifelong Guideline or LIFESKILL. Here are but a few. Remember to think of changes you would make for your own students and your own sources of literature.

- Character Web: Read a book that exemplifies one of the Lifelong Guidelines or LIFESKILLS. Write the name of one main character in the center of a piece of chart tablet paper. Draw a circle around the name. Add rays coming out from the circle, similar to a child's drawing of the sun. (For very young students, consider using a felt story board with images rather than words.) Have your students identify a Lifelong Guideline or LIFESKILL that this story character used to solve problems and reach his/her goals. Write the target word on the ray and the action below the ray. For example, based on *Charlotte's Web*, put the name Wilbur in the center circle. Add a ray; above it write Perseverance; under the ray write the descriptors of action from the text, e.g., "He thought and thought until he created a plan to help save his friend Charlotte, the spider." (See an example of such a character web on the next page.)

- Identify three Lifelong Guidelines or LIFESKILLS that were used to solve a problem in the story. Identify two Lifelong Guidelines or LIFESKILLS that were not used and thus resulted in problems.

- Read a traditional story such as *The Three Little Pigs*. Rewrite the ending as if the pigs had used the Lifelong Guideline of Personal Best to solve their problem with the wolf.

- After reading a biography or autobiography, label three or more Lifelong Guidelines or LIFESKILLS that the person had. Link them to actions from the book. Next, invite members of your learning club to share their experiences in developing these same three or more Lifelong Guidelines or LIFESKILLS. Using a Venn diagram, identify the behaviors associated with the selected LIFESKILLS that the book character and your learning-club members have in common and which behaviors are different. Again using a Venn diagram, compare two LIFESKILLS you use to do your personal best with those used by a character in the story.

- After completing several stories, play "Who Am I?" Choose a character from a previously read book. Share the Lifelong Guidelines/LIFESKILLS used along with one or two related actions to carry out the Lifelong Guidelines/LIFESKILLS. Invite other students who have read the book to guess who the character is.

- Compare three LIFESKILLS used by two well-known people. Select people from different time periods and settings (e.g., Madame Curie and Rosa Parks). List three LIFESKILL strengths they have in common. List three weaknesses that each one has. Discuss whether or not the LIFESKILLS are unique to the time period/setting of the story.

- Find local newspaper articles that reflect the Lifelong Guidelines being used or problems occurring because they were not used. Read the articles with your students and have them determine which Lifelong Guideline or LIFESKILL was or wasn't used. Ask students to share their thinking with other members of their learning club.

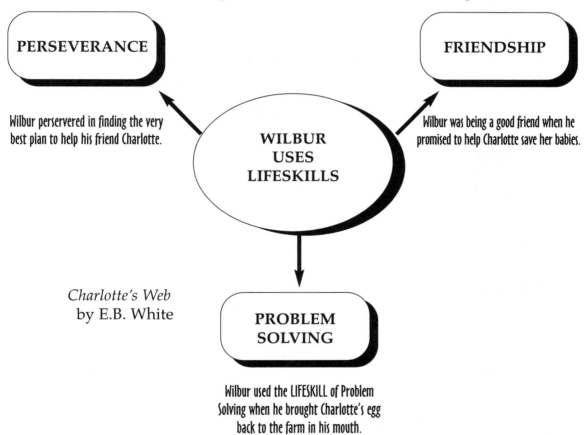

PERSEVERANCE

Wilbur perservered in finding the very best plan to help his friend Charlotte.

WILBUR USES LIFESKILLS

FRIENDSHIP

Wilbur was being a good friend when he promised to help Charlotte save her babies.

Charlotte's Web
by E.B. White

PROBLEM SOLVING

Wilbur used the LIFESKILL of Problem Solving when he brought Charlotte's egg back to the farm in his mouth.

Hopefully these few ideas will have you thinking in many different directions. Perhaps you remember a favorite biography and think, "Of course, why didn't I ever mention perseverance when we read about Thomas Edison or Rosa Parks?" Or, perhaps you recall a link to humor using *Charlotte's Web*? How about the courage shown in *The True Story of Ruby Bridges*? Eventually, you'll wonder why you ever thought it would be hard to make connections. They'll be popping up everywhere!

T-Charts

An excellent way to introduce a Lifelong Guideline or LIFESKILL, and to do an in-depth refresher course if needed, is to brainstorm pictures of what a particular Lifelong Guideline or LIFESKILL looks like, sounds like, and feels like *and* what it does **not** look like, sound like, or feel like.

How to Use T-Charts. Using a large chart tablet, write the name of a Lifelong Guideline or LIFESKILL across the top of the page and create three columns. Label the first column "Looks Like," the second "Sounds Like," and the third "Feels Like." Ask students to think of personal experiences at school or situations from stories they have read that will fit into each category. Allow them sufficient think time so that they can fill in the spaces with only minimal prompting. Let them use their own words (for younger students, draw simple pictures to illustrate the meaning). Students' intuitive understanding of the Lifelong Guidelines and LIFESKILLS is often surprising.

The example below illustrates a beginning chart for the Lifelong Guideline of Trustworthiness.

TRUSTWORTHINESS

Looks Like	Sounds Like	Feels Like
students sharing ideas	"I've got a secret!"	safe
people working together	"Will you teach me how to do that?"	comfortable
student running an errand	"Please take this to Mrs. X down the street."	I'm trusted
students helping one another	"Would you help me?" "Yes."	friendliness
student turning in found object	"I found this. It belongs to someone else."	honesty

Next, create a second chart with what the Lifelong Guideline or LIFESKILL does **not** look like, sound like, or feel like.

Save both charts and add to the columns daily throughout the first week of study and at least monthly thereafter as students identify more attributes. The more pictures students have for each of the Lifelong Guidelines and LIFESKILLS, the more adept they will become in applying them in social and personal settings.

The chart on the next page illustrates how to contrast pictures of what it is and is not.

TRUSTWORTHINESS

Looks Like	Sounds Like	Feels Like	Doesn't Look Like	Doesn't Sound Like	Doesn't Feel Like
going on an errand alone	"You can do it!?	special	somone supervising you	"I know you can't get there without getting into trouble."	sarcastic
borrowing a library book	"I know you will take good care of it."	honored	losing a library book	"I think somebody stole it!"	distrust
finding money	"Thank you for bringing the money to the Lost and Found."	trusted	pocketing found money	"Finders keepers! Losers weepers!"	suspicious
going to a friend's house	"Be home on time."	someone depends on me	sneaking out of the house	"I wouldn't do that. Trust me!"	lying

Discussion

The more you and your students refer to and use the Lifelong Guidelines and LIFESKILLS, the more natural they will feel and the more spontaneous your responses and those of your students will become. Think through in advance ways to:

- Identify the Lifelong Guidelines/LIFESKILLS and their power to direct the course of our lives (e.g., "Do you think _____'s life would have turned out differently if he/she had used more of the LIFESKILL of _____? If so, how would it have been different?"

- Give succinct and memorable behaviors consistent with the Lifelong Guidelines/ LIFESKILLS (e.g., discussing a local newspaper article: "The five-year old boy saved his family's lives because he was the only one who put his flashlight in a place he could remember and find in his room at a moment's notice. Without his LIFESKILL of Organization, he and his family would not have been able to see well enough to gather together and escape the fire."

- Avoid value judgment; allow students to make the judgments of value for themselves, thus internalizing the behaviors (e.g., "Three students at the high school were just arrested for selling drugs. How will this affect the course of the rest of their lives? What do you think motivated them to do what they did? What Lifelong Guidelines/ LIFESKILLS could they have used to accomplish the same thing over the next 15 years (the probable length of the prison term)?

- Identify other ways people use the guidelines, both in and out of school (e.g., "What Lifelong Guidelines and/or LIFESKILLS does your best friend have? Which do you like about him/her the most? How do his/her Lifelong Guidelines/LIFESKILLS make your life happier and better?"

Discussion should be part of your formal introduction and on-going teaching of each Lifelong Guideline and LIFESKILL. It can occur during your "lesson" and it should also carry over to classroom conversation at the cafeteria; it should also "pop" up during the day as part of interactions to solve a problem or correct behavior.

Give considerable thought to discussion as a way to capture the "teachable moment" as discussed in Chapter 3. For example, having two of your students sit in the office waiting for the principal to discipline them for fighting on the playground doesn't have the teaching value that stopping them at the moment and holding an impromptu class meeting. Discuss with them what Lifelong Guideline or LIFESKILL they didn't use (that caused the problem) and what Lifelong Guidelines and LIFESKILLS they could have used to have prevented the fighting. This, of course, should then be followed up with having both parties "clean up the problem" (apology plus whatever is appropriate) as the teacher applies the appropriate consequences for such a severe breach of behavior.

For an excellent resource for structuring discussions and other forms of group work, see *TRIBES: A New Way of Learning and Being Together* by Jeanne Gibbs and *Cooperative Learning* by Spencer Kagan.

Role Playing

Role playing is highly appealing to students; there is action to watch, dialogue to hear, and a story line to follow. Often because of the emotional impact, the moral or lesson just "pops" out making it easier for students to make connections to real life. Therefore, consider role playing to illustrate the Lifelong Guidelines and LIFESKILLS.

Role playing can be formal—with time allowed to invent and rehearse an assigned scenario— or spontaneous. Both are powerful. It's especially effective for teaching students alternative responses. For example, set up a simple situation: "Instead of ____ [hitting Jack], role play what Lifelong Guideline or LIFESKILL you could have used."

Conversely, if a story or incident worked out well, ask the question, "What if Kenny had not used the Lifelong Guideline or LIFESKILL of _____? Role play what would have happened then."

Have students act out the options. Be playful. Know that for many students, hearing about something is seldom as powerful as seeing it. And, because education is about giving students options in life, what better way than to have them experience those options now through role playing.

Journal Writing

Journal writing is an excellent device to help students process what *they* think about something. With no one looking over their shoulder or judging what they say, they can be reflective about what they truly think. And, because writing is thinking on paper, the act of writing requires students to sort through their thoughts and sift down to the bottom line.

Encourage students to keep a journal and to write in the journal about experiences that relate to the Lifelong Guidelines and LIFESKILLS. Remember, a journal differs from a diary which primarily records what occurs from day to day.

Social and Political Action Projects

Social and/or political action projects—midway into study or as a culminating activity—put learning to the test. They require students to apply what they have been learning to personal use in the real world. What we know from brain research is that locking knowledge and skill into long-term memory takes practice—multiple uses in varying situations. Test-taking is usually performed from short-term memory. In contrast, social and political action projects immerse students in in-depth projects that extend over time, thus giving rich, engaging, practice that ensures mastery and long-term memory storage of a wide range of skills and knowledge.

Therefore, if studying the LIFESKILL of Caring, encourage your students to act upon it—to assist at a home for the elderly (sing, help with a Christmas party, write letters, go outdoors for fresh air and conversation, and so forth), volunteer at a soup kitchen (cook, serve, help organize provisions), offer to help a neighbor just home from the hospital (take care of his/her yard for a month, feed pets, do dishes, and so forth).

Connect projects to the study of a Lifelong Guideline or LIFESKILL. For example, if studying the LIFESKILL of Resourcefulness, have your students start a business (walking pets for a neighbor, mowing lawns, washing windows, teaching others how to use the Internet or make a web page, delivering newspapers). If studying the LIFESKILL of Initiative, look around the neighborhood. What political action is needed? A crosswalk light at a dangerous intersection, pollution to be cleaned up, an empty lot to be made safe, drug pushing outside the school to be cleaned up, low voter registration in the neighborhood?

The projects don't have to last a lifetime. Two to four weeks is enough to make the learning memorable.

Young citizens of a democratic society should start learning the gears and levers of democracy as preschoolers. Several good resources for helping you guide your students through planning and carrying out social/political projects include: *Enriching Curriculum Through Service Learning*, edited by C.W. Kinsley and K. McPherson, and *The Kid's Guide to Service Projects: Over 500 Service Ideas for Young People Who Want to Make a Difference* and *The Kid's Guide to Social Action: How to Solve the Social Problems You Choose—and Turn Creative Thinking into Positive Action* by Barbara Lewis.

Celebrations

How will you celebrate your accomplishments as a class family and as individuals? Pride—personal satisfaction in a job well done—is an important source of motivation to do one's personal best the next time. Do note that celebration of accomplishments is vastly different than receiving a reward. While rewards, such as ice cream treats, a trip to McDonald's, and so forth, work in the short run, they are extremely detrimental in the long run. Your goal is to instill in your child the desire to do what is needed because it needs to be done and to feel a sense of personal satisfaction from doing his/her part.

For a hair-raising discussion of the dangers of rewards, see Alfie Kohn's book, *Punished by Rewards: The Trouble with Gold Stars, Incentive Plans, A's, Praise, and Other Bribes.* Surprisingly enough, external rewards work against us; they extinguish the behavior that is rewarded. The key to development of character, values, and attitudes implicit in the Lifelong Guidelines and LIFESKILLS in the long run is having students internalize them rather than externally rewarded for them.

Celebration, on the other hand, is taking time to acknowledge students' success in implementing the Lifelong Guidelines and LIFESKILLS and to experience that deep sense of personal satisfaction that comes with doing so. The feedback is thus internal, not external; the sense of pride internally generated—and earned.

Examples of Celebrations include:

- Planned and scripted drama skits performed by students for special gatherings of other students (younger buddies and/or same age or older students). These skits replicate and/or demonstrate the results of students' favorite inquiries/projects about the topic of study just concluded

- A LIFESKILLS Fair for Parents, a special evening during which your students plan LIFESKILL "booths"—demonstrations of what his/her favorite LIFESKILLs mean and how to use them. Students can work as a learning club, in partners, or individually.

- A LIFESKILL Day planned for the entire class during which students, as members of a small group of 2-5 students, carry out their plans to practice that Lifelong Guideline or LIFESKILL for the entire day (or whatever time period is chosen). Projects can be carried out on campus (Caring and Friendship with younger buddies, reading to them, helping them learn to use the library), at a nearby public park (Effort and Cooperation, clean up projects, trail restoration), or at a museum or aquarium (Curiosity, a behind the scenes tour). The possibilities are endless. On return to class, have each group give a 3-5 minute presentation of how the LIFESKILL of the day helped make that day special for them— more interesting, more fun, more friendship.

Celebrate the day by day triumphs. Learn to appreciate them as everyday miracles in the life of your students. And celebrate, celebrate, celebrate. Let your love and joy in your students grow as they grow.

Chapter 5

Trustworthiness

"Others have confidence in me."

> **trustworthiness** *n* **1a:** worthy of confidence: dependable
> **trust** *n* **1a:** assured reliance on the character, ability, strength, or truth of someone or something **b:** one in whom confidence is placed

Trustworthiness: To act in a manner that makes one worthy of confidence and trust

WHAT IS TRUSTWORTHINESS?

If we were artists commissioned to paint a masterpiece representing the Lifelong Guideline of Trustworthiness, we would choose for our model a mother rocking her infant child, the baby's eyes intently studying her mother's face, a tiny hand reaching up to touch her mother's cheek. The purest form of trust in life is child to mother. The parent provides food when the child is hungry, warmth when cold, and comfort when hurt. This relationship between mother and baby is a child's first experience with trustworthiness.

Yet we know there are other pictures in which food is late or lacking, comfort is in short supply, and warmth is missing. What do such babies begin to learn about trustworthiness? They learn that "people in my world are not reliable." Such early experiences with family and caretakers impair a child's ability to have confidence in other people.

Trustworthiness: An Umbrella in Stormy Weather

Trustworthiness, identified by specific attributes such as reliability and dependability, is vital because it is an umbrella under which we protect ourselves from stormy weather. Each one of us needs at least one such umbrella for protection—if not a trustworthy friend, at least a parent or close family member with whom we can talk and know that our words will go no further. We need to trust that those close to us will adhere to the Lifelong Guidelines and LIFESKILLS. Likewise, we need to be the umbrella of protection for other people by providing confidentiality, steadiness, and support during those occasional drizzles, steady rains, and torrential downpours that life presents.

Trustworthiness Is a Double-Sided Coin

But trustworthiness is more than an umbrella in stormy weather for us as we seek out those who are trustworthy, safe, and comfortable to be with. Trustworthiness is a double-sided coin, a two-way street. It isn't just what we receive; we in turn must be trustworthy for others. Students must be taught that they can't expect the gift of trustworthiness from others if they are not trustworthy in return.

The Lifelong Guideline of Trustworthiness requires that parents and teachers teach both sides of Trustworthiness—how to give it and how to receive it. To do so, we must teach children the sign posts for recognizing this characteristic in others. Who is really deserving of their trust so others don't take advantage? How do they extend their trust so that relationships of all levels can deepen and enrich their lives.

WHY PRACTICE TRUSTWORTHINESS?

The Lifelong Guideline of Trustworthiness forms the basis of relationships—effective working partnerships, close friendships, healthy family bonds, and the long-lasting intimate relationship of husband and wife. Simply put, if people can't trust us, they don't want to be around us—it's too risky. The lower the level of trustworthiness, the more distant people remain. And, because few pursuits in life are solitary, most goals require the participation of others. If we are to succeed in our goals, we must become a trustworthy person.

For Staff

The higher the stakes become, the more crucial trustworthiness becomes. Designing seal rings for the space shuttle booster rocket, problem-solving safety design issues on the Boeing aircraft assembly line, doing customer service in a small business whose owner has just invested his entire life savings into his business are examples of everyday work environments in which our trustworthiness and ability to work as a team can have life-and-death or life-changing impact.

Can your colleagues feel secure that you are dependable (the job gets done), consistent (high quality of work), and reliable (follows directions and meets deadlines)? Does our level of trustworthiness evoke a degree of credibility? Does our supervisor feel confident and secure when assigning tasks to us, working on projects with us, or discussing confidential information with us?

As trust-building skills improve, we are more likely to be included in upper-level planning and decision making. Such involvement is a key element in satisfaction in the workplace.

For Students

Close relationships of any kind, including teacher-student and student-student, cannot exist without trustworthiness. It is the cornerstone of respect and liking. One can love someone without liking and respecting them—a common burden of children abused by their parents. It is also the source of one's sense of security, safety, and confidence.

A key ingredient in the Lifelong Guideline of Trustworthiness is emotional consistency —that the student knows the teacher loves him/her and that the teacher's emotional and physical behaviors are consistent with that love, that no matter what happens, the student knows he/she will be fairly treated.

When students feel safe and secure in the classroom, learning becomes paramount because the bodybrain can focus on learning. The atmosphere in the classroom, instead of tense and fraught with suspicion, is calm and steady. The teacher can be relied on to keep her word when students share problems. Consistency is the standard for student actions, both in application and outcome.

For Families

When a teacher is known to be trustworthy, relationships with students' families will flourish. A teacher who consistently and fairly applies rules and consequences wins respect from both students and adults. Family members recognize that we are working with them, not against them, in the education of their child. Generally, the more we know and understand about a child's circumstances, the greater the possibility that the teacher can provide emotional support, which in turn will promote academic learning. The parent-teacher relationship exudes confidentiality, whether relating to family or school concerns; this raises the level of trustworthiness for all involved, leading to additional exchanges of pertinent information.

Note: The only time a teacher must divulge confidential information from a student is when some form of abuse is apparent. Many states have laws requiring that this information be disclosed, and indeed, the penalties are severe if this type of action is not reported. A student sharing this type of information is crying out for help and trusting that we will provide guidance, backing, and support.

HOW DO YOU PRACTICE TRUSTWORTHINESS?

We practice being trustworthy by not abusing others' trust; we don't share confidences, ignore deadlines, spread rumors, talk behind backs, lie, cheat, steal, or exhibit any of the other behaviors that would abuse trust.

The beginnings of trustworthiness lie deep within our childhood experiences. As infants, was food consistently there when we felt the pains of hunger? Were we changed when wet and uncomfortable, rocked when ill, comforted when frightened? If the answers to these questions are yes, then we felt trust in our caretaker. On the other hand, were we left to wonder if food would come or if someone would take care of us when we were ill or frightened? Did our caretakers keep their word? Did they model good judgment and integrity? Clearly, the development of trust in the classroom comes more quickly for some students than for others. Whatever it takes, however, it is our job as educators to develop future citizens who are trustworthy and who are capable of trusting in those who have earned their trust.

Making Wise Choices

Trustworthiness is the result of making wise choices over time—some wise, others not so wise. The ability to do so, however, isn't automatic. It takes practice, in the midst of which we make mistakes—lots of them! For instance, when sent to deliver a message, does the student attend to the task at hand or slowly meander through the hallways disrupting other learners by waving in classroom windows? Do you remember some of these situations from your own child-hood experiences? One friend shares a secret with another, who promises not to tell. The two are part of a trust-building pact. Did the secret get told as soon as another warm body was in sight or remain private? Remember going to a friend's house and *promising* to return home by dinner time? Were you at your place at the dinner table or nowhere to be seen? Remember finding money around the house or at school? Did you search for the owner or pocket the cash? These are all examples of early trust-building opportunities.

At school, does a trip to the bathroom take a few minutes or is it necessary to dispatch an escort to accompany the unreliable student back to class? Can the child be trusted to complete her own work and not to copy someone else's work? Will the child tell the truth even though negative consequences may result? Does the student return forms and homework on time, turn in "found" objects and money, work hard to eliminate put-downs from his vocabulary, and do his personal best consistently?

As adults, every action we take, every deed we accomplish, every word we utter, creates the person others see us to be. People either believe us or don't. Building trust is a definitive example of actions speaking louder than words because all of the good intentions and promises in the world will not be able to compensate for jobs not done, deadlines ignored, secrets revealed, and promises broken. Therefore, tell the truth, work to your personal best, keep your word, exceed expectations—be a person viewed as reliable, dependable, and believable.

Building a Reputation Takes Time

A reputation of trustworthiness is slowly earned since it is based on a collection of positive experiences among people over time. Consistency, reliability, and honest actions all typify a person who is worthy of our trust. The same is true for each of us. Our actions and reactions will be watched for awhile, before we are known to be trustworthy.

Adults must recognize that trustworthiness develops in stages. Expectations of trustworthiness for five-year olds should be more basic than expectations for fifteen-year olds. Students must understand that each time trust is broken, it takes longer to be restored; sometimes it can be irrevocably broken.

What Does Trustworthiness Look Like in the Real World?

We

- Honor promises made to customers and clients

- Follow traffic laws at all times, not just when there are police cars in the vicinity

- Stop after vehicular accidents and provide insurance information

- Respect confidentiality of family and friends

- Follow the guidelines of contracts and agreements even when we are not being monitored

- Research political candidates' platforms and voting records to verify honest fulfillment of intentions

- Behave in a friendly and sincere way to all people, without regard to race, religion, or skin color

- Say what we mean and mean what we say

- Share honest emotions with family members and friends

- Work to rid our community, country, and world of practices that are harmful to life on earth

What Does Trustworthiness Look Like in School?

Staff

- Rely on one another to work together to create an atmosphere free of threat and conducive to learning

- Refuse to spread rumors and unfounded allegations

- Complete all assignments accurately and on time

- Respect confidentiality of students, parents, and fellow workers

- Share honest feelings about educational and professional issues

- Develop respectful relationships with students so that they speak of us as a person of integrity, someone who is fair and consistent

- Make promises sparingly and only when they can fulfill them

Students

- Follow the Lifelong Guidelines and LIFESKILLS for "guest" (substitute) teachers, visitors, and the general school community

- Support class members who are going through a troublesome time or experience

- Share honest emotions during class meetings and community circles

- Promise only what can be honored

- Follow school and classroom procedures

- Respect school property at all times

INQUIRIES TO DEVELOP TRUSTWORTHINESS

Whole Group Inquiries

- Listen to the story *Stellaluna* by Janell Cannon. Draw a picture illustrating a part of the story where Stellaluna is being a trustworthy friend.

- Experiment with being trustworthy on a "Trust Walk." Take turns leading a blindfolded friend through an obstacle course using verbal directions. Discuss how it feels to have to rely on someone else to move around the room.

- Write "Guest Teacher Procedures" with four or more ideas for polite and helpful behavior that will promote a sense of trustworthiness. Practice using the procedures before they are needed.

- Read a story/novel (e.g., *Charlotte's Web* or *My Side of the Mountain)* with the theme of trustworthiness. Identify two characters (one trustworthy and one not) and write their names at the top of a piece of paper. List six or more attributes under each name that explain why one character is trustworthy and the other is not. Use the words from your list to create a word search puzzle. Trade papers with a classmate and find his/her hidden words.

Small Group/Individual Inquiries

- Find a cardboard box larger than two pairs of boots. Cut off the cover. Ask an adult for help if the cardboard is too strong. Paint the sides of the box a favorite color. Add some designs and create a sign that reads, "Lost and Found Box." Put it in a convenient place in your classroom. Use it to hold lost and misplaced items that belong to students. Volunteer to make one for the school secretary to place in her office.

- Listen to the story *The Velveteen Rabbit* by Margery Williams. Share a time when one of the characters was being a trustworthy friend. Draw a picture illustrating that part of the story and hang it up in your classroom on the TRUSTWORTHINESS bulletin board.

- Design a chart with three pictures that illustrate trustworthy, polite, and helpful behaviors that you will use when a substitute, the "guest teacher," is teaching your class. Show this to your teacher. Then place it in your learning-club binder or notebook. Share it with the guest teacher when he/she comes to your class.

- Read the story of *Little Red Riding Hood*. Identify and describe two strategies that the wolf used to convince Little Red Riding Hood to trust him. Design a "WANTED" poster educating the public about the dangerous "big, bad wolf." Include a drawing of him, his description, and two sentences explaining why no one should trust him.

- Choose four different community helpers. Compare and contrast how each one builds trust in your community. Design and make a public service chart illustrating each helper at work.

- Write procedures for students to follow when delivering notes/materials to someone in the building. List three behaviors to guide the messenger in performing his/her job. Add graphics to illustrate the words. Share this plan with your teacher.

- Design a collage of photographs and drawings that illustrates trustworthy people in your life. Write each person's name next to his/her picture. Add a sentence explaining why you trust that person. Hang the finished product up in the class art gallery.

- Create actions to portray the meaning of the lyrics in the song "Trustworthiness" (*Spread Your Wings* by Jeff Pedersen*). Teach the song and the movements to the class. Explain why you chose those movements.

- Brainstorm three or more ways that you earn the trust of community members while playing, selling products for fund-raisers, or participating in organizations such as Cub Scouts, Brownies, Girl Scouts, Boy Scouts, and 4-H. Create a poster that will help a new member become a trustworthy member of a group or organization. Include strategies that will help foster trustworthiness in the community.

- Design a "Guest Teacher Day" self-evaluation form for class members to use for rating personal behavior on the days the regular classroom teacher cannot be in school. Review the completed form with your learning-club members and set three goals for the group before the next guest teacher's visit.

- Compose a pledge that will help your learning-club members understand that they are part of a special family. Include words such as: trustworthy, truthful, friendship, and pride. Print the pledge on an overhead transparency and share it with another learning club. Recite this learning-club pledge every Monday and Friday as you begin and end the week together.

- Volunteer to be a kindergarten buddy. Identify five ways your buddy will know that you are trustworthy. Design a picture dictionary to teach these five descriptors to your buddy. Add more descriptors as you work with your buddy. When the school year ends, donate the book to the classroom library or present it to your buddy as a farewell gift.

* Available on video, audio tape, and compact disc through Books for Educators, Inc., Kent, WA.—888/777-9827; email: books4@oz.net; www.books4educ.com

- Identify actions that would cause your learning club to lose trust in a member or members. Create a list of three or more positive alternative actions that will help rebuild the trust. After trying these actions, reflect on any changes in actions or feelings that you have. Write about your feelings in a journal. Share the results with the teacher.

- Create a skit about trustworthiness and trust building. Choose one situation and write two different endings—one where trust is misused and one where trust is honored. Perform your skit for the class twice showing each ending. Invite your classmates to think of additional ways to end the skit so that trust can be rebuilt.

- Design an "Emotions Chart" with two categories. Write "Trustworthiness" at the top of the first column and list three or more feelings that you have when people trust you. Print "Untrustworthy" at the top of the second column and list three or more feelings you have when people believe you cannot be trusted. Illustrate each emotion. Compare your feelings from one column to the other by writing a journal entry. Place the chart in your notebook and add more words as you think of them.

- Identify three people in your neighborhood who are trustworthy citizens. Create the front page of a newspaper to honor these people. Write a short article explaining what each one has accomplished. Use real photographs if they are available to you for your article.

- Interview a manager/CEO/president from the business community about trustworthiness in his/her company. Explore at least three examples of trustworthiness that he/she expects from employees. Write a classified ad of 25 words or less that might attract the kind of person needed for a position in this company.

- Study a copy of the U.S. Constitution, including the Bill of Rights and all amendments. Choose one section and determine what basic rights it affords to the citizens of the United States. Research the penalties that may be imposed when a citizen and/or the government abuses this "trust" agreement. Prepare and present a TV documentary to teach others about this topic.

SIGNS OF SUCCESS

Congratulations! Students are showing signs of Trustworthiness when they

- Keep a secret or a confidence

- Choose to follow the Lifelong Guidelines and LIFESKILLS both in and outside school

- Identify and eliminate behaviors, words, and actions that destroy a relationship built on trustworthiness

- Complete all assignments to the best of their ability and turn them in when due or early

- Return materials in the same, or better, condition than when they were first borrowed or offer to replace them if they are damaged or lost

- Meet or surpass expectations and promises made to others

- Are invited to share their opinions about crucial ideas/issues relating to the school community

Keep trying! Students need more practice when they

- Make numerous promises and honor few or none

- Accept more responsibilities than they can manage

- Spread rumors with delight as though the words are true

- Can't be relied on to carry out tasks and assignments in an accurate and timely fashion

- Aren't trusted to plan or participate in events that require dependability

- Don't search for the owners of lost items they have found

- Sneak around the room taking other people's belongings

- Offer to do something but don't do it

LITERATURE LINK ~ TRUSTWORTHINESS

Primary Grades

Abuela's Weave	Castaneda, Carlos
Certain Small Shepherd, A	Caudill, Rebecca
Dexter	Bulla, Clyde Robert
Gentle Ben	Morey, Walt
House for a Hermit Crab, A	Carle, Eric
Love You Forever	Munch, Robert
Make Way for Ducklings	McCloskey, Robert
Never Trust a Squirrel	Cooper, Patrick and C. Walters
Real Thief, The	Steig, William
Stone Soup	McGovern, Ann
Sweet Clara and the Freedom Quilt	Hopkinson, Deborah
Velveteen Rabbit, The	Williams, Margery

Intermediate Grades

Charlotte's Web	White, E. B.
Dog Called Kitty, A	Wallace, Bill
Josefina Saves the Day	Tripp, Valerie
Never Trust a Sister Over Twelve	Roos, Stephen
Question of Trust, A	Bauer, Marion Dane
Slake's Limbo	Holman, Felice
Summer Story, A	Tibbles, Jean-Paul
Too Many Tamales	Soto, Gary
Trust Me	Blackman, Malorie
Trust Walk, The	Ekberg, Susan
Trust-T: Solving Problems Through Creativity	Ekey, Barbara N.
Who Can You Trust?	Day, Lauren

Middle School and High School

Behind the Secret Window: A Memoir of a
   Hidden Childhood During World War II   Troll, Nelly S.

Bless Me, Ultima   Anaya, Rudolfo A.

Canyons   Paulson, Gary

Dicey's Song   Voigt, Cynthia

I Am the Cheese   Cormier, Robert

TEACHER'S RESOURCES

The Peaceful Classroom: 162 Activities to
   Teach Preschoolers Compassion
   and Cooperation   Smith, Charles A., Ph.D.

Tribes: A New Way of Learning
   and Being Together   Gibbs, Jeanne

Date _____

Dear Family,

For the next few weeks, our classroom community will be discovering and noting all of the attributes of the Lifelong Guideline of

~ Trustworthiness ~

We have defined the Lifelong Guideline of Trustworthiness as "to act in a manner that makes one worthy of confidence and trust." Through our class discussions and projects, the students will associate such words as dependable, honorable, and responsible with being trustworthy. Working together, we intend to create a safe environment in which active learning can take place.

Some of the activities we might do include:

- Defining the word "promise"

- Reviewing bicycle safety rules as a trust agreement between parent and child

- Discussing the Pledge of Allegiance—its words and their meaning

- Reading the United States Constitution and Amendments as an agreement of trust between a government and its people

As parents, you are working with your child everyday to inspire truth, honor, and respect. Some ways to do this include:

- Discussing pertinent news stories that deal with a loss of trust (an employee who steals, one person hurting another, a bank robbery, swindlers cheating people out of their money) and discussing how such people would be viewed by their friends and family

- Listening to your child's responses (laughter, comments, sadness) to favorite TV programs and situations, always reinforcing the most effective choice that a trustworthy person would make

The quote we are using is "Others trust your judgment and your word. Listen to what is right and good in your heart and mind."

Sincerely,

_____

Your child's teacher

Chapter 6

Truthfulness

"Friends expect the truth."

truthfulness *n* telling or disposed to tell the truth
truth *n* **1a:** constancy **b:** sincerity in action, character, and utterance
2a: (1) the state of being the case: FACT   (2) the body of real things, events, and facts

Truthfulness: To be honest about things and feelings with oneself and others

WHAT IS TRUTHFULNESS?

Truthfulness has many aspects; its complexity unfolds as students mature. It is a difficult Lifelong Guideline to practice. Its attributes are complex and often dependent upon circumstances. The definition of truthfulness that follows is the result of brainstorming by a class of teachers and administrators at U.C. Davis, California.

"To be truthful means being honest about things and feelings . . . being honest with ourselves and with others. Being truthful is not always easy because truth is not absolute (black and white) and two seemingly contradictory statements could both be the truth depending upon the perspectives of the observers (for example, the blind men discovering the elephant). It takes courage to be truthful because others may disagree.

"Being truthful requires good judgment about:

• what to say (possible risk to our source of information)

• when to say it (in private or before others)

• to whom to say it (to the person responsible for the problem/situation or as a complaint to anyone who will listen)

• how to say it (with sensitivity and tact or intended to hurt)

"Truthfulness is a critical building block for human relationships and therefore has significant consequences for each of us, both short-term and long-term."*

* Karen D. Olsen, instructor, extension course in brain-compatible learning at the University of California, Davis, 1993.

Preserving the Truth

Preserving the truth depends on each one of us refusing to exaggerate, change, or vary the facts we are sharing. This requires careful observation and clear thinking as we perceive and analyze a situation; it also requires precise communication when sharing about it.

Whether it's the policeman asking, "What happened here? Which driver caused the accident and how?" or the parent asking, "How did this happen? Who started this?" the situation calls for the truth. How well did we observe the incident? Do we stick to the facts or make inferences that may or may not be true? Are we committed to telling the truth despite consequences?

WHY PRACTICE TRUTHFULNESS?

Most people will believe what they hear *unless* the information is proven to be inaccurate. After that, the informant's word is not as good as it used to be; people then listen with a sense of disbelief or the feeling that they should check another source. Recall the story from *Aesop's Fables* about the boy who cried wolf. The boy lied so many times about the wolf being after the sheep that when the wolf really did attack, none of the villagers responded to his cries for help. If we aren't truthful at all times, people—especially family and friends—will be suspicious when we share stories; they'll want proof or verification from other sources. The greater the number of lies and careless statements that pass through our lips, the more corroboration our listeners will need.

It is important, sometimes even a matter of life or death, that people believe us. Nothing is as precious as our reputation that we say what we mean and mean what we say. Truthfulness is the bedrock of trustworthiness.

Effective Relationships Rely on Truthfulness

Based on a survey of more than 15,000 people, 88 percent chose honesty as the key trait of effective leadership.* Honest people have credibility; credible leaders gain the trust and confidence of their followers. They keep their promises and follow through on their commitments. In contrast, people who consistently lie are shunned, have few friends, and have fewer options for well-paying employment.

In personal relationships, if we can't be trusted to tell the truth with even insignificant information, how can anyone believe that our important ideas are true? By always telling the truth, friends, family, and co-workers will believe what we say. We become respected and valued members of our families and communities.

When the Lifelong Guidelines of Truthfulness and Trustworthiness are present, a sense of community develops. Then, all members are less likely to be dishonest because each is genuinely cherished for who he/she is. When we belong, we have something to lose if we break the norms of our group. When we belong, there is no need to create some persona bigger and better than in real life.

---

* See *The Leadership Challenge* by James M. Kouzes and Barry Z. Posner, Jossey-Bass, Inc., San Francisco, CA, pp. 21-22.

Benefits to Telling the Truth

According to Dr. Abraham Kryger, DMD, MD, there are real benefits to telling the truth. Among them are: greater success/personal expertise, an increased sense of grounding/confidence, less anxiety/worry/guilt, increased ability to deal with crises/breakdowns, improved problem-solving abilities, improved interpersonal relationships, greater emotional health/control of one's emotions, increased ability to influence others, better sleep, better health, increased ability to think well/reason soundly, less need to control, good humor, and greater self-expression and self-satisfaction.* Do those sound like qualities you'd like in your life? Truth—and its dark twin, lies—drive world events, nudge the fall of civilizations, and sculpt our lives like no other character trait.

Consequences of Not Telling the Truth

There are also consequences that result from not telling the truth. Some of these consequences according to Dr. Kryger are: more frequent failures/frustrations in life, being distrusted by others, lack of self-esteem/self-confidence, dysfunctional interpersonal relationships, inability to self-correct, and stress of many kinds. Virtually all types of human stress can be traced to not telling the truth at one level or another.**

HOW DO YOU PRACTICE TRUTHFULNESS?

Always tell the truth! It was Mark Twain who said, "If you tell the truth, you don't have to remember anything."*** It is easier to remember what really happened, what words were really spoken than to try to recall a made-up story or a distorted version. You also practice the Lifelong Guideline of Truthfulness by telling the entire truth immediately rather than telling the story a little bit at a time until finally the whole truth emerges. Credibility is easy to destroy with just some simple untruths told in a moment to either create a better impression, deny involvement, or refuse to acknowledge that an incident has occurred. As a teacher, you're on stage; be honest with your class. Remember, what you *do* is more important than what you *say* you do!

Recognize That There are Barriers to Telling the Truth

When teaching students about the Lifelong Guideline of Truthfulness, we must admit to ourselves and to them that there are formidable barriers to telling the truth in our society. Perhaps the biggest is refusing to accept that it is possible to tell the truth. A widespread but false belief held by many is that it isn't humanly possible to tell the truth. That is just a handy excuse that absolves us of the need to question our lack of truthfulness.

---

* *Benefits of Telling the Truth* by Dr. Abraham Kryger, DMD, MD http//www.wellnessmd.com/tellingtruth.html
** The lie detector test is based on physiological evidence of the body's reaction to lying—more rapid pulse and rise in blood pressure. Also see *The Orman Health Letter* published monthly by TRO Productions, Inc., Baltimore, MD, and http://www.wellnessmd.com/tellingtruth.html
*** Mark Twain, *Notebook, 1984.*

A second powerful barrier is fear of consequences of telling the truth. For example, fear the boss will fire us, someone close to us will lose respect for us, or people will retaliate for our having challenged their belief system.*

Practice, Practice

Have students share stories and repeat information as accurately as possible. Teach them to write terms and facts on paper so they can refer to them if needed. Show them the importance of being willing to recheck any data that seem to lack credibility by going back to the source of the information. Teach students many problem-solving strategies; when logical, natural choices are available, a student is less likely to lie. Avoid setting a trap for a student as when you already know the answer but ask the question anyway. All you accomplish is "catching" him/her in a falsehood. Why not "catch" someone when telling the truth and thus reinforce the desired, rather than the negative, behavior.

Seek Work Places and Friendships That Value Truthfulness

Telling the truth isn't always easy. Often, telling parents, friends, the boss, and co-workers the truth brings unpleasant consequences. However, telling a lie under these circumstances almost always has far-reaching consequences, too often of greater severity than if we simply spoke the truth up front and accepted the consequences, as unpleasant as they might be. Once we're caught lying, people lose faith and confidence in us. In work relationships and with friends, this is devastating.

One final caution. Sometimes people in power will ask for our "honest" opinion about plans, choices, and situations. If the level of trust in that business or organization is high, we feel comfortable in sharing our thoughts. If it's low, our risk is much greater, particularly if our true beliefs are not what the person in power wants to hear. Rather than be part of a lie that will have unwanted consequences for us and others, we should look for work settings where truthfulness is truly valued. During interviews, ask questions that will reveal the level of truthfulness in that culture. By gathering as much information as possible before accepting a position, we can make more informed decisions.

WHAT DOES TRUTHFULNESS LOOK LIKE IN THE REAL WORLD?
We

- State accurate figures to the Internal Revenue Service on our yearly income tax forms
- Admit to being a participant in misdeeds
- Say "No!" when we have no time to add anything more to our calendar

* *Benefits of Telling the Truth* by Dr. Abraham Kryger, DMD, MD http//www.wellnessmd.com/tellingtruth.html

- Return money for items overcharged at the store

- Return extra items from the grocery bag that we weren't charged for

- Turn in to the "lost and found" or police station money or items that don't belong to us

- Give honest reasons for absences and lateness

- Report accurate losses to insurance companies

- Refuse to gossip about other people and situations

- Take responsibility for traffic tickets and vehicular violations

WHAT DOES TRUTHFULNESS LOOK LIKE IN SCHOOL?

Staff

- Offer genuine feelings and sincere opinions at staff meetings without being judgmental of others' offerings

- Share precise observations of incidents

- Provide accurate reasons for being late or not showing up

- Abide by contractual agreements

- Ignore rumors and verify the truth

- Support children and co-workers when they make "learning" mistakes

- Eliminate back-stabbing and put-downs in the teachers' room and throughout the school

Students

- Explain their own misbehavior

- Turn in found money and belongings so the true owner can be found

- Tell the teacher "I forgot . . . " or "I did . . . " instead of making up a story

- Learn tact

- Verify information about other people and not spread rumors or hurtful stories

INQUIRIES TO DEVELOP TRUTHFULNESS

Whole Group Inquiries

- Choose a tune that you know (e.g., "Twinkle, Twinkle, Little Star" or "Row, Row, Row Your Boat") and write two or more verses with new lyrics about the importance of telling the truth. Sing the song for another class at your school.

- Create a class T-chart with the title of "Truthfulness." Write these headings for the three columns: Looks Like, Sounds Like, and Feels Like. Brainstorm words and phrases with the class for each category. Then create a second Truthfulness chart and list words/phrases for what it does not look like, sound like, or feel like.

Small Group/Individual Inquiries

- Ask one of your teachers or the principal to share a childhood "life" story about when he/she told a lie, got into trouble, and learned a lesson. Find out what lesson he/she learned. Be prepared to share the lesson.

- Listen to/Read the book *Little Red Ridinghood* by Trina Schart Hyman. In your own words, explain whether or not you would have believed the wolf. Brainstorm two or more questions you think Little Red Ridinghood should have asked the wolf before believing everything he told her. Share with a partner.

- Think about the actions on the list below. Discuss with your learning club which actions you feel show honesty and which ones show dishonesty. Decide if all the members can agree.

  — You take a dollar bill from a classmate's desk.
  — You choose an ice cream bar in the school cafeteria and pay for it.
  — On the way to school, you find a wallet. Looking inside, you see many dollar bills and an identification card. Once you arrive at school, you give the wallet to the school secretary.
  — On the way to school, you find a wallet, pocket the money, and then toss the wallet into a trash can. At lunch, you offer to buy all of your classmates ice cream.
  — Your friend has some Pokemon cards. When he/she isn't looking, you take them and put them in your backpack.
  — The teacher is giving a math test. Even though you have studied, there are three number facts that you don't know. During the test, you peek at a neighbor's paper and copythe answers.

- Listen to the story *The Boy Who Cried Wolf.* Choose three or more positive ways the boy could have received attention when he was lonely. Create a puppet for each of the main characters and practice retelling the story at least five times, or until you remember the words with ease. Visit another classroom and perform the story. Invite the audience to share the morals (lessons) of the story.

- Construct or design a visual representation (such as diorama, mobile, collage, illustration) of people to whom you would feel safe telling the truth. Share it with an adult in your school.

- Read *Sam, Bangs and Moonshine* by Evelyn Ness. Choose two examples of "moonshine" from the story and explain to your learning club how you knew the words were not the truth. Write two statements, one "moonshine," one real. Ask 10 classmates to identify the true statement and the "moonshine" one. Share your results with a partner.

- Reflect how you feel about telling the truth in words and/or pictures or as a PMI chart (columns for ideas that are Plus, Minus, and Interesting).

- Play the Pantomime Game. Identify and list six or more emotions such as love, joy, remorse, sadness, disgust, happiness, sorrow, fear, or fright. Write each one on its own index card. Ask one person in your learning club to choose a card, not to look at the word that is written on it, and give it to you. Act out the feeling and invite others to guess it.

- Identify five or more quotations containing the word "truth" or "truthfulness." Write a fable (a short story, often told with animal characters, intended to teach a moral lesson) about truth. Choose one of the quotations as the moral of the story. Read it to a friend.

- Discuss the following questions with your learning club. Are there situations in which lies are acceptable? What should you do if you catch someone telling a lie? How do you get people to believe you after you lied? Does the truth ever change? Is there such a thing as a "good" lie? Tape record your discussion and give the tape to the teacher. Also, write some of your reflections in your journal.

- Investigate two or more famous people or leaders from the business world who have lied to the public and only admitted wrongdoing after they were caught. Research two or more famous people or company executives who told the truth even when they knew it might damage their image/business. Write a news report comparing and contrasting the reactions of the public to the two different situations. Tape record your discussion and give the tape to the teacher.

- Research the tobacco industry's relationship with the public about the dangers of smoking. Investigate both sides of the story, that of cigarette makers and of cigarette smokers. Take a position—tobacco industry representative or smoker with serious medical problems such as cancer or emphysema. Debate your position with a classmate representing the opposite view.

SIGNS OF SUCCESS

Congratulations! Students are showing signs of Truthfulness when they

- Tell the truth even when the consequences may be harsh

- Explain their true feelings to family, friends, and coworkers

- Find something and look for the rightful owner

- Distinguish right actions from wrong

- Listen to their conscience telling them what is right

- Correct misinformation and stop gossip from spreading

- Tell the truth with tact

Keep trying! Students need more practice when they

- Lie to avoid trouble

- Make up stories and pretend they're the truth

- Tell the truth only when it benefits their situations

- Bend the facts or exaggerate to make themselves sound "bigger and better" than life

- Realize they can't remember what version of a story they have told before

- Tell lies that hurt their family, friends, and/or fellow students

- Use a person's color, religion, or beliefs as a measure of his/her true worth

LITERATURE LINK ~ TRUTHFULNESS

Primary Grades

Adventures of Pinocchio, The	Collodi, Carlo
Berenstain Bears and the Truth, The	Berenstain, J. and S.
Emperor's New Clothes	Burton, Virginia Lee
Lilly's Purple Plastic Purse	Henkes, Kevin
Little Red Riding Hood	Hyman, Trina Schart
Polar Express, The	VanAllsberg, Chris
Sam, Bangs and Moonshine	Ness, Evelyn
Tasty Taffy Tale and Super-Stretching the Truth: A Book about Honesty, The	Scieszka, Jon
Three Sacks of Truth	Kimmel, Eric A.
True Story of the Three Little Pigs, The	Scieszka, Jon

Intermediate Grades

Apple Island: Or the Truth About Teachers	Evans, Douglas
Dear Mr. Henshaw	Cleary, Beverly
Josefina Saves the Day	Tripp, Valerie
Lies, Deception, and Truth	Weiss, Ann E.
Lily's Crossing	Giff, Patricia Reilly
Nothing But the Truth: A Documentary Novel	Avi
Ring of Truth, The	Bateman, Teresa
Shiloh	Naylor, Phyllis
Terpin	Seidler, Tor
Truth About Mary Rose, The	Sachs, Marilyn
Truth About Stacey, The	Martin, Ann M.
Whoppers: Tall Tales & Other Lies	Schwartz, Alvin

Middle School and High School

Black Water	Bunting, Eve
First Honest Book About Lies, The	Kincher, Jonni
Nothing But the Truth	Avi
Speak	Anderson, Laurie Halse

Teacher's Resource

Teaching Your Kids About Truth and Consequences:
  Helping Them Make the Connection Between
  Choices and Results
	Hahn, Daniel

Date _____

Dear Family,

Today we begin our investigation of another important Lifelong Guideline by focusing on …

~Truthfulness~

According to many parenting books, most young children tell the truth all of the time. It is just not in their nature to lie—they tell things as they see them. However, as children grow older and begin to discern the consequences for actions and observe the reactions of some adults, they may decide to lie believing that it's the easier course to take.

During the next few weeks, our class will be sharing thoughts on some of these topics:

- Why do people lie?

- When do people lie?

- What are short- and long-term consequences of lying?

- How do I determine what choices I have?

- What is good about the truth?

If you are interested in pursuing this topic further with your child, visit the local library and check out a book or two on the topic. A few excellent books to consider include:

Children's titles

- *Sam, Bangs and Moonshine* by Evelyn Ness

- *The Adventure of Pinocchio* by Carlo Collasi

- *Whoppers: Tall Tales and Other Lies* by Alvin Schwartz

Adult title

- *Teaching Your Kids About Truth and Consequences: Help Them Make the Connections Between Choices and Results* by Daniel Hahn

Sincerely,

_____

Your Child's Teacher

Active Listening

"LISTEN WITH YOUR HEAD AND HEART, THEN TALK."

active *adj* **1** characterized by action rather than by contemplation or speculation
listening *v* **1** to hear something with thoughtful attention: give consideration

Active Listening: To listen with the intention of understanding what the speaker means to communicate

WHAT IS ACTIVE LISTENING?

Hearing is an inactive, involuntary process that occurs when the ears pick up sound waves being transmitted by some kind of vibration and forward them to the brain. Listening, however, is an active, voluntary process which includes recognizing, understanding, and correctly interpreting messages received. Listening requires participation, patience, energy, and the intention to "get it"—not just what the speaker said but what he/she intended to communicate.

To actively listen, the brain must be physiologically active. Not only must it perceive the sounds correctly but it must also compare words to emotional nuances for consistency, then convert words into images that can be analyzed, compared, and stored for future reference. This is an extremely active process requiring neural wiring that one out of four students haven't developed by the time they start school.* However, such wiring can easily be developed in the classroom. For more information, contact Lindamood-Bell Learning Processes Center, San Luis Obispo, California, 800/233-1819.

Most people listen passively. That means the sound acts on them—enters their ears—but they don't actively and consciously participate in the process; they don't exert effort in order to listen and attend to what they are hearing. An example is listening to a music tape or book tape while driving or a CD while cleaning the house. In contrast, active listening is more complex than passive listening because it demands that we listen with our eyes, ears, heart, and undivided attention as

---

* Not surprisingly, the more hours spent in front of a television, the less time spent developing language. See *Visualizing and Verbalizing for Improved Language Comprehension* by Nanci Bell, p. 21.

YOU

EAR

EYES

UNDIVIDED
ATTENTION

HEART

TRIBES: A New Way of Learning by Jeanne Gibbs, p. 93

illustrated in the TANG,* a Chinese character for "to listen."* An active listener not only hears but also pays close attention, focusing on the words, ideas, and emotions of the speaker.

The active listener is more than a receiver. In many ways, he assists the speaker to deliver his message by providing encouragement, such as attentive body posture, full eye contact, positive body signals, and multi-tiered acknowledgements, such as "Mmm; uhuh; yes; I understand; I agree; yes, interesting; I heard something about that yesterday . . . tell me more." The listener is saying to the speaker, "I understand. Your ideas and message are important to me and to others in the room. I will listen while you communicate with me and then I will ask questions if I disagree or don't understand. Above all, I respect your opinions and your right to speak."

WHY PRACTICE ACTIVE LISTENING?

Active listening is critical because it is the doorway to understanding. Whether in social settings, at work, or with family and friends, not "getting it" can cause serious problems. At best, it is embarrassing and makes us feel like outsiders. All too often it is also costly in terms of our relationships with others and expensive for our employers when we misinterpret instructions. Furthermore, it is difficult to be successful in life if we are not taking in accurate information about the world and how it works.

---

* For a wonderful discussion of the meaning of the Chinese symbol for "to listen," see *TRIBES: A New Way of Learning and Being Together* by Jeanne Gibbs, 1999, pp. 93-94 . The book also provides many ready-to-go activities for students to practice the Lifelong Guideline of Active Listening. See also *ITI: The Model* by Susan Kovalik, 1997, 1994 edition, pp. 26-27.

On a daily basis, our sense of hearing collects a wide range of information that we need to protect ourselves and to enhance our problem solving. What might happen, for instance, if a jogger, wearing head phones and listening to music, is crossing the street against the walk sign and can't hear a persistent honking horn? Or, if a worried parent is unable to focus on the doctor's directions for the baby's medicine and care? Wouldn't you feel sad if you missed your plane to Disney World because you didn't hear the final boarding call? Since one of the ways we stay safe and make informed decisions includes listening to sounds collected from the real world, isn't it common sense to concentrate on what we hear?

Unlike reading, we can't regulate the pace of someone else's speech, replaying it again to check an unfamiliar word. Thus, we may miss important information reported to us and respond in a peculiar way. To immediately understand what we hear, it's crucial that we perfect the skill of listening well. We can only talk intelligently about a topic when we can grasp what is said to us. To be able to listen well gives us confidence when communicating with others. Listening in the real world is an everyday skill.

Spotlight on Brain Research.
Most educators don't realize that active listening—turning words into mental images that can be processed and stored in short- and long-term memory—requires neural wiring that over 25 percent of the population does not have or has not developed sufficiently to succeed in school. Nanci Bell, author of *Visualizing and Verbalizing for Improved Language Comprehension*, describes typical symptoms of oral language processing difficulty, any one of which would increase difficulty and frustration in learning as well as in social settings. Unfortunately, most people who have difficulty with language processing display more than one of these symptoms. It is a sobering list:*

1. *Individuals may frequently not understand jokes.* Language humor depends on imagery, whereas sight humor (pie in face) does not and is more easily understood. Almost everyone gets sight gags but not everyone gets language-based humor.

2. *Individuals may not understand concepts of cause and effect.* To process cause and effect relationships you must be able to process a gestalt from which to judge an effect.

3. *Individuals may not respond to explanations given in language.* If a student's performance needs correcting, a "talking to" may be only partially understood or not understood at all because the student is connecting to only a part of the oral explanation.

4. *Individuals may ask and re-ask questions that have already been answered.* The individual hears the answer but is unable to process and connect to the given information and will therefore ask the same question again, only phrased differently. Such individuals are often not aware that they are asking the same question over and over, only with modified language.

5. *Individuals may not grasp the main idea or inferences from television shows or movies, although they may get a few details.* The individual may seem to miss concepts or nuances from movies they've seen. In discussions with them, they don't interpret the movie or story sequence well.

---

* See *Visualizing and Verbalizing for Improved Language Comprehension* by Nanci Bell, Gander Publishing, Inc., Palo Alto, CA, 1991, page 21. Available through Books For Educators, Inc. at www.books4educ.com or by calling 888/777-9827.

6. *Individuals may lose attention quickly in conversation or lectures.* Students who are unable to connect to the gestalt of language will find that in a few minutes, often less, they are "lost" and may drift away mentally and/or physically.

7. *Individuals may have weakness in auditory memory and in following directions.* These symptoms may be severe and labeled as aphasia . . . [or] be subtle weaknesses that cause others to suspect lack of intelligence or lack of motivation. In fact, individuals with these symptoms will frequently doubt their intelligence.

Ms. Bell also points to a link between listening difficulties and oral language expression:

"The oral language comprehension weakness is often accompanied by an oral language expression weakness. Individuals experience difficulty organizing their verbalizing and expressing themselves easily and fluently or they are verbal but scattered, relating information out of sequence. For example, a student on academic probation, with severely impaired auditory and reading comprehension, frequently interjected irrelevant comments in conversation. His comments were disjointed both unto themselves and to the topic. Consequently, he was often viewed as mentally disabled."*

Every teacher can list students who have exhibited these frustrating symptoms. There is more to being an active listener than most people realize.

HOW DO YOU PRACTICE ACTIVE LISTENING?

If these listening difficulties sound familiar, you owe it to yourself and your students to read Nanci Bell's book. Use it as a teacher's manual with your entire class every day for 30 minutes for at least six weeks. You'll be astounded at the transformation in academic capability of individual students and the class as a whole.

Once the necessary neural wiring is in place, more traditional classroom strategies for teaching students to pay closer attention, try harder, focus more, and so forth, can be used with greater success.

Proficient listening requires the neural wiring to process language plus the social skills our society has come to expect of listeners. There are many ways for students to practice these social-based listening techniques.

Using the Chinese Symbol for Listening

The Chinese symbol which depicts "to listen" as an act involving ears, eyes, heart, and undivided attention is a good place to start. It offers a handy visual and expands the meaning of the verb "to listen." In addition, teach children that the intention to "get" what the speaker intends to communicate is a critical element. Listening with intention helps the listener "hear" with an open mind and rid him/herself of any prejudicial notions that would corrupt the speaker's message. Many poor listeners get so involved in the speaker's style of delivery they miss the message. Listening with ears, eyes, heart, undivided attention, and with the intention to receive the intended message are keys to active listening.

---

* See page XXI, *Visualizing and Verbalizing for Improved Language Comprehension* by Nanci Bell, 1991, Gander Publishing, Inc., Palo Alto, CA.

Social Expectations

In Western culture, certain behaviors are expected of a good listener, including "attending skills" and "follow-up skills." Attending skills include not interrupting the speaker, listening for what he/she intends to say rather than what we want or think he/she will say, holding eye contact, using open body language, and offering some encouraging responses ("Wow!" "Then what happened?" "Really?" "I understand") and actions (nodding, smiling, and so forth).

Personal Behaviors

To form a more accurate impression of a speaker's intended message, we must pay constant, careful attention. When we lose our concentration, we also lose much of the information. There are a number of ways to help ourselves focus on listening and collecting information.

- Limit distractions. Change places to promote concentration.

- Look at the speaker. Observe body language (open versus closed), listen to the tone of voice (pitch, quality, and timbre), and note facial expressions as clues to emotions. In many instances, the medium is the message—most of the message is communicated non-verbally.*

- Focus your attention on the meaning of words used; use signals (head nodding, smiles) to indicate you understand.

- Create pictures in your mind of what you're hearing.

- Visualize how this information fits with what you already know and what it means to you. Expect to act upon what you are hearing.

WHAT DOES ACTIVE LISTENING LOOK LIKE IN THE REAL WORLD?
We

- Visit doctors who listen to our symptoms

- Retain lawyers who listen to our problems

- Attend concerts, plays, movies, and shows

- Listen to guest lecturers and ask pertinent questions

- Focus on what family members are sharing

- Listen carefully to new tax laws explained by our accountant

---

* "The Importance of Effective Communication," Northeastern University, College of Business Administration, October, 1999. http://www.cba.neu.edu/~ewertheim/inter/commun.htm

- Learn how to operate the computer, VCR, and the newest technical wizardry from our children

- Evaluate politicians' speeches and promises

- Pay attention when customers return broken, damaged, or unsatisfactory merchandise

- Offer solace by being present and quiet while others share their tales of sorrow or distress

- Discuss problem-solving strategies with others who care

- Watch news programs and evaluate the information for accuracy, helpfulness, and problem-solving opportunities

- Stop to listen when adults and children share ideas, concerns, and problems with us

WHAT DOES ACTIVE LISTENING LOOK LIKE IN SCHOOL?
Staff

- Pay attention during faculty meetings, in-service presentations, and conferences

- Put paperwork/materials down while a student is talking to us

- Arrange conferences for all parents/guardians and listening for input before providing output

- Look at other school community members when they talk to us

- Respond to information by commenting and asking questions

- Share thoughts and feelings yet remain open to other ideas

Students

- Wait patiently while another student gives his/her side of the story

- Use active listening skills and strategies during direct instruction time

- Listen to the story being read

- Hear and follow directions and procedures

- Use attentive behaviors during class meetings, community circles, learning-club discussions, and other collaborative activities

- Ask thoughtful questions of a guest speaker or expert presenter

- Follow agreed upon procedures during performances and shows (such as sitting still, remaining silent, listening to the words, songs, or speeches, and showing appreciation by applauding when appropriate)

INQUIRIES TO DEVELOP ACTIVE LISTENING

Whole Class Inquiries

- Listen to the story *Listening Walk* by Paul Showers. Take a listening walk with your class. Record with drawings or words five or more sounds you hear on the walk. Compare sounds with a classmate. Count how many you both have that are the same and how many sounds are different. Share which sound from the walk is your favorite.

- Record a variety of sounds found in your house or school. Play these sounds for your class and have them try to identify each one. (Hint: Some sounds to tape include a squeaky door opening or closing, popping a soda can, opening a can using the electric can opener, different washing machine cycles, sawing a board, chalk on a blackboard, cafeteria trays being stacked, etc.)

- Listen to three different kinds of music. Choose from classical, jazz, country/western, new age, disco, reggae, Celtic, and rock and roll. Take three pieces of drawing paper and write the categories of these selected songs at the top of the sheet, one to a page. Illustrate your feelings for each of the separate selections on the appropriate paper. Share the results with your classmates.

Small Group/Individual Inquiries

- Memorize two favorite nursery rhymes. Illustrate each one using crayon and paper. Teach them to a friend and recite them for your class. Ask classmates to name rhyming words they heard.

- Play a guessing game. Record some sounds from around the house, e.g., door opening, computer game, mechanical toy, washing machine cycles. Keep a list of each sound's source as you record it. Play the tape for your learning club and ask them to identify the sounds.

- Design a symbol or picture to represent the Lifelong Guideline of Active Listening. Label it and write a descriptive sentence explaining your reasons for choosing the symbol you did. Share and use the sign for one week with your learning club. Discuss the sign's effectiveness with your group members.

- Sing and demonstrate the sign language for "active listening" whenever those words occur in the song "Five Things" (*Spread Your Wings* by Jeff Pedersen).

- Discuss the miscommunication problems that occur in the story *The Cat Who Wore a Pot on Her Head* by Jan Slepian. [Teachers: Substitute appropriate titles for your students.]

- Dramatize six different audience behaviors. Invite the class to label these actions as non-active listening or active listening.

- Create a poster that illustrates at least two skills needed for active listening. Display your poster outside the classroom door or at another visible location.

- Videotape some of the experts who talk to your class. Write four questions about active listening that can be answered by watching and listening to the tape. Provide a copy of the questions for viewers. Show the videotape and ask them to write or draw their answers. Provide the correct answers after the video is completed and allow them to check their work for accuracy.

- Experience non-active listening with a partner by choosing a topic that you feel comfortable talking about. Ask your partner to demonstrate non-active listening skills while you talk for thirty seconds on the topic. Next, using a second topic, repeat this process but ask your partner to demonstrate active listening skills as you share. Then, reverse roles. Repeat the exercise (using similar topics). Share your reactions as a speaker when your listener was and was not using active listening. Create a chart comparing three or more attributes of non-active listening to those of active listening.

- Create an active listening self-evaluation form that you and your classmates can use to evaluate yourselves on a regular basis. Include four or more attributes of an active listener. Discuss your progress with an adult in your school.

SIGNS OF SUCCESS

Congratulations! Students are showing signs of Active Listening when they

- Restate the speaker's ideas showing a high recall rate

- Focus on the speaker, remain silent, ask questions at the proper time, demonstrate appropriate body language, and use encouraging responses

- Pay attention, especially when there are distracting elements in the room

- Stop whatever they are doing to listen to someone share a story or situation

- Actively listen in a variety of situations, such as with a friend or acquaintance sharing a problem or during direct instruction, individual/group presentations, a news broadcast, fine arts performance, or formal lecture

Keep trying! Students need more practice when they

- Interrupt the speaker

- Ignore the person who is talking

- Continue working on something else while someone is talking to them

- Use unfriendly body language (signs, gestures, facial distortions)

- Refuse to make eye contact with the speaker

- Cannot list or state the important points

- Overlook the speaker's feelings

- Create a disruption while someone is speaking

- Expect everyone to listen to them but don't listen in return

- Act rudely or don't pay attention during a performance or presentation

Literature Link ～ Active Listening

Primary Grades

Good Day for Listening, A	King, Mary Ellen
Hullabaloo ABC, The	Cleary, Beverly
I Can Hear the Sun: A Modern Myth	Polacco, Patricia
Listen, Buddy	Lester, H. and L. Munsinger
Listen to Me	Neasi, Barbara J.
Listening Walk	Showers, Paul
Listening with Zachary	Slater, Teddy
Shrinking of Treehorn, The	Heide, Florence Parry
Silver Morning	Pearson, Susan
Story of Danny Three Times, The	Leibel, Estrin
Who's Listening?	Armstrong, Beverly

Intermediate Grades

Bizarre and Beautiful Ears	Santa Fe Writers' Group
Blue Willow	Conrad, Pamela
Brother Eagle, Sister Sky	Jeffers, Susan
Cheshire Moon	Butts, Nancy
Deafness	Taylor, Barbara
Ears: Adaptation for Survival	Savage, Stephen
Gabby	Cosgrove, Stephen
Gluskabe and the Four Wishes	retold by Bruchac, Joseph
Listening for Leroy	Hearne, Betsy
Listening to Crickets: A Story About Rachel Carson	Ransom, Candace F.
One TV Blasting and a Pig Outdoors	Abbot, D. and H. Kisor
Tuck Triumphant	Taylor, Theodore
Yang the Youngest and His Terrible Ear	Namioka, Lensey

Middle School and High School

Dogwolf	Carter, Alden R.
Nothing But the Truth: *A Documentary Novel*	Avi
Speak	Anderson, Laurie Halse

Teacher's Resources

How to Talk So Kids Will Listen and *Listen So Kids Will Talk*	Faber, A. and E. Mazlish
Visualizing and Verbalizing for Improved *Language Comprehension*	Bell, Nanci

Date _____

Dear Family,

The Lifelong Guidelines are the behavior guidelines that our class community will be practicing this year. These five guidelines are based upon a respect for others and self and, when faithfully followed, provide for a safe environment in which learning can take place. The next guideline that our group will be focusing on is

~ Active Listening ~

Some of the ways that we can explore the Lifelong Guideline of Active listening include:

- Practicing note-taking skills

- Listening to different forms of music

- Listing the characteristics of an active listener

- Attending an in-school or community performance to practice active listening skills

In addition to modeling Active Listening for your child, there are ways that parents can help to improve their children's listening skills. You can support your child by:

- Reading aloud increasingly longer stories, starting with picture books and working up to chapter books (one or two chapters a day) and asking him/her to share what pictures come to mind as the story progresses

- Asking him/her to retell and evaluate TV programs (including some news segments)

- Providing opportunities for your child to remember and follow increasingly difficult, multi-step instructions

- Identifying nature sounds during a walk in the woods, a romp in the field, or while strolling along the beach

Please let us know of any other ideas that have worked for you. We will include them in a future letter to families or in a class newsletter.

Sincerely,

_____

Your child's teacher

No Put-Downs

"CARE ABOUT OTHERS."

no put-downs *v* **1a:** not to degrade   **b:** not to disparage or belittle
c: not to disapprove or criticize   **d:** not to humiliate or squelch

No Put-Downs: Not to use words, actions, and/or body language to degrade, humiliate, or dishonor others

WHAT ARE PUT-DOWNS?

Put-downs are words and body language that imply, "I am better than you. I have more money than you, I am smarter than you, or I have more options than you." The objective is to elevate the speaker's social standing and power. By creating a laugh at someone else's expense, the speaker gains power in the situation by controlling the behavior of others and undermining relationships among those in the audience and with the targeted person. Put-downs are also a way of avoiding the real issues of the moment. They often mask unconscious feelings of jealousy, anger, fear, or inadequacy. Whether from one person or a group, the goal of put-downs is always the same—humiliation, power, control, and increased social status.

The body language of put-downs—actions and body movements, such as rolling the eyes, tapping the forehead, caricaturing, and so forth—are honed to an art form in sitcoms and other popular media in our society. They are every bit as powerful as words.

Sometimes put-downs affect us more deeply than usual. For example, when they're spoken by people we like and trust or by people we want to like us, the results are devastating. We feel betrayed. If the people whose opinion we so value express something negative about us, then it must really be so. Also, if the comments are aimed at a sensitive area (e.g., physical changes during puberty, being overweight or underweight, being an immigrant with beginning English skills, and so forth), students often feel shame about something over which they have little or no control. Similarly, when we receive put-downs in front of our peers, the humiliation and shame deepen as we lose face.

WHY PRACTICE NO PUT-DOWNS?

Put-downs among adults produce a lack of trust which is extremely detrimental to an educational agency, especially when it trickles down to influence students' attitudes and behaviors. If a staff is to pursue efforts to improve the school program, put-downs must be eliminated.

Also, to be open to learning is to be vulnerable. We're open to snickers when we make mistakes or admit we can't answer a question. Every student should be able to approach new opportunities and learning experiences without dreading verbal abuse.

When we refuse to allow put-downs in the classroom, we're teaching respect for all people, ideas, and situations. We're building a positive emotional climate in our classroom so that our students feel comfortable enough to risk an answer, offer a thought, and try some new skill without worrying about mocking remarks or gestures. This is particularly important for students in the middle position of sibling birth order whose skills and knowledge can't match the older sibling but who don't have the safety of "being the baby." Prohibiting the use of disparaging remarks is akin to constructing an invisible shield that protects and nurtures.

HOW DO YOU PRACTICE IT?

To change a negative habit to a more positive one, we first must recognize the negative behavior that needs to change. And, because put-downs are so pervasive in our mass media and society, we must first teach students to recognize put-downs and become sensitive to their effects. Many students look on the word plays of put-downs as a form of humor, overlooking that it's at the expense of others.

Next, we must create an action plan to eliminate put-downs and encourage respect for others.

Recognizing the Need to Change. Select a video clip ripe with put-downs. Have your students identify and count the put-downs he/she hears and sees. Discuss with your students how they would feel if they were on the receiving end of these put-downs. Next, focus on comments heard in the classroom and school common areas. Ask your students to observe the participants. Who is handing out the put-downs? Who is the brunt of the put-downs? Who has power and social position and who doesn't? Refer to Glasser's needs list: belonging, power, fun, and freedom.* Which of these fundamental human needs is the speaker missing? If put-downs occur in your classroom, what's missing from your classroom environment? Look for patterns that demand change and then, with your students' help, create an action plan.

The Importance of Modeling. Creating an environment free of put-downs requires constant modeling by all adults. The entire school staff (administrators, teachers, aides, custodial workers, cafeteria staff, and parent volunteers) need to understand their positions as role models for students. It

---

* See *Choice Theory: A New Psychology of Personal Freedom* by William Glasser MD, HarperPerennial, New York, 1998, pp. 31-41.

cannot be a "Do as I say but not as I do" atmosphere. Post the Lifelong Guidelines and the LIFESKILLS around the school for all to see and follow. Initiate discussions about the harmful effects of put-downs. If a put-down is heard, deal with it immediately using a calm, rational manner before the situation escalates.

Taking Responsibility for Eliminating Put-Downs. Everyone plays a part in eliminating put-downs. To begin cleansing your classroom of put-downs, eliminate the put-down banter that is passed off as humor. Recall a comment that had dual interpretations and then the speaker quickly said, "Just kidding!"—but you never knew the intent for sure. As the saying goes, "Many a true word is said in jest."

Second, agree on a "cancel" signal. Whenever someone says a put-down, other family members simply say, "Cancel." The hurt is canceled, the "power play" is canceled.

Practicing the Lifelong Guideline of No Put-Downs requires a concerted effort from all members of the school community. Otherwise, the realization of a caring, risk-taking, nurturing, fellowship of learners has little chance for success.

WHAT DOES NO PUT-DOWNS LOOK LIKE IN THE REAL WORLD?

We

- Offer constructive criticism without the addition of demeaning terms

- Refrain from racial slurs, disparaging remarks about ethnic groups, and negative comments about religious views that differ from our own

- Support learners by providing encouragement and assistance until they are successful

- Provide emotional support for others who receive put-downs

- Decry the use of put-downs from TV programming, movie producers, politicians, and others in the public arena

- Refuse to become victims and instead empower ourselves to be strong enough to ignore put-downs

- Act professionally; ban the put-down mentality from conferences, meetings, and the work place

- Nurture family members by supporting their learning experiences

WHAT DOES NO PUT-DOWNS LOOK LIKE AT SCHOOL?

Staff

- Use humor that does not "bite" or leave the listener wondering exactly what your message was

- Remind a colleague or student of the "No Put-Down" policy

- Teach students ways to counteract the use of put-downs

- Ensure that all members of the school community are trained in the "No Put-Down" policy

- Build a strong sense of community where everyone feels special, wanted, and a part of the group

- Eliminate the use of put-downs in our presence

- Value each person—adult and student—as an individual and a "work in progress"

Students

- Identify words and phrases that are put-downs and replace them with statements of respect (terms that are positive and affirm the self-worth of other individuals)

- Provide encouragement for classmates practicing new skills

- Refuse to give others power by believing the put-downs they deliver

- Acknowledge that every individual has unique gifts and talents that make for a well-rounded community

- Explain the reasons behind the "No Put-Downs" policy to visitors and guests

INQUIRIES TO DEVELOP NO PUT-DOWNS

Whole Class Inquiries

- Draw a picture of a smiling face. Listen to your teacher read *Chrysanthemum* by Kevin Henkes. Demonstrate recognition of a put-down by tearing off a portion of the face every time you hear a put-down in the story. Replace one piece each time you hear a statement of respect.
OPTION TWO: Listen to your teacher read the story of *Chrysanthemum*. Every time you hear a put-down, point your thumb down. Each time you hear a statement of respect,

point your thumb up. With a partner, practice some strategies to use the next time someone zaps you with a put-down.

- Watch a segment of a Charlie Brown movie. Tally the number of put-downs that are used. Watch the segment again and determine which characters are using the put-downs and which characters are receiving them. Explain to a partner why you think a writer would use put-downs in a story.

Small Group/Individual Inquiries

- Listen to the stor, *The Ugly Duckling* by Hans Christian Anderson. Write a short note to the duckling sharing your thoughts on his appearance before he became a swan. Show your note to another person to see if you have no put-downs.

- Think about saying, "You can't tell a book by it's cover." Discuss with your learning club what this quotation might mean. Visit the school library and observe the different book covers. Choose two favorite books that have unattractive covers. Check out the books, read both stories and design a colorful, exciting bookmark for each one. Recommend the books to a friend and offer the bookmarks as a preview of the stories.

- Create a skit (short play) of five minutes or less to teach about the hurtfulness of using put-downs. Invite other learning-club members to play parts. Use puppets, stuffed animals or action dolls to tell the story. Include the song, "No Put-Downs" (*Spread Your Wings*, Jeff Pederson). Practice your skit at least three times. Present your play for the rest of the class.

- Design an appreciation card for someone in your class. Create an attractive cover on colored construction paper. Write the appreciation on the inside and sign your name. Read and give it to him/her during community circle or class meeting time.

- List four or more put-downs you have used. Reflect on why you said those words. Illustrate your list of put-downs with a face that shows how you would feel if someone said those words to you. Place the paper in the class "No Put-Downs" box. When the box is full, take the box (you, your teacher, and classmates) to the school yard; have a burial ceremony for the put-downs and bury the box in the ground. After you return to the classroom, write four statements of respect that you will practice using for the next week.

- Interview an adult about the use of put-downs at their workplace. Ask such questions as: Why do you think people use put-downs at work? What are some signs that your employer treats you with respect? How does your boss discourage or encourage the use of put-downs? Are there some people that seem to be the targets for put-downs? In what ways does the use of put-downs at work affect you? Afterward, write two or three paragraphs about what you learned and share them with your class.

- Learn to "sign" the phrase, "No Put-Downs." Practice until you can repeat it from memory. Teach the class to sign the phrase and show them when to do it during the singing of "Don't Put Me Down" (*Spread Your Wings*, Jeff Pedersen). Or, OPTION TWO: Learn the signing for "Don't Laugh at Me" (*Wish You Were Here*, Mark Wills).

- Design a brochure explaining the Lifelong Guideline of No Put-Downs. Add graphics to illustrate this policy. Make copies of the pamphlet available for visitors/new families so that they will understand this guideline.

- Write a skit showing a situation in which put-downs are used. Rewrite the skit eliminating put-downs and inserting statements of respect. With a partner, perform the skit both ways for your classmates. Ask them to brainstorm other statements of respect that would be appropriate for another version of the skit.

- Study commercials and advertisements for subtle forms of put-downs against males or females. OPTION ONE: Choose one example and compose a letter addressing the issue. Educate the agency about the personal and emotional hurts caused by the use of put-downs. Send the letter to the company.
  OPTION TWO: Create a new commercial/ad that sells the product or service without the use of put-downs. Perform your version for the class.

- Read the following quotation, "No one can make you feel inferior without your consent" by Eleanor Roosevelt. Write a paragraph about what this quotation means to you, explain your feelings and experiences. Share your thoughts with your teacher.

SIGNS OF SUCCESS

Congratulations! Students are showing signs of not using Put-Downs when they

- Compliment others' accomplishments

- Feel uncomfortable in the presence of others who are using put-down terminology

- Extend themselves to become acquainted with someone in school who, in the past, has received put-downs because he/she is considered unique or different

- Teach family members about the bad effects of put-downs

- When they recieve a put-down, say "cancel" and consciously stop themselves before any negative words pop out of their mouths

- Apologize when they do use a put-down and take action to make it up to the person

- Understand that other people trust them to make appropriate, positive comments

- Include all class members in various activities

- Stand up for someone who is receiving put-downs by others

Keep trying! Students need more practice when they

- Use put-downs against others in the school community

- Laugh at put-downs

- Encourage people to use put-downs

- Hear put-downs but do nothing

- Repeat put-downs that they've heard

- Deny/Ignore their family's heritage because others might make fun of them

- Can't give genuine compliments to classmates

- Constantly use put-downs related to another's race, religion, nationality, or economic status

LITERATURE LINK ~ NO PUT-DOWNS

Primary Grades

Adventures of Connie and Diego, The	Garcia, Maria
Charlie, the Caterpillar	Deluise, Dom
Chrysanthemum	Henkes, Kevin
Did You Carry the Flag Today, Charlie?	Caudill, Rebecca
Drinking Gourd, The	Monjo, F. N.
Hue Boy	Mitchell, Rita Phillips
Hundred Dresses, The	Estes, Eleanor
Ida Early Comes Over the Mountain	Burch, Robert
Talking Eggs, The	San Souci, Robert D.
Ugly Duckling, The	Anderson, Hans Christian

Middle Grades

Best Christmas Pageant Ever	Robinson, Barbara
Blubber	Blume, Judy
Coping with Cliques	Peck, Lee and Ruth Rosen
Crow Boy	Yashimo, Taro
Daring to Be Abigail: A Novel	Vail, Rachel
Freckle Juice	Blume, Judy
Harriet, the Spy	Fitzhough, Louise
James and the Giant Peach	Dahl, Roald
Joshua T. Bates Takes Charge	Shreve, S. and D. Andreasen
Mrs. Fish, Ape, and Me, the Dump Queen	Mazer, Norma
Rag Coat, The	Mills, Lauren
Whipping Boy, The	Fleischman, Sid

Middle School and High School

Autobiography of a Face	Grealy, Lucy
Light in the Forest, The	Richter, Conrad
Warriors Don't Cry: A Searing Memoir of the Battle to Integrate Little Rock's Central High School	Beals, Melba Patillo

Teacher's Resource

Free to Be You, Free to Be Me	Thomas, Marlo, L. Pogrebin and G. M. Steinam

Date _____

Dear Family,

As we move forward towards building a strong, healthy classroom community, the Lifelong Guidelines continue to provide a firm foundation for behavior. The next Lifelong Guideline that we will focus on is

~ No Put-Downs ~

Put-downs, which have become a part of many TV programs and everyday conversations, are comments that are hurtful or demeaning to either a person or group. While often meant to be humorous, the words or gestures are usually biting, scornful, and contemptuous. To help rid put-downs from conversations in the classroom, we will:

- Practice giving and receiving compliments

- Learn more about the cultural heritage of classmates

- Tally put-downs read or heard in books, movies, or TV programs

- Provide support for a local service organization

As your child's primary teacher, you can help develop the Lifelong Guideline of No Put-Downs by:

- Not allowing your child or visiting students to use put-downs in your home

- Sharing how you feel when you've been put-down

- Discussing put-downs that you and your child hear on TV and how these words might affect relationships among friends and family members

Thank you for your continuing support for the development of Lifelong Guidelines.

Sincerely,

_____

Your child's teacher

Chapter 9

Personal Best

"DO YOUR BEST."

personal *adj* **1:** done in person without the intervention of another
2: relating to an individual, or his character or conduct
best *adj* one's maximum effort

Personal Best: One's best possible performance given the time and resources available

WHAT IS PERSONAL BEST?

For those using the ITI model, the Lifelong Guideline of Personal Best is defined by the 18 LIFESKILLS: Integrity, Responsibility, Common Sense, Problem Solving, Organization, Resourcefulness, Effort, Perseverance, Sense of Humor, Initiative, Curiosity, Courage, Flexibility, Patience, Friendship, Caring, Cooperation, and Pride (see definitions of LIFESKILLS on page 9.4). To pursue one's personal best means working to develop and strengthen each LIFESKILL.

Quality work is never an accident; it is always the result of combining clear goals, high standards, knowledge and skills, and genuine effort. It represents the wisest choice among many options matched with commitment, perseverance, and wise use of time, talents, and resources. There is no one way to achieve a sense of fulfillment but doing one's personal best on a consistent basis is the best road we know of to reach that end.

The Lifelong Guideline of Personal Best is not about treats, rewards, or bonuses; it's about a deep sense of personal satisfaction for a job well done, mastering a skill, or making a contribution.

Personal Best Is Not a Fixed Standard

Personal Best is not about perfectionism. Personal best is the result of our consistent pursuit of a moving target within an ever-changing terrain. Our performance in the same activity looks different over time. As our competence grows, our performance improves. As the tools, time, and resources available to us improve, our performance improves.

For example, while supporting your family (emotionally, financially, and physically), you might take up jogging. You may try hard to improve your running technique but you struggle to complete the course. You're doing your personal best in both areas—family life and jogging—but your jogging skill and capabilities in no way compare to those of a professional athlete who can and does devote full focus and time to his/her athletic pursuits. Personal best is using the utmost effort possible and striving for a heightened stage of excellence. This may or may not translate into being Number 1, the winner, the hero; in the real world, such status is rare. But all of us can achieve our personal best.

The Lifelong Guideline of Personal Best is one's best possible performance at the time, under the circumstances of the moment, and using the tools, time, knowledge/skill, and resources available at the moment. This, of course, takes into account the LIFESKILL of Resourcefulness!

PERSONAL BEST IS A MINDSET

What drives you to do your personal best? The most important element is a clear vision of your goals and personal performance standards and love of what you are doing. When such vision and love are united, you want to do your best! The secret about goals is to make them personal—to focus on your performance, not on the status or glamour of the project, job, or assignment. Athletes strive to surpass their previous personal accomplishments. This provides a vision that pushes them to constantly improve. Then, love the process of working toward your goals, celebrating each step toward your vision.

Doing one's personal best is a way of life, not an isolated incident.

WHY PRACTICE PERSONAL BEST?

Aristotle wrote, "We are what we repeatedly do. Excellence, then, is not an act, but a habit."* The LIFESKILL of Personal Best is transferable from one sector of life to another—in family and social life, on the job, in religious experiences, and during recreational activities. You can't work on excellence in one area and not have it show up in other areas. But the converse is also true: Refusing to do your personal best in one area will show up as laziness or avoidance in other areas.

Some people start out by thinking, "Doing my personal best is too difficult! I'll have to work really hard." But think of the opposite—do you really want to work toward personal worst or mediocrity? You may have to expend the same amount of effort to achieve less. Does that make sense? Self-respect—and the respect of others—depends heavily upon performing consistently at our personal best.

---

* *Nicomachean Ethics* by Aristotle, 350 BC, translated by W.D. Ross. *The Internet Classics Archives/Works by Aristotle,* http://classics.mit.edu/Browse/browse-Aristotle.html

HOW DO YOU PRACTICE IT?

As I'm sure the Army has discovered, the slogan "Be all that you can be!" is far easier said than done. Not that it is a mystery. But to achieve our personal best requires a broad range of personal and social skills that need to be learned early and practiced daily until they become dependable habits of mind rather than now-and-then skills we pull up when we get in a pinch.

The Lifelong Guideline of Personal Best is defined by 18 LIFESKILLS as shown on the following page. To the surprise of many, children seem to have an intuitive grasp of the LIFESKILLS. The word and concept of "perseverance," for example, is no hurdle at all for kindergarteners. And they seem delighted to be let in on the secret of how to succeed at things—when they want something, they know how to go about getting it. A wonderful gift so early in life. One might say that the road to success in life is paved with 23 yellow bricks: the 18 LIFESKILLS and five Lifelong Guidelines.

In addition to keeping our feet on the yellow brick road, we must also:

- Identify a vision, set personal goals

- Continuously self-evaluate in order to improve as needed (attitude, performance, or goal-setting) and to revise or completely redesign our plans as needed

- Welcome suggestions from others with a different perspective and who may have unique experiences to share.

- Understand that we will make mistakes but that we can turn them into life lessons; accept the realization that we have discovered a way *not* to do something, a necessary fine-tuning of our thinking. Thomas Edison discovered over 2,000 ways not to make the light bulb before he found a way that worked.* We should expect to refine our methods, thinking, and techniques—any variation that might improve us or our product. Feel pride in our heart when all of these LIFESKILL efforts combine as one and provide us with the experience of doing our personal best.

Does this sound like a recipe for adults only? Not true. Even five year olds can set a vision of what they would like to be when they grow up although it may and often does change weekly. At five, many of the skills being learned have feedback built into the learning event; they don't have to ask, "Teacher, is this right?" They are able to judge for themselves. As for welcoming suggestions from others, they are used to getting plenty of advice from grown ups! And when it comes from learning from mistakes, young children do it with much more grace than adults do.

Can children younger than five learn these aspects of doing the LIFESKILL of Personal Best? In their own age-appropriate ways, absolutely! It may in fact be more difficult for high school students and adults to learn the LIFESKILL of Personal Best because there is a lot of unlearning of old attitudes and habits of mind that must first be shed.

---

* *A 2nd Helping of Chicken Soup for the Soul: 101 More Stories to Open the Heart and Rekindle the Spirit* by Jack Canfield and Mark Victor, Health Communications, Inc., Deerfield Beach, Florida, 1995, p. 253. See also *Thomas Alva Edison Home Page,* http://www.thomasedison.com. Webmaster: Gerald Beals, October, 1999, Online AOL.

LIFESKILLS

CARING: To feel and show concern for others

COMMON SENSE: To use good judgment

COOPERATION: To work together toward a common goal or purpose

COURAGE: To act according to one's beliefs despite fear of adverse consequences

CURIOSITY: A desire to investigate and seek understanding of one's world

EFFORT: To do your best

FLEXIBILITY: To be willing to alter plans when necessary

FRIENDSHIP: To make and keep a friend through mutual trust and caring

INITIATIVE: To do something, of one's own free will, because it needs to be done

INTEGRITY: To act according to a sense of what's right and wrong

ORGANIZATION: To plan, arrange, and implement in an orderly way; to keep things orderly and ready to use

PATIENCE: To wait calmly for someone or something

PERSEVERANCE: To keep at it

PRIDE: Satisfaction from doing one's personal best

PROBLEM SOLVING: To create solutions to difficult situations and everyday problems

RESOURCEFULNESS: To respond to challenges and opportunities in innovative and creative ways

RESPONSIBILITY: To respond when appropriate; to be accountable for one's actions

SENSE OF HUMOR: To laugh and be playful without harming others

WHAT DOES PERSONAL BEST LOOK LIKE IN THE REAL WORLD?

We

- Guarantee services from our business and products from our company

- Recall unsafe and dangerous products

- Offer money-back guarantees

- Donate money, time, and materials to help disaster victims

- Volunteer time for service organizations such as the Red Cross, American Cancer Society, and Ronald McDonald House

- Work, sometimes two and three jobs, to provide for our family

- Provide bonuses for a job well done

- Accept awards for outstanding achievement

- Persevere until we complete a project or task

- Dedicate extreme amounts of time to obtain excellence

WHAT DOES PERSONAL BEST LOOK LIKE IN SCHOOL?

Staff

- Volunteer to serve on committees that aim to improve student performance

- Develop skills and extend knowledge base by attending workshops and taking college courses

- Use administrative and peer evaluations as guidelines for growth

- Read professional journals for reports of current educational research

- Write curriculum using a variety of strategies to more effectively teach all learners

- Present a smiling, welcoming face at the classroom door each morning

- Tackle tough tasks and follow through to completion

- Perform duties to a personal high standard of excellence

Students

- Say "I can!" rather than "I can't!"

- Take on and complete challenging projects

- Persevere to master a skill or to reach a goal

- Complete work that indicates intense personal investment, a high level of accountability, and continuous growth

- Learn for the love of learning, not for an extrinsic reward

- Adopt and apply the Lifelong Guidelines and LIFESKILLS in school and the world beyond

INQUIRIES TO DEVELOP PERSONAL BEST

Whole Group Inquiries

- Write "Audience Procedures" with your teacher. These are the behaviors you will use when you are a guest at a performance, presentation, or show. Include what kind of voice to use (indoor, outdoor, 24" inch), how you will move (tip-toe, walk), what you can touch (nothing, nonbreakables, ask for permission), and manners to follow (ask permission, please, thank you, may I?). Illustrate these procedures and practice them in your classroom before you attend a performance.

- Create a portfolio of your best work. Every week, choose an example of additional "personal best" work to place in the folder/box. Once a month, organize the papers by date. Look for improvement in your work as the year progresses. Plan to share this portfolio with your parents during conference time. Share your favorite example of personal best with a partner.

- Invite representatives from different fields of work (e.g. medical, engineering, computers, education, advertising, food service, maintenance) to visit your class and share the attributes of the Lifelong Guideline of Personal Best in their job/profession with your classmates. Identify five common attributes that appear in most of the occupations. List three or more ways you can use what you learned to improve your own personal best performance.

Small Group/Individual Inquiries

- Make a "Personal Best" folder by folding a 12"x18" piece of paper in half the short way (hamburger fold). Using your favorite color, print the words "PERSONAL BEST" near the top of the folder. Draw a picture of yourself doing your personal best in school. Print your name across the bottom of the folder. At the end of each week, choose one or two papers that you feel show you have tried your personal best to learn something new. Date and place these papers in your folder. Share them with your parents at conference time.

- Write a poem with two verses or more that will explain what personal best is and how it looks. Accent the rhythm of your poem with a clapping and finger-snapping routine. Teach the routine to the others and perform it for the class.

- Identify a family member, friend or other acquaintance who always demonstrates the Lifelong Guideline of Personal Best. Create a card, badge, or write a letter explaining to this person what you have learned from observing him/her and how you plan to use this information to do better on any task.

- Research four people who have had to overcome obstacles/disabilities to enable them to contribute to the world (e.g. Helen Keller, Christopher Reeves). Determine the personal best attributes for each subject. Compare and contrast their characteristics, looking for similarities and differences. Share your findings with your learning club.

- Read a minimum of three biographies. Choose one of the individuals. Create a Venn diagram comparing the individual's personal best to your own. List at least three ways you are similar and three ways you differ. Share your diagram with a partner, in learning clubs, or during community circle time.

- Choose a LIFESKILL (e.g., responsibility, caring, friendship) that you feel you need to practice more. Establish a time frame for improving this skill. List three or more practical steps to reach your goal. When you feel that you have improved, reflect on the process of goal setting and record your thoughts in a journal to read during community circle time.

- Identify four or more local or national companies that bear the founder's name. Write to the company and ask for information about the founder, including personal qualities and professional characteristics. Present the information to your class. Offer your own ideas about why the company succeeded.

- Read the biography of a successful athlete. List two training techniques taught to him/her by coaches that led to success. Invite a trainer/coach to speak to the class on improving personal sports skills. If possible, also invite a sports player (perhaps one who graduated from your school) now playing for a high school/college/professional team to explain his/her own process for reaching personal best.

- Research four local businesses or companies, their work standards and customer satisfaction policies. Choose which you would work for or buy from because of its employment policies or customer service record. Share your reasons with your learning club.

- Invite a local politician to visit the classroom and discuss his/her concept of the Lifelong Guideline of Personal Best. Ask for personal information about attendance at meetings, voting record, and introduction of new legislation.

SIGNS OF SUCCESS

Congratulations! Students are showing signs of Personal Best when they

- Work, work, and do more work to complete a project in ways that meet high personal standards

- Are willing to redo any task that does not meet, or even exceed, the specified criteria

- Look at some of their work and judge the results as, "Yes, this is my personal best!" or "No, this is not my personal best; I have more work to do!"

- Practice self-evaluation and use these observations as guidelines for setting goals and working on the next tasks

- Feel a deep sense of personal satisfaction and pride in their hearts and minds when they've done their personal best

Keep trying! Students need more practice when they

- Show no interest in improving skills or work habits

- Don't do their share of the work on cooperative projects

- Refuse to listen to suggestions from parents, friends, and teachers

- Speed through an assignment just to be the first one done

- Can't feel honest pride in what they are doing

- Do sloppy, incorrect work and try to pass it off as their personal best

- Set goals but don't work toward accomplishing them

- Only use personal best when it suits their own interests

LITERATURE LINK ~ PERSONAL BEST

Primary Grades

Art Lesson, The	dePaola, Tomie
Friends from the Other Side	Anzaldua, Gloria
Giving Tree, The	Silverstein, Shel
Knots on a Counting Rope	Martin, Bill Jr.
Miss Rumphius	Cooney, Barbara
Now One Foot, Now the Other	dePaola, Tomie
Patchwork Quilt, The	Flourney, Valerie
Peppe the Lamplighter	Bartons, Elisa
Samuel Eaton's Day	Walters, Kate
Through Grandpa's Eyes	MacLachlen, Patricia

Intermediate Grades

Anne Frank	Epstein, Rachel
Cesar Chavez: Leader for Migrant Farm Workers	Gonzales, Doreen
Charlotte's Web	White, E. B.
Circuit: Stories from the Life of a Migrant Child, The	Jiminez, Francisco
Helen Keller	Graff, Stewart
Jackie Robinson	Bergman, Irwin B.
Sara Crewe	Burnett, Frances
Stone Fox	Gardner, John Reynolds
Wilma Unlimited: How Wilma Rudolph Became the World's Fastest Woman	Krull, Kathleen
You Want Women to Vote, Lizzie Stanton?	Fritz, Jean

Middle School and High School

Hug a Thousand Trees With Ribbons: The Story of Phyllis Wheatley	Rinaldi, Ann
Lyddie	Patterson, Katherine
Nightjohn	Paulsen, Gary
Zach	Bell, William

Teacher's Resource

Punished by Rewards: The Trouble with Gold Stars, Incentive Plans, A's, Praise, and Other Bribes	Kohn, Alfie

Date _____

Dear Family,

Aristotle wrote, "We are what we repeatedly do. Excellence, then, is not an act, but a habit." We all realize that a habit is nothing more than hard work in disguise—practicing a task over and over until it can be done with ease and accuracy. This next Lifelong Guideline is very important because it encompasses all of the LIFESKILLS in action. The guideline is

~Personal Best~

We define personal best as "one's best possible performance at the time, under the circumstances of the moment, and using the tools, time, knowledge/skill, and resources available at the moment."

In school, we will practice determining personal best by:

- Creating portfolios in which "personal best" work, chosen by each student, will be filed

- Learning how athletes set personal goals

- Comparing the personal best performance of a famous person and that of a student

- Practicing self-evaluation and goal setting to improve personal standards

Parents are steady supporters of the Lifelong Guidelines. Perhaps you often say, "Just do your personal best!" The "best" is very personal. It varies from person to person, can depend on available resources, and changes over time. You can support your child's efforts by:

- Encouraging him/her to bring home paperwork from school. Compare different assignments in relation to: organization, cooperation (if a group project), patience, and pride

- Pointing out (to your child) situations in which you feel he/she has done his/her personal best

- Encouraging your child as he/she works through a project or skill toward personal best

- Sharing personal best stories from the real world: athletes, presidents, scientists, doctors, fathers, and mothers

Together, you and I will do our personal best to educate a responsible, caring, hard-working child.

Sincerely,

_____

Your child's teacher

Caring

Chapter 10

"Show you care."

caring *vi* **1 a:** to feel trouble or anxiety on behalf of another's situation; to feel concern or interest; **2:** to give care **3:** to have a liking, fondness, or taste **4:** to have an inclination

Caring: To feel and show concern for others

WHAT IS CARING?

Caring is a visceral feeling arising from empathy for another's situation when we detect their distress or anxiety. The feeling prompts us to provide support for others in day-to-day living experiences or during crisis situations. Caring is a gift from our bodybrain's "information substances"* that detect and transmit information about the emotional status of those around us.

Caring and empathy are innate qualities in humans; we are born with a sensitivity to the plight of others. Consider, for example, the infant who bursts into tears because another child in the room is crying. Unfortunately for some, hard circumstances conspire over time to freeze caring and empathy up inside.

WHY PRACTICE CARING?

Caring is a key ingredient for our personal and social lives and for citizenship.

Caring As a Glue. Caring is a critical glue that binds us to family, friends, and community. Without it, we would interact like ships passing in the night—indifferent, detached. Without it, community—even on a small scale within family life—would be impossible. In family life, healthy and enduring relationships depend on caring.

---

* For a fascinating and understandable yet scientific explanation of our inner emotional life, see *Molecules of Emotion: Why You Feel the Way You Feel* by Candace Pert.

Life in the work place would be a nasty experience without the element of caring. There would be no cohesiveness, nothing to look forward to when showing up in the morning. It would amount to 40-hours a week spent with strangers. In contrast, effective teamwork is built on two foundations: Genuine caring for members in the group plus an interest in what is to be accomplished coupled with concern about what might happen if the task isn't accomplished.

Caring says: "What happens to you matters to me," "I want the best for you," "I am here for you," "I am willing to help provide support when you cannot stand alone." It is important that we practice caring because we are models for those around us. This is especially important for those students who do not know how to care or how to show caring. A nurturing relationship with even one other caring person can spell the difference between despair and success.*

Caring As Antidote to Egotism and Prejudice. Egotism—the well-known "me first" attitude that has flourished over the past 30 years—and prejudice, in all its many forms, are real threats to society and citizenship. Caring is perhaps our best antidote to both. Caring lowers the expression of egotism and prejudice and speeds healing for those who bear the brunt of them.

As caring and empathy increase, we begin to see each individual as unique and valuable; in so doing we begin to unlearn prejudices.

Caring As Key Ingredient for Citizenship. Caring is also a key ingredient for citizenship. When we go to the polls, we must vote for the good of the many, not the special interests of the few. The search for solutions that work best for all concerned requires that we genuinely care about the welfare and happiness of others. The attitude of "Not in my backyard" must be widened to a concern about that issue in other communities as well.

HOW DO YOU PRACTICE IT?

The motto for practicing caring could be John Donne's statement "No man is an island; every man is a piece of the continent, a part of the main."** That is true from birth onward.

Caring comes from our deepest-held convictions about the value of the human race and of the individual. To model caring, it must be lived.

Start Early

Nurturing a child's innate sense of caring starts in the home. To no surprise, the number one strategy is modeling. Caring must be experienced; it is based on emotions, not intellectual thoughts. And, it must be nurtured; encourage the child's gentle, empathetic nature. With boys,

---

* Coontz, Stephanie, *Phi Delta Kappan,* March, 1995, p. 16.
** "Devotions Upon Emergent Occasions," *Meditation XVII,* 1624. *John Donne Society Home Page* http://www.csus.edu/org/

guard against society's pressures to be macho, the tough guy.* With girls, focus on the ability to care and detect the feelings of others as a key skill for leadership—in the community and on the job as well as within the family.

At School

There are several ways teachers can help students practice caring. Modeling is, of course, the most important. Next come curriculum content, guided practice, friendships, and community work.

Curriculum Content. The LIFESKILL of Caring, as the other LIFESKILL Lifelong Guidelines, must become part of the formal curriculum of the classroom. The content of this chapter is intended to give you a place to start teaching the concept and practice of caring. Content can be tailored to students' needs and environment by taking advantage of related topics from social studies, science, and literature.

In addition to planned curriculum embedded in a lesson plan, don't overlook the power of the teachable moment.

Guided Practice. The practice of caring requires thoughtful observational skills. Who is hurting? What steps will provide support but not dependency? What problem-solving strategies will be most effective? In day-to-day relationships, help students discern opportunities that will enable them to extend their heartfelt concern. When they show, share, and shoulder concern for others, they are caring.

The inquiries on pages 10.6 to 10.7 provide opportunities for lots of guided practice which will in turn open up many golden teachable moments for modeling, target talk, and processing the process.** Also, an inappropriate remark can open up in-depth discussion about caring; learning how to "clean up" our insensitive words is an important skill.

Caring Through Friendship. Help your students develop their childhood friendships into the kinds of caring interactions that will last a lifetime. These special relationships—with their intense feelings of camaraderie, their secrets, codes, clubhouses, and long hours spent together—are the perfect vehicle for developing caring.

Listening to a friend's problems is one of the simplest ways to feel caring at a visceral level and one of the best opportunities to show caring. Not only do we listen but we also feel and respond with phrases like, "I understand," "Is there something I can do to help support you while you sort this out?" and "Explain it to me." Although the friend may not need advice or should be left to figure it out on his/her own, just having someone listen and empathize provides release from stress. Make sure that community circle times focus on expressions of caring as well as resolution of issues. Think of community circle time as an opportunity to deepen positive behaviors as well as resolve negative behaviors.

---

* Michael Gurian, *The Wonder of Boys: What Parents Can Do to Shape Boys into Exceptional Men*, Los Angeles, CA: J.P. Tarcher, 1997. See also James Garbarino, *Lost Boys: Why Our Sons Turn Violent and How We Can Save Them*, New York, New York: Free Press (Simon & Schuster), 1999.

** "Processing the process" is an important instructional strategy, especially for extending and enriching the Lifelong Guidelines and LIFESKILLS. See *TRIBES: A New Way of Learning and Being Together* by Jeanne Gibbs, p. 403.

Caring Through Serving the Community. Since the average life span keeps increasing, assisting elderly relatives and neighbors who can't navigate on their own is a humbling look at our own future. Many of us are part of the "sandwich generation," caught between growing children and aging parents. Tasks that the older generation once handled automatically now require monumental effort and must be taken over by a younger population with flexible knees, a steady heart, and sturdy limbs. If we are unwilling to care now, what would make us think that others would be willing to care about us later?

Neighbors form another link in the caring chain. We should be there to help each other celebrate and grieve, laugh and cry, and cheer and admonish. We should band together for common causes and concerns.

Make community service a weekly or biweekly activity. We can serve our community and live the LIFESKILL of Caring by volunteering to work with the homeless, Red Cross, a food bank, a Ronald McDonald House, or the Special Olympics.

And, in the really big scheme of life, we must also care about our planet and learn ways to express that caring. Global caring is a necessity, not a luxury. Our very existence is at stake— environmentally, socially, and economically. Help students create action plans meant to improve the quality of life for all citizens in our neighborhoods and the world.

WHAT DOES CARING LOOK LIKE IN THE REAL WORLD?
We

- Shovel the snow from an elderly neighbor's sidewalk

- Organize a fund-raiser to pay medical bills for a seriously ill friend or fellow worker

- Help to clean litter and trash from the streets around the neighborhood

- Volunteer time at a local food bank or soup kitchen

- Welcome a new family to our neighborhood

- Listen to a friend who needs support

- Write a note to provide strength when there's a serious illness or death

- Provide support for those who feel overwhelmed with demands on their time, energy, and emotions

- Practice the 4 R's of waste management—Refuse~Reduce~Reuse~Recycle

WHAT DOES CARING LOOK LIKE IN SCHOOL?

Staff

- Work cooperatively to plan activities

- Help one another in times of need or stress

- Offer professional support for each other

- Share the challenges and demands of assignments and tasks

- Show an interest in the lives of those at your school

- Assist each other to evaluate his/her teaching performance

- Set teaching/learning goals to assure that each classroom works for every student

- Establish a formal mentoring program in which all participate

Students

- Inquire about the welfare of a classmate

- Help fellow students be more effective learners

- Volunteer to be a cross-age tutor

- Serve as a buddy for a new student

- Share materials and ideas

- Offer help with everyday tasks in the classroom

- Talk with and listen to classmates

- Bring cans of food for school service projects

- Take care of classroom pets

- Notify an adult who can assist when a student is angry or crying

- Inquire about the teacher or a fellow student when he/she has been absent

INQUIRIES TO DEVELOP CARING

Whole Group Inquiries

- Illustrate three or more ways to show friends you care about them. Title your drawing, "Caring for Friends." Share your drawing during community circle.

- Read the daily newspaper. Find an article recognizing someone's efforts to help others. Design an appreciation card for a local resident who demonstrates caring actions towards other people in the community. Mail the card to the newspaper then ask that they forward it to the resident.

Small Group/Individual Inquiries

- Design a special card for Mother's Day, Father's Day, Grandparents Day, or someone's birthday. Use markers, paints or crayons to color a picture of yourself on the front of the card. Write a two-line poem on thw inside of the card, e.g., "I just want to say, Have a Happy Mother's Day," sign your name and give the card to that (those) special person (people).

- Create a "how to" handbook that explains the care and feeding of the classroom pet. Include a drawing of the pet, a description of its classroom home, the kinds of food it eats, the amount of water to provide for good health, and how to provide exercise. Design a cover, staple the care pages inside, and leave it next to the cage (container) for guests to read.

- Make a class video with funny jokes, happy songs, short skits, and good wishes for a classmate who will be absent from school for longer than three weeks. Gift-wrap the case and deliver it to his/her house or to the family.

- Research two pets that could live in your classroom (such as a gerbil, goldfish, hamster, hermit crab, or mouse). Determine the food each eats, the kind of shelter each creates or requires, and any unusual habits each has. Survey your classmates to determine which two pets they prefer in the classroom. Then write a "how to" book about caring for the two animals that received the most votes. Include cage, shelter, food, water, and sleep requirements. Exhibit the book in the school library.

- Design a pop-up "get well" card for an absent classmate. Practice first using scrap paper. Write a short note explaining one thing that has happened while he/she was away and one reason why the person is missed. Show the card to your learning club and then give it to the teacher to mail.

- Collect newspaper stories about people helping animals. Research one local organization that cares for animals that are mistreated, abused, and/or abandoned. Organize a class fund-raiser and donate the money to that organization for food and toys for animals that are waiting to be adopted.

- Create "caring" posters for area service organizations (Red Cross, United Way, etc.) that extend help to community members on a regular basis. Using a familiar tune, write new lyrics to teach the public about one organization. Record your class singing the song and send the posters and tape to them in appreciation of their caring for others.

- Call your local Red Cross, the Salvation Army, or a similar group. Ask them what supplies are needed for disaster victims. Organize a disaster relief collection center at your school. Tally the items as they are donated. Deliver them to the organization with the help of an adult.

- Design a card recognizing Veterans' Day (November 11th), Flag Day (June 14th), or Memorial Day (last Monday in May). Learn to sing some patriotic songs such as "America," "It's a Grand Old Flag," "Anchors Aweigh," "My Country 'Tis of Thee." Add appropriate motions to help explain the meaning of one of the songs. As a class, deliver the cards and provide entertainment for the members of an American Legion Post or a local veterans' hospital.

- Investigate a local food bank. Interview the director to learn the amount of food needed each month, the number of people/families served, and where the food comes from. Write a 30-second public service TV commercial to teach audiences about the work of this organization. Practice and then video tape the commercial. Play it for the class. Answer any questions afterwards.

- Research a community resource (such as a food pantry, homeless shelter, Salvation Army) that helps people with food, shelter, and clothing. Invite a representative from the organization to visit your class. Ask him/her to share the group's philosophy and strategies for helping others. Write thank-you notes sharing one thing you learned about the organization and one way you believe that you can personally help them to provide for those in need.

- Organize a collection of food bank items from your school community. Design posters advertising the collection. Visit other classes to explain this service project. Provide decorated containers for the goods. Arrange to have the items delivered to a local food bank.

- Research the community's efforts to reduce the amount of trash that is sent to dumps, landfills, or trash burning facilities. Explain which materials can be recycled in our area. Provide a plan to organize, collect, and dispose of trash collected in our classroom. Design "Care About Our Earth" posters to teach your classmates and teacher what items can be recycled. Predict how many pounds or items will be recycled from our classroom in one week. Record the different kinds and amounts of materials collected and compare with your prediction. Dispose of the items properly.

- Design a brochure encouraging citizens to vote in the next election. Propose two reasons why a caring citizen should exercise his/her constitutional duty to vote. Contact the League of Women Voters for their voter pamphlet; offer your brochure for educational purposes or possible distribution to the parents of our school.

SIGNS OF SUCCESS

Congratulations! Students are showing signs of Caring when they

- Share their own feelings and also care about the feelings of other people

- Notice someone needing help and volunteer assistance

- Inquire as to why someone is upset/crying/angry

- Feel upset over another person's unfortunate circumstances or situation

- Work to save local stray animals or an endangered species

- Organize services (food, shelter, clothing) for people experiencing hard times

- Write notes appreciating the good deeds of others

- Think less about themselves and more about other people

- Right an injustice

- Offer to help a classmate

Keep trying! Students need more practice when they

- Need reminders to think of others' feelings

- Ignore someone in need

- Choose not to help

- Think it is funny that someone else is different from themselves

- Toss trash directly on the ground instead of using a trash can; won't recycle

- Disregard others' obvious signs of distress and need for care

- Overlook an opportunity to ensure fair play/justice

- Use put-downs

- Put their own wants ahead of the pressing needs of others

- Abuse an animal or physically hurt another person

Literature Link ~ Caring

Primary Grades

Beyond the Ridge	Goble, Paul
Chicken Sunday	Polacco, Patricia
Do You Love Me?	Gackenback, Dick
Family Pictures: Cuadros de Familia	Lomaz Garza, Carmen
Key into Winter, The	Anderson, Jeanie
Legend of the Bluebonnet, The	dePaola, Tomie
Miss Rumphius	Cooney, Barbara
Mufaro's Beautiful Daughters	Steptoe, John
Pearl's Promise	Asch, Frank
Somewhere Today: A Book of Peace	Thomas, Shelley Moore
Stellaluna	Cannon, Janell

Intermediate Grades

Calling the Doves	Herrera, Juan Felipe
Cricket in Times Square	Seldon, George
Day No Pigs Would Die, A	Peck, Robert Newton
Grandma Didn't Wave Back	Blue, Rose
Mrs. Frisby and the Rats of N.I.M.H.	O'Brien, Robert
Muir of the Mountains	Douglas, William O.
Pablo's Tree	Mora, Pat
Rabbit Hill	Lawson, Robert
Sadako and the Thousand Paper Cranes	Coerr, Eleanor
Taste of Blackberries, A	Smith, Doris B.
Velveteen Rabbit, The	Williams, Margery

Middle School and High School

California Blues	Klass, David
Chicken Soup for the Teenage Soul: 101 Stories of Life, Love and Learning	Canfield, Jack (Ed.), Mark Victor Hansen (Ed.), and Kimberly Kirberger (Ed.)
Door Near Here, A	Quarles, Heather
Puppies, Dogs, and Blue Northers: Reflections on Being Raised by a Pack of Sled Dogs	Paulsen, Gary

Teacher's Resources

Giving Book: Creative Classroom Approaches to Caring, Valuing, and Cooperating, The	Stanish, Bob
Peaceful Classroom, The	Smith, Charles A.

Date _____

Dear Family,

An African proverb says, "It takes a whole village to raise a child." You and I are part of that village. Currently, as part of our school's effort to help students develop strong, positive, lifelong behaviors, we are highlighting the LIFESKILL of

~Caring~

We will be discovering the attributes of caring by using some of the following strategies:

- Participating in group projects

- Reading literature that shows examples of caring

- Discussing current events

- Studying environmental issues

- Generating class outreach projects

- Interviewing caregivers such as parents, teachers, nurses, doctors

At home, you can provide reinforcement of the LIFESKILL of CARING by encouraging your child to:

- Visit a sick or injured relative. (If distance is a factor, encourage your child to write a letter, create a card, or phone the person.)

- Read stories and play games with a younger sibling

- Include a new classmate in neighborhood activities

- Visit and help an elderly neighbor

- Help care for any family pets

Together we are creating the caregivers of the future.

Sincerely,

_____

Your child's teacher

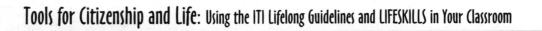

Common Sense

Chapter 11

"Take a practical approach."

common sense *n* **1:** the practical opinion of ordinary people **2:** sound and prudent but often unsophisticated judgment **3:** intuitive application of natural principles

Common Sense: To use good judgment

WHAT IS COMMON SENSE?

Look at the people around you. Some seem to have a natural inclination toward making common-sense decisions. Even as youngsters, they were able to choose the down-to-earth, straightforward solution without much effort. When asked how they did that, these children might have answered, "It's just the way it's supposed to be. How else would you do it?" They are known by family, friends, and co-workers for their sensible, workable solutions.

Common Sense Isn't Common

In truth, common sense is not common. It requires the use of five LIFESKILLS: Curiosity (look closely at the problem and see it in its entirety), Flexibility (approach the problem with an open mind; don't get attached to a prescribed approach or easy solution), Organization (keep a clear head; be thorough), Patience (have faith that there is a solution), and Resourcefulness (work with what you have; the best solutions are often the most simple, economical, and/or low-tech).

Common sense doesn't stop there. It in turn is a prerequisite for the LIFESKILLS of Initiative and Problem solving. Initiative without common sense is going off half-cocked; problem solving without common sense creates more problems.

In short, people with the LIFESKILL of Common Sense are extraordinary people and invaluable in any environment—at home, work, and in our community. They are also astute and effective citizens.

It's the "Not-So-Obvious" Obvious

One of the hallmarks of a common-sense solution is that, once it's been found, it appears perfectly obvious. It's the simple solution to a complex issue, a low-tech solution to a high-tech problem. It's one the farmer can see but the college professor can't. It is often the most time-efficient, the quickest, and the least costly.

Sometimes the common-sense solution is based on ordinary, everyday experiences and knowledge. Sometimes it's based on data from similar previous problems. At other times, however, the solution comes from a simple, straightforward examination of the problem, an analysis unclouded by prior knowledge or expectations.

It's Intuition at Its Best

Some people believe that common sense is an accidental "Aha!" by the uneducated or unsophisticated. Sometimes this is true but more often common sense is the intuitive application of natural principles. Contributing editor, Karen Olsen, tells of her farmer stepfather, Henry Miller, whose high school physics, geometry, and chemistry stuck with him for a lifetime, not just long enough to bring him an "A" on tests. Henry practiced the principles of those subjects daily; his common-sense solutions to problems were renowned throughout the area. For example, when he needed a more efficient disk and harrow, he designed one, bigger than anything on the market. A representative from John Deere came out, took a look, and patented it (how to patent an invention wasn't taught in his high school!). If he had a runaway harvester that broke its header in a ditch, he combined a little physics and geometry to bring together several tons of metal for a welding job out in the field. When Mother Nature dumped too much rain during a 24-hour a day seeding operation, he got creative; he asked a crop-duster friend to modify his plane to fly seed on and became the first in the area to prove the economic feasibility of aerial seeding. When he thought Cargill Grain and the other giant grain conglomerates had him and the other little guys by the neck, he figured out how to hold grain several months after harvest until the prices went back up. He designed and built a set of truck scales, a grain elevator and pit, and half a dozen storage tanks from the brief instruction manuals from the manufacturers.

Karen Olsen's mother had a favorite motto: "If you really think about it, you can figure it out." To Karen's mother, not coming up with a common-sense solution was unthinkable, even inexcusable. If "build it and they will come" rings a bell, try "Think and you will know"! Both stepfather and mother were powerful models and common sense was expected of their daughter, whatever the setting. We need to hold the same expectations for our students. Common sense is in them. We need to draw it out and insist on it.

It's a Solution That Works

However we arrived at it, the common-sense solution is one that works. It's immediately recognized as workable; "Aha," says the onlooker, "Now, why didn't I think of that?"

A Comical Example of No Common Sense!

Do you remember the fairy tale about Foolish Jack, a young boy and his mother? She is always sending him on errands which he muddles up each time. Now, being a good mother who is trying to instill common sense into her son, she carefully explains what he should have done in each situation. Jack then conscientiously applies her words of wisdom to the next problem but, of course, the situations are never the same. He is always one lesson behind and quite off the mark.

As the story moves from one ridiculous scene to another, children howl with laughter. Once the children recognize the pattern, they love to predict what Jack will do next. While Jack lacks common sense, he is great at following directions!

WHY PRACTICE COMMON SENSE?

Common sense helps us choose practical solutions. Our lives are easier if we can apply sound judgment early in the thinking process, thereby eliminating chaotic and hasty solutions. This is vital during a crisis when poor solutions escalate the very problem we're trying to solve.

Common sense opens doors which allow us to go places and to do things we would otherwise only dream about. It also keeps us grounded in what's real.

HOW DO YOU PRACTICE IT?

Strengthening the LIFESKILL of Common Sense builds upon the LIFESKILLS of Patience, Flexibility, and Problem Solving and requires lots and lots of practice solving problems and dilemmas of consequence. We must, therefore, be willing to risk the consequences of solutions that are off the mark (so long as they aren't life-threatening or catastrophic) and be willing to learn from the results, both good and bad.

Model

As with all of the Lifelong Guidelines and LIFESKILLS, modeling, including "talking out loud" as we go, is critical. To develop common-sense, modeling is all the more important because, when it comes to common sense, there are no rules or pat formulas to follow. The only way to help students develop the LIFESKILL of Common Sense is to involve them in the process of solving problems, problems, and more problems. Attitude, a belief in "I can do," is everything when it comes to conjuring up common sense.

Provide Practice

Opportunities for students to practice Common Sense can be provided in two areas: through the curriculum content you design and through your instructional strategies.

Curriculum. In addition to the inquiries you design to practice applying common sense (such as those on pages 6 and 7 of this chapter) regular subject area content can become your most powerful source for providing practice of the LIFESKILL of Common sense.

First, eliminate factoids and express the content as conceptually as possible. Concepts allow students to generalize from one situation to another. Such a rich, deep, and easily flexed knowledge base invites solving problems and making choices.

Second, develop multiple inquiries for each concept, inquiries that invite students to apply those concepts in real-world situations that are diverse and integrate subject areas in a natural way. Your goal is not only helping students wire the knowledge and skills into long-term memory but providing practice in applying what they learn in flexible, creative ways. This helps students learn to take their academic learning out of its silver box and come to expect their education to unlock mysteries in the real world.

Third, give science a central focus. Use its concepts as the central organizers for your integrated curriculum.

Instructional Strategies. It is important to involve yourself and your students in joint decision-making. Teach them to listen to those around them who are in the process of using their common sense to resolve problems or dilemmas. Be a model for them; share your thinking out loud as you think your way through a problem. Give them process prompts such as: "What's the key issue or idea here?" "What is it that you really want to happen? What would that look like?" "What are your choices?" "Has something like this happened before? What solutions did you try then?" "Which one(s) worked best?" "Is that a reasonable solution for your current problem?"

Practice Reflection

Students should reflect on the results of their solutions and evaluate if they were effective and practical. Did their solutions really deliver what was hoped for or did they compromise what they wanted to achieve? Did it make the most sense? Is it practical? Was the choice developed in a thoughtful way? Did it resolve or intensify the circumstances?

The answers to such questions increase our ability to reach wise, common-sense decisions.

WHAT DOES COMMON SENSE LOOK LIKE IN THE REAL WORLD?

We

- Find the most practical and economical way to complete a task or solve a problem

- Learn from one experience and transfer that knowledge to another situation

- Think through assignments, tasks, and events before we begin to make sure we're prepared

- Seek advice from someone who has experience in the area and knows what works

- Watch how other people problem solve and learn from their thinking processes

- Read manuals and "how-to" books for practical problem-solving advice

- Practice common sense when caring for our bodies by eating the right foods, sleeping an adequate amount of time, exercising both body and mind, and wearing clothing appropriate for the climate and weather

WHAT DOES COMMON SENSE LOOK LIKE IN SCHOOL?

Staff

- Keep the "big" picture in the forefront of their thinking

- "Live" the Lifelong Guidelines and LIFESKILLS

- Treat parents and students with respect

- Show good judgment when making decisions

- Model a variety of effective problem-solving skills

- Recycle materials because it saves money and is good for the environment

- Brainstorm strategies and lessons because they know that "two heads are better than one"

Students

- "Live" the Lifelong Guidelines and LIFESKILLS because they make school a safe and welcoming place to be

- Schedule time so assignments are completed by the due date

- Ask for advice when stuck solving a problem

- Wear appropriate clothing for the weather

- Learn from previous lessons

- Share personal experiences to help classmates solve problems

- Apply skills and strategies that will strengthen learning

- Say "I know if I think this through I can find a good, workable solution"

INQUIRIES TO DEVELOP COMMON SENSE

Whole Class Inquiries

- Listen to the story *Silly Jack* by Laurence Anholt. Choose two of Jack's silly responses and come up with your own common-sense choices that Jack could have followed. With your learning club, write a "Silly Jack" skit with your own characters, setting, situations, and props. Practice and present the story for your classmates.

- In your learning club, write procedures, each with four to five steps, for each of the following: group work, partner work, and choice time. Use a separate piece of paper for each one. Include who will be in the group, what area of the room you will be working in, how you will go to the work area, what behaviors you expect, and the sound level in each place (e.g., six-inch voices, 12-inch voices, silence). Think of common-sense routines to make movement around the classroom easier. Compare your procedures with another learning club. Work with the teacher to create the final version for student use. Use the "Procedures for Intrapersonal Work" as a pattern to guide you.

> ### Procedures for Intrapersonal Work
>
> 1. Remain in your own space.
>
> 2. Work alone. If you must talk, use an eight-inch voice.
>
> 3. Raise your hand for the teacher's help.
>
> 4. When finished, do something from the "choice" list.

Small Group/Individual Inquiries

- Choose a classroom jigsaw puzzle of 25 or more pieces. Invite a friend to put the pieces together with you. Set the box top with the puzzle picture standing where you can see it. Decide what steps you will follow to do the puzzle (outside edges first or inside center part first). Organize the pieces in some common-sense way. Put the puzzle together. Explain to your teacher the easiest and the hardest part of doing a jigsaw puzzle with someone else.

- In your learning club, brainstorm practical ways for the class to experience a "special class" such as art, music, physical education, or computer when that teacher is absent for the day. Design two or more classroom activities that will work in your classroom, provide for some movement, include music/art, and will let the class do something special. Share your ideas with the teacher.

- Check all of your materials (notebooks, crayon/marker box, books) and clothing to make sure each thing is labeled with your first and last name. Ask the teacher or a family member for help with some of the harder items. Keep your materials in your desk and backpack. If something is missing, design a small "Lost" poster and hang it from the side of your desk until the object is found.

- Find a real life "Silly Jack" story in the newspaper. Read the whole article to a partner and discuss the silly choices made. Brainstorm wiser choices. Record your favorite choices in your journal.

- Create a procedure chart (one with four to five steps) to help fellow students effectively use our "Peace Table" (a place to settle disputes). Include who should be at the table, when, what they should do, and how they should do it. Write your final list in capital letters on a chart tablet. Add graphics. Share the final project with the teacher or class.

- Collect three newspaper articles demonstrating problem-solving situations. Highlight examples of following common-sense choices/decisions and ignoring them. Draw a political cartoon illustrating a lack of common sense by people in one of the articles. Share it with your teacher and then submit it to your local newspaper for possible publication.

- Select a problem from a list provided by your teacher. Brainstorm three or more solutions for the problem and share them with a partner. Then test each solution by asking, "If I do "x" then it seems likely that "y" will happen." Rate your answers from "Most Common Sense" to "Least Common Sense." Explain each of the three choices to your learning club and provide an explanation for your ratings. Illustrate the problem and your highest rated solution on a piece of drawing paper. Share this work with a friend. *(Note to teachers: be sure that the list of problems is appropriate for your students' age level.)*

- Choose a current long-term assignment. Schedule how you plan to complete the work by the due date. Include at least six mini-deadlines (dates for choosing a topic, researching material, gathering materials, meeting with teacher, completing the project, and presenting your product to either your learning club or the class). Follow your plan. Evaluate its effectiveness with your teacher and adjust it before you begin the next project. Record in your journal your thoughts and feelings about this experience with time management.

- Research four examples of common law in our legal system. Determine how the laws evolved and if/how they were influenced by common sense. Write to the editor of the local newspaper explaining what you learned from this task.

- Locate two or more outrageous examples of lack of common sense by people in local, state, and/or federal government. Share the information with the class. Brainstorm common-sense answers for the problems. Write letters to the appropriate elected officials sharing your thoughts on the topic.

SIGNS OF SUCCESS

Congratulations! Students are showing signs of Common Sense when they

- Think and plan before they speak or leap into action
- Weigh choices for possible positive and negative results
- Prioritize choices in a common-sense way
- Make simple decisions with ease
- Understand the humor in stories that emphasize foolish decisions
- Understand cause-and-effect relationships
- Use prior experiences and knowledge as a basis for current and future decisions

Keep trying! Students need more practice when they

- Have a hard time finding common-sense solutions for simple problems
- Refuse to analyze the problem before trying to solve it or ignore alternative ideas
- Choose solutions that have worked in the past but are unrelated to the current problem or choose solutions that haven't worked in the past for similar situations
- Neglect to weigh options but instead go with the first idea
- Don't understand the humor in stories that is based on characters demonstrating a lack of common sense

Literature Link ~ Common Sense

Primary Grades

Absolute Zero	Cresswell, Helen
Alvin's Swap Shop	Hicks, Clifford
Amelia Bedelia	Parish, Peggy
Freckle Juice	Blume, Judy
Gone Is Gone	Gag, Wanda
It Could Always Be Worse	Zemach, Margot
Ma'ii and Cousin Horned Toad	Begay, Shonto
Miller, Boy, and Donkey, The	La Fontaine, Jean de
Thundercake	Polacco, Patricia
Wagon Wheels	Brenner, Barbara

Intermediate Grades

Ears, Tales, and Common Sense: Stories from the Caribbean	Sherlock, Philip Manderson
Eighteenth Emergency, The	Byars, Betsy
Flight of the Fox, The	Murphy, Shirley Rousseau
Hey, What's Wrong with This One?	Wojciechowska, Maia
Roll of Thunder, Hear My Cry	Taylor, Mildred
Shoeshine Girl	Bulla, Clyde Robert
Sign of the Beaver, The	Speare, Elizabeth George
Snowbound	Mazer, Harry
Take It or Leave It	Molarsky, Osmond
Tales of a Fourth Grade Nothing	Blume, Judy
Where the Red Fern Grows	Rawls, Wilson

Middle School and High School

Ballad of Lucy Whipple	Cushman, Karen
Canyons	Paulsen, Gary
Day No Pigs Would Die, A	Peck, Robert Newton
Into the Wild	Krakauer, Jon
Joyride	Olson, Gretchen

Teacher's Resource

101 Things You Can Do for Our Children's Future	Louv, Richard

Date _____

Dear Parent/Guardian,

When it comes to the LIFESKILL of Common Sense, parents always seem to agree—children need more of it! While it sounds like the simplest LIFESKILL to acquire, some people believe you either have it or you don't and that no amount of practice will help. Actually, this LIFESKILL is no different from any other; the more we practice and apply it, the more it becomes an intrinsic part of us. Our emphasis is on

~Common Sense~

During the next few weeks, our study will include:

- Learning to look for the not-so-obvious elements in a situation in order to solve a problem

- Brainstorming various solutions to problems and rating their potential effectiveness

- Role playing predicaments and exploring problem-solving skills to resolve them

- Listening to stories about ridiculous situations that occur because a character has no common sense

You can help at home by encouraging your child to:

- Welcome problems as an opportunity to use his/her common sense

- Participate in solving problems around the home that you and other family members are trying to solve

- Support friends and siblings as they try to solve problems in a common-sense way

Together, home and school will help your child develop the important LIFESKILL of Common Sense.

Sincerely,

_____

Your child's teacher

Chapter 12

Cooperation

"Work with others."

cooperation *n* **1:** the act of cooperating: common effort
2: association of persons for common benefit

Cooperation: To work together toward a common goal or purpose

WHAT IS COOPERATION?

Cooperation is a working relationship that develops between two or more people as they perform certain tasks. It is characterized by a sense of "give and take" among the group members, of shifting smoothly between the roles of leader and follower, of agreement on goals being pursued.

In *TRIBES: A New Way of Learning and Being Together,* Jeanne Gibbs defines the phases of collaboration as inclusion, influence, and community. If you haven't discovered this book,* it is a "must have" resource, filled with ready-to-go activities that develop each of these stages as well as explanations of the research behind them.

Attributes of Cooperation

Certain attributes or qualities of interaction help us identify the LIFESKILL of Cooperation as people work together. Participants share goals, brainstorm solutions, listen to each others' ideas, delegate duties, readily volunteer assistance, accept responsibility for gathering and organizing information, for creating the product or service, and, finally, for presenting the final project. If the group works together cooperatively for a long time, especially on a highly-charged topic that promotes emotional bonding, a strong sense of camaraderie develops.

Cooperation requires a delicate balancing act or dance in which members alternate between the role of leader and follower as the tasks of the group require different expertise, knowledge, and skills. Through this natural shift in roles, each person in the group comes to feel that his or her contribution is important and essential for a completed project or goal; any one person working alone would probably find it difficult, if not impossible, to complete the entire task. In true cooperation, the whole is greater than the sum of the parts.

* This invaluable book is not generally available through bookstores. However, it can be ordered through Books for Educators, Inc. at www.books4educ.com or call 888/777-9827.

WHY PRACTICE COOPERATION?

Many children possess fewer personal and social skills for cooperating than ever before, yet we live in a time when such skills are vital for current and future success.

Changes in Technology

There are many reasons why children are less adept at cooperating but two significant culprits are overuse of TV and computers.

Television. The popularity of television, and its frequent misuse as baby sitter and educator, has hindered the development of a range of social skills, not just cooperation. According to James Garbarino, "Besides teaching that violence is an acceptable means of conflict resolution, television has another and more insidious effect on human development. By crowding out activities that used to be shared with family and friends, thus substituting passive observation for real interaction, television deprives people of lessons in living together. The less experience people have with face-to-face interaction, the more they distrust one another; and the more hostile and defensive their social maps become, the more toxic the environment becomes."*

Computers. A second technological advancement that, if used incorrectly, can hinder children's socialization is the computer, now found in an increasing number of homes. Again, time before the computer screen is primarily a solitary act, thus limiting opportunities for conversation and interaction. Recent studies have shown that the greater the time spent on the computer, the greater the sense of isolation and deterioration of family interaction**—all of which is counter-productive to developing cooperation.

So, technology, while for many years considered a great gift for all of us, may instead be compared to the Trojan Horse because of the hidden consequences of misuse and overuse. To compensate for these effects of technology, we must actively teach cooperation skills that were formerly picked up from more comprehensive social interactions. We can no longer assume that children will have sufficient opportunities to pick them up on their own.

On the Job

It is hard to imagine a job or occupation today that does not require some form of cooperation. Workers in the future will, more often than not, need to know how to produce new knowledge and ways for making things happen rather than being able to draw upon a previously developed bank of knowledge and old ways of doing things.

---

* See *Raising Children in a Socially Toxic Environment* by James Garbarino, San Francisco: Jossey-Bass Publishers, 1995, p. 35. Also see *Smart Moves* by Carla Hannaford, pp. 93 and 171-172.

** See *Failure to Connect: How Computers Affect Our Children's Minds—For Better and Worse* by Jane Healy, pp. 194-196 and pp. 273-274. Also see *Smart Moves* by Carla Hannaford, pp. 66-67.

Reinventing the wheel by oneself is very inefficient and costly to businesses and organizations. It is expedient to brainstorm, debate, and make decisions based upon a pool of ideas, rather than upon one person's experience and ideas. Working with at least one other person enriches the experience base for shared decision-making, conflict resolution, and life-long learning. Cooperation provides an opportunity to do just that.

For Family Life

Cooperation is fundamental to harmony in the home. Control (it has to be like this), autocracy (my way of the highway), ego (me first) are killers. A sense of family depends upon all being fully included, having influence, and liking as well as loving other members. Cooperation is a must.

For Citizenship

Cooperation skills are also essential for citizenship, especially in an increasingly diverse national population.

HOW DO YOU PRACTICE IT?

We practice cooperation by working in harmony with other people towards a mutual goal. This means creating necessary conditions for group work such as: basic understandings of what it takes to make groups work, procedures to follow, how to create meaningful group jobs,* individual responsibilities, and projected time lines. Your students may totally lack experience in cooperating. If so, start small; set up procedures for partner and group work, keep the beginning projects uncomplicated, model the process, continue to provide adequate support, and include time at the end of each collaborative work period for students to "process the process"—to reflect on the growth of cooperative skills and their ability to achieve goals through cooperation. Again, *TRIBES: A New Way of Learning and Being Together* by Jeanne Gibbs is an excellent source of activities for processing and reflecting.

Start Slowly and Plan for Many Experiences

Start slowly; don't assume students have the social and personal skills to succeed working in groups of four or five at the beginning of the year. Start with partners—groups of two—and then gradually increase group size and the complexity of the tasks. At first, problem solving with other students may be difficult. But with discussion, modeling, and practice, students develop the skills that make it easier. Pursuing the LIFESKILL of Cooperation takes time and effort, by both teachers and students, but it is time well spent when we see the positive, harmonious results.

---

* See *Designing Groupwork: Strategies for the Heterogeneous Classroom,* by Elizabeth Cohen, Teachers College Press, New York, NY, 1994.

Role playing provides opportunities for immediate feedback when a skill is modeled correctly. Please realize that any one experience is not going to provide enough practice for cooperation to happen. Only daily opportunities with different situations over an extended period of time and with a variety of classmates will build the skills students need.

WHAT DOES COOPERATION LOOK LIKE IN THE REAL WORLD?

We

- Volunteer to improve local conditions by being active members of neighborhood watch, the PTA, hospitals, community action groups, and other nonprofit and governmental organizations

- Share information to create a true sense of security for our community

- Work together on a variety of projects, such as "Earth Day," to provide a cleaner, healthier, and safer environment

- Provide materials and assistance during times of disaster (e.g., tornado, flood, fire, earthquake, and severe storms)

- Work together toward a common goal to provide a product or service for the general good

- Avoid trying to control situations and people in order to allow all members of the group to contribute fully

- Support, rather than sabotage, changes to improve our schools and community

- Work with others to research, present, and lobby for needed legislation

WHAT DOES COOPERATION LOOK LIKE IN SCHOOL?

Staff

- Work together to create and provide a strong curriculum for all students

- Create curriculum that helps students develop conceptual ideas and knowledge

- Share materials and supplies among classrooms

- Increase the amount of time for developing a sense of community among class members by providing inclusion activities (*see TRIBES: A New Way of Learning and Being Together* by Jeanne Gibbs), encouraging cooperative learning activities (see *Cooperative Learning* by Spencer Kagan), and including time for family meetings (see *Positive Discipline* by Jane Nelson)

- Reorganize their school day to provide adequate time for pattern recognition and the development of mental programs for long-term memory

- Offer assistance to new staff members as they learn the school routines, policies, and schedules

- Grow professionally and personally by coaching others and allowing themselves to be coached

- Mentor new co-workers and offer support to others who are experiencing difficulty in their work assignment

Students

- Assist classmates in acquiring, learning, and reviewing curriculum

- Work together for greater understandings of social, emotional, and learning differences

- Organize and use materials cooperatively

- Offer help to other students

- Work in harmony with classmates and teachers

- Include every classmate in work, study, or play groups

- Mediate differences

- Participate in a play, musical group, student council, school safety patrol, and/or team sports

INQUIRIES TO DEVELOP COOPERATION

Whole Class Inquiries

- Pick up your puzzle piece from the teacher. When the music starts, you must be silent. Walk around the room and locate the other people who have pieces to complete the puzzle your piece fits into. Work cooperatively to put the puzzle together. Glue the completed puzzle onto another piece of poster paper. Decide on a name for your group and write that on the poster.
[*Directions to teacher for putting children into new groups or learning clubs*] On paper, arrange the children into groups of four or five students. Use one sheet of construction paper (same color) for each group. Divide each sheet into jigsaw pieces, one for each child in that group. Write one name per piece (a group of four children will require one piece of construction paper cut into four jigsaw pieces). Just before starting the activity, hand each child the piece with their name on it. Play music. Check the completed puzzles for accuracy of group members.

- Listen to the words of the song "Cooperation" on the LIFESKILLS tape/CD by Russ and Judy Eacker. Create pictures in your mind of what the words mean. Listen to the song again. Create movements that would help someone understand the meaning of the LIFESKILL of Cooperation. Perform them for your learning club.

- Name an early spring day as "Clean Up the Playground Day." Gather rakes, shovels, garden gloves, wheelbarrow, and trash can with plastic liner. First, take some "before" photos of the playground/schoolyard. Then organize learning clubs for different tasks.

   — Learning Club #1: Walk around the schoolyard. Carefully pick up papers and place in a recycle bin.
   — Learning Club #2: Pick up cans and bottles; place them in the trash can.
   — Learning Club #3: Rake up old leaves and place in leaf bags or follow your community's laws for garden waste.
   — Learning Club #4: Put twigs, branches and other debris in the wheelbarrow. Move them to a place designated for pick up.
   — When the schoolyard looks neat and clean, put away all of the tools and admire the result of your own personal "Clean Up the Playground Day." Take some "after" photos. Add all of the pictures to your class scrapbook.
   — Assign each learning club one day a week for any quick pick ups to keep the playground looking neat.

Small Group/Individual Inquiries

- Write three or more procedures with your learning club that describe the actions you will all follow at the end of the day to get your area neat and clean before leaving for home. Add some illustrations that will remind you of the actions needed. Place the procedures in your learning club binder for easy reference.

- With your learning-club members, plan to make some fruit salad for a snack. Decide the following: which fruits will be included, who will bring each, what kind of container and serving cups will be used, and whether or not the fruit needs to be cut before coming to school. Assemble the salad, serve and taste your "Friendly Fruit Salad."

- Organize the learning club materials (such as markers, scissors, crayons, colored pencils, rulers, glue sticks) in a container so that the members may use them in a cooperative way. Write three or more polite ways to ask for materials when someone else is using them.

- Brainstorm five or more attributes of a cooperative group with your learning club. Choose three of those qualities and include them in a pledge that describes how the class can work together. Present your pledge to the class.

- Research two people who work cooperatively in your community. Illustrate three examples of how they work together to get the job done.

- Write "Cooperative Group Procedures" to help your learning club work together in a productive way. Describe at least four steps. Use color and graphics. Give each member of the learning club a copy to use. Review and change the steps as needed.

- Design a spelling/math board game for two to four players that teaches about cooperation. Write two or more rules to help the players understand the goal and how to play. Create the board, choose some tokens for the players, add dice or a spinner, and create some game cards. Play the game with a partner and ask for feedback on the game's purpose (teaching cooperation).

- Interview an adult who works at your school. Invite him/her to describe the job and ways it requires cooperation. Produce a classified advertisement of 25 words or less about the position. Ask 10 classmates if they would like this job some day. Share the survey results with another learning club. Design and send a thank-you note to the person you interviewed, sharing one idea you have learned from him/her about cooperation.

- Choose one of the class jigsaw puzzles with 100 or more pieces. Divide the pieces among your learning-club members. Work silently to complete the puzzle. Show the completed picture to the teacher. Brainstorm with your club members three strategies that helped you to complete the task. Place this list in the procedure binder and use the strategies for the next group project.

- Invite a school business partner representative to visit your classroom. Plan three or more questions, at least one focusing on cooperation, to help you and your classmates understand the reasons behind this particular business-school partnership. Write your questions down and be prepared to share them during the visit. Design a billboard/commercial/advertisement for the company to explain the partnership. Mail this drawing to your school's business partner along with a short thank-you note.

- Develop an annotated list of eight or more books about cooperation that a boy or girl your age would enjoy reading. Include title, author, publisher, and a short description of each book. Include both fiction and non-fiction stories. Be sure that you have read each book before you share the list with your classmates. Survey those classmates who read a book on your list; ask them what they learned about cooperation from the story.

SIGNS OF SUCCESS

Congratulations! Students are showing signs of Cooperation when they

- Work collaboratively

- Solve problems in learning clubs

- Learn to "give and take" in the relationship

- Shift roles between leader and follower

- Accept responsibility for gathering information

- Feel that their contribution is important and necessary for the completion of the task

- Understand that the "whole is greater than the parts"

- Show signs of good citizenship by working with students of all races, religions, and ethnic origins

Keep trying! Students need more practice when they

- Involve themselves in power struggles

- Talk but forget to follow the Lifelong Guideline of Active Listening

- Refuse to work with other children because of their race, religion, or ethnic origin

- Believe their part is more important than anyone else's

- Feel that their contribution is NOT important and needed

- Argue and bicker over every little item

- Refuse to share materials

LITERATURE LINK ~ COOPERATION

Primary Grades

Ant and the Elephant, The	Peet, Bill
Aunt Harriet's Underground Railroad in the Sky	Ringgold, Faith
Changes, Changes	Hutchins, Pat
Church Mice Adrift	Oakley, Graham
Garden of Happiness, The	Tamar, Erika
Harriet and the Promised Land	Jacob, Lawrence
King Wacky	Gackenbach, Dick
New Coat for Anna, A	Ziefort, Harriet
Patchwork Quilt, The	Flourney, Valerie
Thousand Pails of Water, A	Roy, Ronald
Wheels on the School Bus, The	DeJong, Meindart

Intermediate Grades

Bridge to Terabithia	Paterson, Katherine
Cay, The	Taylor, Theodore
Cricket in Times Square	Seldon, George
Dunc and Amos Get Famous	Paulson, Gary
Follow the Drinking Gourd	Winteer, Jeannette
I Speak English for My Mom	Stanck, Muriel
Little House on the Prairie	Wilder, Laura Ingalls
Not-Just-Anybody Family, The	Byars, Betsy
Secret Garden, The	Burnett, Frances Hodgson
Sign of the Beaver, The	Spear, Elizabeth George
Whipping Boy, The	Fleischman, Sid

Middle School and High School

Endurance: Shackleton's Legendary Antarctic Expedition, The   Alexander, Caroline

Lord of the Flies   Golding, William Gerald

Snowbound   Mazer, Harry

Steal Away Home   Ruby, Lois

Teacher's Resources

Cooperative Learning   Kagan, Spencer

Creating Community Anywhere: Finding Support and Connection in a Fragmented World   Shaffer, C. and K. Anundsen

TRIBES: A New Way of Learning and Being Together   Gibbs, Jeanne

Date _____

Dear Family,

Once again we are beginning the study of a new LIFESKILL. This time we are focusing on

~Cooperation~

Webster's Ninth New Collegiate Dictionary defines cooperation as follows:

1. the act of cooperating: common effort

2. association of persons for common benefit

At school we will practice working together in many different ways. Students will:

- Brainstorm the attributes of cooperation

- Write procedures for working cooperatively

- Find examples of cooperation in our local and state governments

Our free public school system was founded to educate students for the role they will play as citizens in a democratic society. Here are some ways that your family can focus on developing cooperation and citizenship at home:

- Interview someone in your family/community who chose to leave his/her homeland to be free. Find examples of governmental cooperation that helped to make this move happen.

- Choose an issue that is important to your community, such as pollution, the condition of roads, or playgrounds. Collect and read some newspaper articles on the topic. Learn both points of view. Ask your children where they stand on the issue.

- Take your child along on Election Day and ask for permission to take him/her into the voting booth with you. Explain a few of your choices and make clear your family's policy on confidentiality.

- Visit your state's legislature while it is in session. Find examples of cooperation between the branches of government.

I welcome opportunities for us to work cooperatively to educate our future citizens.

Sincerely,

_____

Your child's teacher

Chapter 13

Courage

"BELIEVE IN YOURSELF AND JUST GO FOR IT."

courage *n* mental or moral strength to venture, persevere, and withstand danger, fear, or difficulty

Courage: To act according to one's beliefs despite fear of consequences

WHAT IS COURAGE?

Do you remember the lion from *The Wizard of Oz*? He was afraid all the time and was known as a coward. What he wanted more than anything else from the great Wizard of Oz was the gift of courage. What he eventually learned is that courage is not something you can get from someone else; instead, it comes from within—from a belief that what you're summoning your courage to do is the right thing to do and that you are committed to do it.

Courage is having the mental or moral strength to do what needs to be done despite problems, fear, danger, or consequences. A courageous person is one who repeatedly faces the difficulties and challenges that life delivers and perseveres no matter what the barriers or consequences may be. When we hear the word "courage," other terms such as bravery, heroism, determination, and risk-taking come to mind; each one of these implies a sense of strength, both physical or moral, that empowers an individual to move beyond fears when confronting any dilemma.

Courage Begins Early in Life

By our very nature, humans are born courageous. Think of a baby taking that first step without holding on to anything. Does fear of falling prevent further attempts? No, the baby just gets up and tries again. Do you remember your first day of school at the tender age of four or five? The butterflies in your stomach? Wondering if you would ever have any friends? Wondering if you would ever learn to read? Courage helped you meet new people, learn new skills, and appreciate adventure in the real world. Life is full of uncertainties and challenges but courage makes progress possible. Reflect on the words of Eleanor Roosevelt: "You gain strength, courage, and confidence by every experience in which you really stop to look fear in the face. You are able to say to yourself, 'I lived through this horror. I can take the next thing that comes along.'"*

* Eleanor Roosevelt, *You Learn by Living,* New York: Harper & Brothers, 1960.

Kinds of Courage

To understand the LIFESKILL of Courage, it's helpful to identify courage as physical (of the body) and moral (of the mind), although many demands for courage call upon both.

There are two kinds of physical courage. One type is chosen by the participant as an exhilarating, personal risk-taking task, such as free-fall parachuting, deep sea diving, rappelling down a mountain. The other is a more spontaneous response to a situation that is thrust upon one with little time for conscious decision-making, such as jumping into raging flood waters to save a child, dashing into a burning building to rescue a trapped person, passing the helicopter's dangling lifeline to a fellow injured airline passenger as you both float in shark-infested waters. In both kinds of courage, the body responds by producing chemicals to help us confront the fear and perform super-human tasks. You feel fear, recognize it, control it, and then make it work for you. While taking the first step may be the most difficult decision, courage grows and expands once the action has begun.

Moral courage includes knowing right from wrong and standing up for your convictions. Moral cowards, those who either give up or give in, never win in the game of life. They might feel they're winning the occasional conflict but their triumphs are seldom glorious, don't last long, nor do they inspire future generations.

Moral heroes face up to ethical challenges in daily life. This same courage over day-to-day issues and events can be drawn upon during times of great stress and controversy. Gandhi and Martin Luther King, Jr. are internationally recognized heroes of moral courage. They remind us that the greatest battleground on which courage is fought is within us. They placed integrity above fear, dread, panic, acute embarrassment, and such to hold true to their visions.

In Western culture, courage is primarily thought of in terms of physical courage rather than moral courage, for example, sports heroes such as football and hockey players, wrestlers, and so forth. In everyday life, however, it is moral courage that carries the day.

WHY PRACTICE COURAGE?

Character development is impossible without the LIFESKILL of Courage for it is not easy to do the right thing; if it were, the world would be a much kinder and gentler place than it is. We have to have courage to act upon what we know to be right.

Courage is a critical element in three important areas of our life: relationships, leadership roles, and teamwork.

Courage in Relationships

In friendships and in the intimacy of marriage and parent-child interactions, it takes courage to say "No" when it's easier to say "Yes"; it takes courage to say "Yes" when the truth is "No"; it takes courage to say what is really so rather than what's expected or what the person wants to hear, especially when it's about our feelings and needs. Where and when we are vulnerable, courage is needed so that we may face situations with integrity rather than with indifference or lies. Courage is not for wimps!

Courage in Leadership Roles

Being a leader requires tremendous courage. Among the many challenges to face are embracing change, committing to personal best, and thinking outside the box.

Embracing Change. Although we may understand that change is inevitable, it still takes courage to embrace change because the outcomes are unknown. Extreme discomfort and disappointment, even failure, could be just around the corner. And heaven help us if we're the one who leads others to failure!

Committing to Personal Best. Leaders in education must have the courage to strive for optimum results by modeling personal best and by not accepting anything less from themselves and others. Think how our lives would change if we modeled the LIFESKILL of Personal Best 100 percent of the time. To do so takes enormous courage because while we are striving valiantly to "walk our talk," we must at the same time accept the reality that our personal best doesn't mean we're perfect. In applying the Lifelong Guidelines and LIFESKILLS we, like our students, are works in progress.

Holding others to their personal best is not a job for shrinking violets either. It flies in the face of the norm of all bureaucracies which pull toward mediocrity. And, to the extent that our personal best is not perfect—and who is?—we're put in the awkward position of telling others to "Do as I say" rather than "Do as I do."

It takes courage to ask the question: How good is my personal best? If we've got areas of weakness, and who doesn't, what are we doing about them? What are we doing to keep improving? And as leaders (administrator or teacher), we can't send others off to inservice training on the Lifelong Guidelines and LIFESKILLS if we too aren't genuinely in the process of working on our own behaviors.

The stakes are high and the process painfully visible.

Thinking Outside the Box. Sometimes tried and true solutions no longer achieve the desired results. We must think "outside the box" for more creative answers and some that may have been rebuffed and rejected by our team. At this point, courage and perseverance go hand in hand as we guide ourself and others out of complacency and into risk-taking. On other occasions, it's essential for leaders to hear and face the truth, especially when it defies their personal beliefs. The willingness to admit the possibility that our viewpoint is fallible, or to change our opinion, requires perhaps the greatest courage of all.

Courage in Teamwork

While all of us hold leadership positions in some areas of responsibility, we also serve as team members—small group and collective whole—for other endeavors. Teamwork requires its own brand of courage—the courage to think clearly under pressure when others don't concur with our ideas and goals, to set out to persuade others when the facts don't speak for themselves, to question decisions that don't make sense, and to mentor someone new to the profession. Teams face difficult decisions, some critical, requiring bravery and boldness to ensure that they're in children's best interests and not simply the most comfortable route for adults.

A common trap for teams is falling into what Glickman* calls congeniality instead of collegiality. In collegiality, teams agree to disagree but focus on professional issues. In congeniality, getting along smoothly is the core value; professional issues that need serious discussion and some head banging are avoided.

HOW DO YOU PRACTICE IT?

Practicing courage takes courage! Compare it to going swimming in a cold, spring-fed lake on the first hot day of summer. Are you the kind of person who, ignoring the frosty temperature of the water, lets out a holler and dives right in, emerging within seconds to declare through chattering teeth, "The water's great! Come on in!" Or, do you cautiously dangle one big toe into the shallow water and slowly begin to immerse one body part at a time, declaring, "It's freezing! I don't know if I want to do this or not!"

You can approach courage the same way. You can either jump right in—and commit yourself to practicing courage in all aspects of your life—or you can start gradually by selecting only a few areas of your life and then expand from there. Either way, the job gets done.

There are some variables, however, that may affect your comfort level and thus your starting point. First, is the issue insignificant or highly-charged for you? Second, are you standing alone or are others standing with you? Third, what are your tolerance levels for things such as uncertainty, risk-taking, nonagreement, or disapproval?

Look for Personal Examples

Think about all of the times you have called upon inner strength and personal conviction to be courageous. Reflect on those experiences. Why did you stand up for your beliefs? What was the driving force behind you? What feelings did you have afterward?

Learn to distinguish nervous excitement from true anxiety. Do some soul-searching; know yourself, your feelings, your beliefs, and your opinions.

Establish and/or clarify your personal goals; these will guide your decision making and will keep you on the path to what is most important in your life.

---

* See *Renewing America's Schools: A Guide to School-Based Action* by Carl Glickman. (San Francisco: Jossey-Bass Publishers, 1993), pp. 22-23.

Act on your moral convictions. Share your opinions with others but, at the same time, listen to theirs. Don't be swayed by ineffective arguments, group size, or fleeting feelings of self-doubt. Know where you stand.

Path of the Warrior

A big part of courage is willingness to give up control of the outcome and stop playing it safe. The world is bigger than we are; a plan for the common good is often larger than our own personal vision for it. If we try to control events, we invariably squeeze them down to less powerful solutions than could be accomplished by teamwork, however messy the process. We can't control events, we can only do our best at playing our part in things.

To practice courage, travel the path of the warrior. First, show up. Second, pay attention. Third, tell the truth. And, fourth, let go of the consequences.

WHAT DOES COURAGE LOOK LIKE IN THE REAL WORLD?
We

- Speak up for ideas and policies that benefit all people

- Take calculated risks

- Develop new products

- Start our own businesses

- Embrace change

- Dare to leave one profession in which we are unhappy and take a different position that may be a better match for our interests and education

- Return to school or college to complete a degree

- Take an unpopular stand when we believe the cause is just

- Ignore the limitations others place on us and always work to personal best

- Speak our minds but always apologize for inappropriate actions and words

- Taste different foods and visit new places

WHAT DOES COURAGE LOOK LIKE IN SCHOOL?

Staff

- Tell the truth

- Create an atmosphere of trust so that all members of the school community feel free to take risks

- Speak up against plans, strategies, and curriculum that may not be age-appropriate for students and/or not based on best knowledge of brain research and best practices to implement the brain research

- Support peers and students when you believe their actions are correct even if such actions are unpopular

- Implement new methods to improve even when others may not understand or agree

- Support worthwhile literature against attacks from those who would censor everyone's reading material

Students

- Are willing to accept new challenges

- Acknowledge when they make a mistake

- Develop strategies to deal with the class "bully"

- Befriend a classmate whom others ignore, tease, or attack with put-downs

- Accept responsibility for their own behaviors and actions

- Ask questions or say "I don't understand. Please explain it to me again."

- Taste new and different foods from the school cafeteria

- Open their minds to learn new ideas, approaches, and skills

INQUIRIES THAT DEVELOP COURAGE

Whole Class

- As a learning club, brainstorm three strategies to deal with someone who bullies. Rank your strategies for their effectiveness. Role play with your learning club how to use the top three strategies until each of you feels that you can use them with ease. Exchange strategies with another learning club in your class.

- Design a "courage" card to present to a local citizen whose outstanding action(s) have improved life for others in our community. Illustrate the card with a drawing that further identifies what he/she did. Mail the card to that person.

Small Group/Individual Inquiries

- Listen to *The True Story of Ruby Bridges* by Robert Coles. Illustrate two or more ways that Ruby showed that she was a courageous child. Illustrate one time that you have shown courage (learning to do something, helping someone when you were scared, helping a friend deal with bullies).

- Listen to the song for courage on the LIFESKILLS tape. Sing it again and again until the words are in your memory. Add motions and facial expressions that will help listeners understand more about courage. Sing the song for your classmates and invite them to sing along on the chorus section.
  OPTION: Write your own lyrics for a tune that you know. The words should offer ideas on how to use courage in everyday life. Teach it to your learning club or classmates.

- Watch the segment of *The Wonderful Wizard of Oz* that introduces the character who is looking for courage. List two ways you are like that character and two ways you are different. Share this with someone you believe has great courage.

- After watching a wildlife video, list 10 situations in which an animal exhibited courage. Decide which you think is the most courageous action. Practice that action and perform it for a partner. Ask him/her to identify the action and an animal that might show courage this way.

- Listen to your teacher read from *The Wizard of Oz*. List five acts of courage that the lion performed before he realized he already was courageous. Create a diorama that illustrates the scene when the lion finally understands he has the LIFESKILL of Courage. Display it in your classroom library.

- Choose a familiar tune such as "Twinkle, Twinkle, Little Star" and compose lyrics that will teach your class five or more attributes of a courageous person. Write at least two verses and transfer the words to overhead sheets. Add motions that will further explain courage. Teach the song to the class.

- Observe a toddler between the ages of one and two years old for at least 30 minutes. List three or more examples of this child using the LIFESKILL of courage. Note what the child does if a courageous attempt fails. Share your observations with the child's mother, your mother, or with the teacher.

- Choose an issue that is important to our community, such as pollution, the condition of parks and playgrounds, or dangerous traffic conditions. Collect and read four or more newspaper articles on the topic. Listen to someone speak about the issue on radio or TV or at a public lecture or governmental meeting. Learn the different points of view. Make a visual aid (sign, poster, video, photo album) to show your classmates how you feel about the issue. Be prepared to answer questions.

- Read a nonfiction book with the theme of courage in your learning club. Choose one part in which one of the characters learns about courage. With your group, act out this part of the story for another group. Explain why your group chose this particular scene.

- Learn 10 phrases in a different language and practice them with a partner. Brainstorm three emotions you might feel if you were visiting a foreign country and weren't fluent in the language. Explain how you would need the LIFESKILL of Courage to handle these emotions.

SIGNS OF SUCCESS

Congratulations! Students are showing signs of Courage when they

- Speak out against injustice and prejudice

- Investigate a new activity

- Practice skills even when the material is difficult

- Analyze how they feel after taking an unpopular but courageous stand

- Use good judgment before taking risks

- Seek relevant data to make informed decisions

- Speak up for themselves and their beliefs

- Stand against the group to follow their conscience

Keep trying! Students need more practice when they

- Don't say what they feel or what they believe because they fear other people's opinions

- Stay silent when they witness incidents of racial, religious, and ethnic prejudice

- Refuse to try a new activity, skill, or project

- Disregard their conscience and ignore "gut" feelings about right and wrong

- Deny personal responsibility for their actions

- Avoid confrontations to take the easy way out

- Avoid an opportunity to be courageous

Literature Link ~ Courage

Primary Grades

Amelia's Road	Altman, Linda Jacobs
Arthur's Loose Teeth	Lillian, Hoban
Brave Margaret	San Souci, Robert
Courage of Sarah Noble, The	Dalgliesh, Alice
Fire Race: A Karok Coyote Tale about How Fire Came to People	Retold by London, Jonathon
Footwarmer and the Crow, The	Coleman, Evelyn
Girl Named Disaster, A	Farmer, Nancy
Knots on a Counting Rope	Martin, Bill Jr.
Minty, A Story of Young Harriet Tubman	Schroeder, Alex
Sheila Rae, the Brave	Henkes, Kevin
True Story of Ruby Bridges, The	Coles, Robert

Intermediate Grades

Be a Perfect Person in Just Three Days	Manes, Stephen
Black Snowman, The	Mendez, Phil
Call It Courage	Sperry, Armstrong
Cat, The	Taylor, Theodore
Grey Cloud	Graeber, Charlotte
Helen Keller: From Tragedy to Triumph	Wilkie, Katharine
It's a Mile from Here to Glory	Lee, Robert C.
Night Crossing, The	Ackerman, Karen
Pink and Say	Polacco, Patricia
Stone Fox	Gardiner, John Reynolds
Women Warriers	Heller, Julek

Middle School and High School

Anne Frank, the Diary of a Young Girl	Frank, Anne
Hold Fast to Dreams	Pinkney, Andrea Davis
I Know Why the Caged Bird Sings	Angelou, Maya
Jemmy	Hassler, Jon
Kids With Courage: True Stories About Young People Making a Difference	Lewis, Barbara A.

Teacher's Resources

Educating Everybody's Children	Cole, Robert W., editor
MegaSkills: How Families Can Help Children Succeed in School and Beyond	Rich, Dorothy

Date _____

Dear Family,

   Webster's Ninth New Collegiate Dictionary defines our next LIFESKILL as the mental and moral strength necessary to persevere in the face of danger, fear, or difficulty. Our class is concentrating on the LIFESKILL of

~COURAGE~

Our exploration of courage will lead us to:

- Research historical events to discover people of courage

- Identify courageous characters in literature

- Analyze actions of people in the news

- Design aknowledgement cards for local people who exhibit courage

You can bolster your child's development of the LIFESKILL of Courage at home when you:

- Share stories of family member's acts of courage

- Nurture your child's interests and endeavors

- Encourage your child to venture out and try new activities

- Help your child accept feedback about their actions—both positive and negative

- Listen as your child shares experiences

- Support and understand his/her attempts to be courageous

   Scientists, writers, artists, inventors, politicians, teachers, and parents—to name just a few—use the LIFESKILL of Courage in everyday life. It is a necessary ingredient for developing character because it allows to continue exploring and growing. In the words of artist, Georgia O'Keefe: "I am afraid every day but I never let it stop me from doing anything."

Sincerely,

_____

Your child's teacher

Chapter 14

Curiosity

"ALWAYS SEEK TO UNDERSTAND."

curiosity *n* **1**: desire to know   **a:** inquisitive interest in others' concerns
b: interest leading to inquiry (intellectual)

Curiosity: A desire to investigate and seek understanding of one's world

WHAT IS CURIOSITY?

Curiosity is a delightful, compelling, and sometimes annoying characteristic of our favorite mammals—puppies, kittens, otters, and, most of all, human children. It guides us to learn about the world and its possibilities and limits, to discover what is fun and what is harmful, to practice old skills and experiment with new ones. Perhaps because we can remember the past and project the future, we're the most curious animals on earth. We are constantly exploring our world and everything that's in it. Human curiosity is a constant search for answers—how things work, why they work. Curiosity is the wellspring of human learning and the inner engine of creativity.

Curiosity Is Innate

Curiosity is a craving, a longing, a passion for knowledge. It is innate in young children. With their passion for exploring and learning new things, babies' drive to explore is taken for granted. Increased neurological connections are created by such exploration and rapidly used as the basis for more curiosity and more learning. Investigating the unusual creates new pathways in the brain. The more pathways, the more connections we can make.

Natural curiosity is easily seen in babies who explore their bodies and immediate environment—toes, fingers, crib, and toys—reaching for everything within sight. When crawling begins, a baby's world expands to include anything within range, creating the need to carefully examine the house for any dangers such as plugs, open doorways, stoves. As the toddler conquers the rudiments of speech, the endless "Why?" emerges as a recurring question.

Curiosity Can Be Fragile

Yet as innate as curiosity is, it can be quite fragile, often diminishing as people are squelched by regimented, sterile learning and living environments that don't satisfy or reward curiosity. For many children, their curiosity slowly begins its spiral descent from wanting to know the "why" about everything to not even caring enough to ask a question. Please note: Boredom is not a natural state for humans. Students who need to be "motivated" to learn are students who have experienced adverse, spirit-crushing circumstances.

Curiosity and Creativity

Creativity often originates from dissatisfaction with the way things are or seem to be. Curiosity—"How could this be made to work better?"—pushes us to investigate and invent. By encouraging and strengthening the LIFESKILL of Curiosity in childhood, we are creating future inventors, scientists, writers, artists, composers, and thinkers. After all, it is curiosity that gives birth to our theories and pushes us to prove, improve, or disprove them. We often use other LIFESKILLS, such as Patience, Caring, Perseverance, and Resourcefulness in conjunction with Curiosity to facilitate our search for answers. Curiosity is the driving force that stimulates and renews the spark needed in our search.

WHY PRACTICE CURIOSITY?

Without the LIFESKILL of Curiosity, life would be very different. An almost endless list of creations would be missing from our lives such as electronic technologies of all kinds, stories, symphonies, buildings, poems, medicine, rock music, cars, planes, and rocket ships. All of these became reality because somewhere along the way, a caring adult took the time to stimulate and encourage a students' curiosity. That student, once grown, rewards us with additional creative efforts.

Lack of curiosity is detrimental to society. When too many of us stop asking questions and seeking answers, human accomplishments will decline. On the other hand, questions about such issues as pollution of the Earth's water can lead to answers that improve the quality of life for all living things. It's vital that we practice the LIFESKILL of Curiosity by continuing to ask "Why."

Lack of curiosity on a personal level is severely limiting. Opportunities pass the uncurious by. Those without curiosity are poor learners. Their knowledge and skill base grows like an inch worm rather than by leaps and bounds. They make poor conversationalists who have little to say that hasn't been heard before. Their personal satisfaction level is low and employment options and income are limited.

Curiosity propels us to ask *what* and *why* and *how* questions to search for meaning, for new ways to do old things. It prompts us to observe more closely, analyze more thoroughly, formulate theories to test, and question the obvious. Curiosity makes us think. For the uncurious, death is a short step away.

HOW DO YOU PRACTICE IT?

It is important to understand that not all students will demonstrate curiosity for the same subject areas because no two brains are the same. We must allow space for students to pursue individual interests. Having said that, however, some things are important to learn for citizenship and family harmony, whether they immediately "tickle our fancy" or not. But a heightened sense of curiosity, like sugar, makes the medicine go down and opens doors to expanding careers, lifelong interests, and hobbies that we might not otherwise have discovered. Nurture curiosity.

Curiosity Is Contagious: Model It

Not surprisingly, the best way to encourage and nurture your students' LIFESKILL of Curiosity is to model curiosity yourself. Are you still avoiding learning how to program the VCR? Are you still avoiding computers and "web-less"? Do you wait for others to figure out new equipment so you can get the quick "explanation for dummies"? If so, you're killing your students' curiosity by example.

Instead, be a lover of books and web surfing. Devote your conversations with others to ideas and "what ifs" rather than gossip about others. Read daily, especially nonfiction, and share what you find exciting and fascinating with your family. Be an active hobbyist—practice your hobby weekly if not daily. Learn at least one new, significant skill a year, such as: play a new instrument, learn to sing, weave, hang glide, sew, cook a new field of ethnic foods, ride a horse.

As educators, we need to nurture our own sense of curiosity. As elementary educators, we must move beyond being a generalist and cultivate special areas of knowledge and expertise. Expect to read at least 20 minutes a day in subject area content and another 10-15 minutes of professional literature. We also need to develop interest in many topics, learn more about the world around us, and model the joy of learning for our students.

Also, we should involve parents in modeling the LIFESKILL of Curiosity for their children. On Parent Night, best held at the first week of the school year, explain the importance of the LIFESKILL of Curiosity and give ideas for developing curiosity at home. Provide a sign-up sheet for family members to list their areas of expertise and skills and ask them to volunteer time as resource people and leaders of special interest groups and clubs. When it comes to the LIFESKILL of Curiosity, modeling is everything. It's a state of mind, a world view that we live, not just talk about.

Formalize Curiosity

As students' curiosity grows, as they learn to use and direct it, teach them formal ways to use it. For example, the so-called "scientific method" is merely a formalized process to channel curiosity. Computer programming is focused effort to satisfy one's curiosity; in contrast computer hacking is curiosity with no bounds.

As we encourage students to exercise their curiosity, help them hone their skills for theorizing, articulating questions, researching data, organizing information, and sharing wisdom. These are the tools of solid thinking in the real world, not just the classroom. Also, teach them to honor the interests of others.

WHAT DOES CURIOSITY LOOK LIKE IN THE REAL WORLD?

We

- Examine the natural world and ask "Why?"

- Wonder, "What if. . . ?" "How can we. . . ?" "Let's try. . ."

- Embrace lifelong learning in vocations and avocations

- Join organizations, clubs, and interest groups

- Are eager to introduce ourselves to new neighbors and welcome them to the neighborhood

- Frequently visit information sources such as the library and World Wide Web for information on varying topics

- Discover new and better ways to accomplish a task

- Experiment in life activities such as cooking, gardening, exercising, traveling, and reading

- Seek answers to the unknown

- Ask theoretical, speculative, and hypothetical questions

- Invent new machines, tools, and products

WHAT DOES CURIOSITY LOOK LIKE IN SCHOOL?

Staff

- Work as a team to create curriculum and lessons that engage the curiosity of all in the school community

- Ask probing questions to understand information

- Develop personal interests, hobbies, and pastimes to share with students and staff

- Encourage student questions

- Open their minds to new ideas

- Implement new strategies and techniques

- Read voraciously and daily; always have at least one book in progress; complete at least one a week

- Read current brain research, educational studies, and subject content to improve classroom and school

Students

- Ask questions to increase knowledge

- Form and test hypotheses when facing new ideas

- Find more than one solution for a problem

- Design new and innovative projects

- Learn outside of the school environment in clubs, groups, and sports

- Experience new activities even if friends show no interest

- Find real-world applications for skills and knowledge learned in class

- Read biographies of scientists, inventors, statesmen, composers, and artists

INQUIRIES TO DEVELOP CURIOSITY
Whole Group

- Listen as the teacher reads *Curious George* by H. A. and Margaret Rey. Make a list of five things that puzzled George. Choose two of them to illustrate. Title your drawing "Curious George." Read the list again and check any items you would like to know more about. Share what you are curious about with a partner.

- Choose one of the following technological products (television, computer, smoke detector, audio cassette player, radio, or VCR) and find out how it works. Ask an adult for help to look inside the product. Draw a diagram of the inner workings. Using recycled materials, create a model that will help others understand how this product works. Display your project for your classmates.

Small Group/Individual Inquiries

- Design a book titled: "MY CURIOSITY BOOK." When you think of an interesting question, write it at the top of a page. Look for information in the library or by investigating in your neighborhood that will help you find the answer your question. Write it under the question. Draw a picture that answers the question for someone who does not read. Share the things your book with the school librarian, your teacher, or a friend.

- Illustrate three or more objects in your school about which you are curious. List where each one is found and what you think it does. Check with an adult who works with each object to see if your predictions were accurate. If they were not, learn all about the object and share the information with one other curious child in your class.

- Study the classroom pet for a few minutes each day for two or more weeks. Write two or more questions you have about this pet. Interview a classroom expert on this animal or visit the library to find answers to each question. Share the information with your parents. Get their permission to baby-sit for the critter during a vacation so you can observe his/her actions for a longer period of time.

- Choose four items from your classroom. Draw a picture of each object on an index card (5" x 8") plus write the object's name on the card. Use a magnifying glass to examine one of the objects. Focus on one special part. Draw what you see on another index card that's also 5" x 8" but do not label what the item is. Do the same for each of the other three cards for which you drew a picture and wrote the name of the item. Ask a partner to match the magnified picture with its matching card that has the original picture and label on it. Provide feedback for your partner on his/her matching skills.

- Create a list of six or more quotations containing the word "curious" or "curiosity." Start with "Curiosity killed the cat. Satisfaction brought it back." Design a banner for each quotation; include both the quote and an illustration on each.Display them outside the classroom door. Explain to your learning club how you interpreted the quotations.

- Choose an insect that you're curious about. Identify five body parts and predict how each one helps the insect. Research the body parts, their design, and their purpose. Use clay or paper to create a large model of the insect. Label the five parts and why they're important to the insect. Make a four-fold title card with the insect's scientific name, the name we know it by, your name, and one more question you have about this insect. Explain what you learned to an interested classmate.

- Browse through a dictionary, newspaper, or magazine to find eight new words that you want to learn. Create vocabulary flash cards by copying each word onto a 5" x 8" index card. On the other side of the card, write a sentence defining each word plus an illustration. Place your cards in alphabetical order. Ask the members of your learning club to check that you understand the correct usage of the words.

- Observe four students in your class when they are showing the LIFESKILL of Curiosity (e.g., during a science lesson or on the playground). Note their activities and actions. Develop a short pantomime skit (no more than four minutes) that uses four or more "curiosity" actions and body movements (one for each of the four students). Ask each person to guess which activity was his/hers and to describe what he/she was doing at the time.

- Brainstorm six or more ways you think school will be different for students in your grade in the year 2050. Build a diorama or model showing the differences. Share your predictions with the class.

- Interview an adult. Invite him/her to share five or more topics they wanted to learn more about as a child. List current topics of interest. Compare both lists to determine if any of the interests match.

- Read a biography about one of the following people: Alexander Graham Bell, Rachel Carson, Madame Curie, Leonardo da Vinci, Thomas Alva Edison, Albert Einstein, or Christa McAuliffe. Write a paragraph of 50 words or less nominating your person to receive the National Curiosity Award. Design the award you think should be presented to the winner. Include in your design key ways your candidate demonstrated the LIFESKILL of Curiosity.

- Design a toy for a student your age. Develop a prototype to use for modeling and demonstration purposes. Produce a commercial (audio/video) of not more than one minute that introduces the toy's name, how it is used, and the proposed cost. Air the commercial for your classmates and survey them to determine how many would purchase the product.

- Choose two items (smaller than your two hands together) from around the classroom. Use a magnifying glass to study each object. Identify three or more ways the items are different and three or more ways the items are the same. Display the information on a Venn diagram and explain to your learning club.

SIGNS OF SUCCESS

Congratulations! Students are showing signs of Curiosity when they

- Relentlessly search for answers to questions

- Improve a new skill or develop a talent

- Create a play, poem, painting, story, or science project

- Acknowledge an interest in many different topics

- Become an expert in a field of interest

- Observe the people, actions, and objects in their world

- Focus on a project from the planning stages to the final product

- Share their interests with others

- Become a mentor

- Express wonder when observing an amazing accomplishment

- Reflect on their ideas and learning

Keep trying! Students need more practice when they

- Are afraid to ask questions or share ideas because others might laugh

- Spend too much time (more than 30 minutes a day) watching TV

- Feel it's a "waste of time" to explore significant questions

- Won't take the time to formulate some ideas and test them for accuracy

- Think that the teacher is asking too many questions

- Stop asking "Why?"

- Are not interested in anything

- Neglect trying any new idea or activity because it will be too hard to do

- State "It's boring!" more than once a week

- Consistently choose not to share ideas with other students

- Put down other people's ideas and projects as insignificant or dumb

Literature Link ~ Curiosity

Primary Grades

Abuela	Dorros, Arthur
Angus and the Cat	Flack, Marjorie
Curious George Series	Rey, H.A. and Margaret Rey
Five Great Explorers	Hudson, Wade
Miss Maggie	Rylant, Cynthia
On the Pampas	Brusca, Maria Cristina
One Morning In Maine	McCloskey, Robert
Pig Who Saw Everything, The	Gackenbach, Dick
Round Trip	Jonas, Ann
Tico and the Golden Wings	Lionni, Leo
Two Bad Ants	VanAllsburg, Chris

Intermediate Grades

Charlotte's Web	White, E.B.
Enormous Egg, The	Butterworth, Oliver
Flight of the Fox, The	Murphy, Shirley Rousseau
Grasshopper and the Unwise Owl	Slater, Jim
Grey Cloud	Graeber, Charlotte
Hubert's Hair-Raising Adventure	Peet, Bill
Hurricane	McNulty, Faith
Mrs. Frisby and the Rats of NIHM	O'Brien, Robert C.
My Side of the Mountain	George, Jean Craighead
Path of the Pale Horse	Fleischman, Paul
Scientist with Determination, Elma Gonzales	Verheyden-Hallard, Mary E.

Middle School and High School

Fahrenheit 451	Bradbury, Ray
Midnight Hour Encores	Brooks, Bruce
To Be a Slave	Lester, Julius

Teacher's Resource

Awakening Your Child's Natural Genius: Enhancing Curiosity, Creativity, and Learning Ability	Armstrong, Thomas

Date _____

Dear Family,

As toddlers are reaching out to learn about their world, parents usually hear a certain question with great frequency. Nearly everything their children observe, hear, touch, or experience generates a "Why?"—sometimes to the point of annoyance. However, one of the greatest gifts we can give to youngsters is the opportunity to ask that question over and over again since it indicates a growing development of the LIFESKILL of

~Curiosity~

As your child's teacher, I will encourage students to:

- Ask thoughtful questions

- Consider many ideas

- Develop areas of expertise

- Wonder about the world around them

- Take an active part in their own learning

As your child's first teacher, your positive response to an inquisitive mind is crucial to fostering the growth of curiosity. Here are some activities that you and your child may enjoy doing together:

- Read with your child but after the first few paragraphs or pages, let the child make up the rest of the story

- Decrease the amount of time for watching television. Instead, take neighborhood walks and look for unusual objects (such as birds, rocks, animals). Discuss your observations and develop questions to be studied

- Visit museums, zoos, historical sites, and natural wonders. In a small notepad, jot down questions that you and your child have. Visit the library to research the answers

Since the LIFESKILL of Curiosity is the lifeblood of creativity and learning, we must nurture it in our children for they are the inventors, scientists, artists, composers, and writers of the future.

Sincerely,

_____

Your child's teacher

Chapter 15

Effort

"Do your best."

effort *n* **1:** conscious exertion of power: hard work **2:** a serious attempt: try
3: something produced by exertion or trying
4: the total work done to achieve a particular end

EFFORT: To do your best

WHAT IS EFFORT?

In ordinary speech and general writing we use "effort" to describe both process and product—the way we work (a serious attempt to attain our goal) and the outcome (something produced by our exertion). For example, "Their effort to get the job done today was commendable." "Our defense worked hard; it was a good effort and carried the day for us."

Effort is both mental and physical. Tasks such as computing, reading, and studying are mostly mental. Shooting hoops, running laps, riding a bicycle, and washing dishes require mostly physical effort. Other tasks, such as performing music, acting (on stage), conducting science experiments, and acting out simulations require both mental and physical effort.

Also, the amount and kind of effort exerted for various activities differ from person to person. Some of our friends, for example, are extremely high-energy people while others are laid back. Effort can also vary with the circumstances. For example, if we lack the knowledge and skill to do a task, it will require much more effort of us than of someone with expertise. Or, if people pretend they want something—they say they want it but make only a half-hearted attempt to reach their goals—effort expended is minimal versus the effort expended by someone passionate about achieving a goal.

Effort can be a solitary endeavor or part of a team project. In either case, it is the willingness to give something our best shot to use all of our energy, skill, knowledge, and commitment to go the extra mile. Both solitary and team efforts are valued in our culture.

Questions To Ask

Effort doesn't automatically result in the desired product—it simply keeps us going. To make sure we're headed in the right direction, we must ask ourselves some questions: What do we want? Why? What plans do we have to make to get there? Setting priorities, choosing goals, reflecting about our progress (or lack of it), are all pieces of the effort puzzle. If one piece is missing, we can't complete the picture; there will always be that little odd-shaped space to remind us that we haven't yet reached our goal. When involved in team efforts, the questions to ask ourselves are the same but we must also define each person's role as well as our own. Once these questions are answered, we can examine how the LIFESKILL of Effort can help us achieve our goals.

Baby Steps

Even when we're babies, the LIFESKILL of Effort is strongly in place. Watch a baby learning to master sitting, crawling, standing, speaking, and walking. "That baby has a one-track mind," someone may say, as the child pushes harder and harder, without a rest, to reach the objective. If he doesn't succeed, the child is even more determined and tries harder. When he succeeds, his glee and satisfaction is obvious in his body language, expressive eyes, and contented look. The joy we see on the infant's face continues into adulthood as a deep sense of satisfaction that arises from concentrating on a goal, putting forth full effort, and, finally, achieving that goal.

It takes effort to explore our world, acquire knowledge, and master needed skills. Too often students define work as an activity beneath their dignity (who wants to be a "school boy" or teacher's pet?) or something for which they should receive a reward (an M & M, a smiley face, or money) rather than something that gives them "a deep sense of personal satisfaction."*

WHY PRACTICE EFFORT?

The best laid plans are worthless if we don't put out the effort necessary to implement them. Effort makes the difference between dream and reality, wishes and accomplishments.

Effort Moves Our Personal Lives and Civilization As a Whole

Think of some examples of effort in action. No doubt your list would include such descriptors as: applies, attempts, uses elbow grease, endeavors, exerts, labors, pushes, strives, and ventures. Lack of effort might be described as: inactive, half-hearted, neglectful, quits, doesn't try, and defeatist. Which list identifies the attributes you want in your doctor, lawyer, car mechanic, child's teacher, airplane mechanic, pastor, friend, and family members?

The qualities associated with effort are those that push civilizations and individuals forward. The efforts of those around us contribute significantly to the quality and success of our own lives.

---

* "A deep sense of personal satisfaction" is a phrase used by Brenda Wycoff, Arizona, to lead students to a recognition that external trappings of money and power aren't as nurturing as the internal reward satisfaction and contentment arising from respect of self and one's accomplishments.

Increased Self-Esteem

Practicing effort is crucial to our self-esteem. A sense of satisfaction and pride springs from deep within when we give our best and strongest effort to complete a task. Such accomplishments are self-perpetuating; the more successful our efforts, the more we want to try.

Effort pushes us to experience, to learn, to excel, and to become. As we do so, our sense of self and our confidence in our capacities increases.

In Times Of Need

Practicing effort is crucial in helping us to work our way through hard times and difficult situations. When the bills are bigger than our paycheck, when family obligations pile up, when we're slogging through our work but don't seem to accomplish anything, when miracles seem few and far between, effort over time will pull us through. By following a strong work ethic and never giving up to failure, we can prevail.

HOW DO YOU PRACTICE EFFORT?

Getting students to embrace the LIFESKILL of Effort may seem like a difficult sell job. Not true. Each day there are a number of opportunities in which to apply effort, some as simple as climbing out of bed on time when the clock radio chimes its wake-up tune. Smiling at the breakfast table, pleasantly greeting co-workers, students, and parents, diligently working to complete one's responsibilities in a timely way, and offering help to others are all examples of effort in action on a daily level.

When teaching students about effort, start small. Don't introduce it as a LIFESKILL needed to complete a 10-page research report. Start small, start with things they care about. Lead them to the experience of a deep sense of personal satisfaction before you significantly increase the complexity and size of tasks to be done.

The American Dream Versus a Pipe Dream

While reading the newspaper's classified section or advertisements, have you ever been tempted by notices that read, "Full-time income! Part-time effort," or "Amazing income! No effort." Don't you find them hard to believe? With little, or no effort, great amounts of money will quietly steal into your pockets. Even with best efforts, wallets often end up short-changed. Do you remember your parents admonishing you as a child, "You don't get something for nothing"?

The first step in practicing the LIFESKILL of Effort is to stop looking for the easy way out, the short cut, the all-American pipe dream to instant riches. Help students distinguish between the dream that can guide a life of accomplishment and satisfaction and the pipe dream that drags its owner through false hopes and fools' gold at the end of the rainbow. Once they're on the right track, the sensible choice is to put forth effort, exert themselves, use elbow grease, and labor over meaningful tasks.

Choose to Try

Implementing the LIFESKILL of Effort means doing whatever it takes to achieve the goal. Phone calls? Letters? Personal visits? Extra hours at work? Either we choose to go for it or we don't. It's as simple as that. If we choose to try, we should give it our best effort. If we decide that we want something, we choose to apply ourselves in ways necessary to attain the goal.

Teach students the importance of the act of choosing and committing oneself to a course of action. Only they can do it, only they can feel it, only they can summon the patience and perseverance to stick to it. Only they can kindle the motivation to sustain the necessary efforts to complete their commitments and reach their goals.

Celebrate Successes

Unfortunately, all too often, even we adults lose the sense of contentment that comes from successful efforts. We become so focused on moving to the next task that we forget to celebrate our accomplishments. This cheats us of an important source of motivation that is essential to maintaining our willingness to apply the LIFESKILL of Effort year in and year out throughout our life. Celebration of success is a powerful antidote to burnout.

Teach children early on to stop and smell the roses, to celebrate success of both the processes and products of their efforts. Teach them to celebrate the fruits of their efforts, to bask in the exhilaration that results from working hard and using effort to attain their goals.

Develop Yardsticks for Self-Assessment

Celebrating success hinges on knowing that we have succeeded—because we believe so, not because someone else says so.* To judge our success, we must develop internal yardsticks that will allow us to measure our expectations. If such yardsticks aren't realistic, they will be too high (so that we are always disappointed in ourselves) or too low (it's what everyone else does). If they are designed by someone else, we won't own them and they won't bring us satisfaction. If they don't grow with us, we will have difficulty adjusting to the world of work and adult-level expertise with any grace; in short, we will have inflated images of our capabilities.

Teach students to assess their own results by learning to apply the 3 C's of Assessment from the ITI model** to their work—especially to inquiries. Include students in parent conferences. Students from third grade and up should lead the discussion about their portfolio.***

---

* See *Punished by Rewards* by Alfie Kohn, 1993.
** See the chapter on the eighth bodybrain-compatible element, mastery, in the ITI book appropriate for your grade level.
*** See *Student-Led Conferencing Using Showcase Portfolios* by Barbara Benson and Susan Barnett, 1999.

WHAT DOES EFFORT LOOK LIKE IN THE REAL WORLD?

We

- Work to discover better ways to design or present a product
- Send out numerous resumes and participate in many job interviews
- Service a new product or replace it if unsatisfactory to a customer
- Learn and practice technological skills
- Improve a process or technique
- Work more than one job when our family is in need
- Choose opportunities for lifelong learning
- Work overtime to complete a task or project
- Strive to do your personal best on every task

WHAT DOES EFFORT LOOK LIKE IN SCHOOL?

Staff

- Acknowledge the efforts of fellow staff members
- Do more than is required or mandated
- Learn new strategies and techniques
- Research current concepts and ideas
- Work with determination and fortitude on each task
- Work as long as it takes to complete a task
- Attend extracurricular activities and events
- Mentor a teacher new to the school
- Seek to know each student personally
- Plan ahead for all materials necessary for the class to run smoothly
- Support team effort

Students

- Offer to assist other students when help is needed

- Persevere in mastering concepts, knowledge, and skills

- Redo work that is less than their personal best

- Make up all work missed because of absence

- Arrive on time

- Keep their space in the classroom neat and clean

- Maintain a positive attitude toward learning and school

- Develop social skills that will enhance the classroom community

- Volunteer for classroom job assignments

- Avoid unnecessary absences

- Meet deadlines in a timely fashion

INQUIRIES TO DEVELOP EFFORT

Whole Group Inquiries

- Read the LIFESKILLS list in your classroom. Choose one LIFESKILL behavior that you want to improve in yourself. Plan two or more ways that you will use the LIFESKILL of Effort to practice the chosen LIFESKILL every day for one week. For example, if you choose to work on the LIFESKILL of Friendship: 1) I will smile and greet two people from other learning clubs every morning; 2) During recess, I will ask _____ to play a game with me and ask questions that will let me get to know him/her better; and 3) Keep a log and write a daily note explaining your progress. Share this with a friend.

- Listen as your teacher reads a biography of Helen Keller. Brainstorm with your learning club three examples of how Helen Keller practiced the LIFESKILL of Effort in her life. Dramatize these examples for your classmates by presenting a short skit (four to five minutes). Include every member in the skit. Tell your learning club which example of the LIFESKILL of Effort you feel showed the greatest effort and explain why.

- During a class meeting, discuss the pleasures of a job well-done and the feelings that accompany its completion.

- List examples of exemplary effort in the classroom and real world. Share these examples in community circles, class meetings, journal writing, or book discussions.

Small Group/Individual Inquiries

- Design an effort banner on 12"x18" colored construction paper. Use colored paper, markers, crayons, and other art materials to enhance your words and pictures. Write the word "EFFORT" across the top of the paper. Write "to do your best" half way down the paper. Browse through magazines and cut out pictures of people using effort to get some job or task done. Paste these pictures on the banner. Explain to a friend how you used the LIFESKILL of Effort to complete the inquiry.

- With your learning club, make a list of one way each member has shown effort at some time during the past week. Copy and fill in the chart. When you are finished, exchange charts with another learning club and look for other ways children show effort.

EFFORT		
Person's Name	Action (what he/she did)	How it Felt

- Bring in a can of fruit, vegetables, a box of rice, or cereal for the food pantry collection. Choose one that is your personal favorite and draw a picture of someone enjoying that food.

- Recall when you have recently used the LIFESKILL of Effort to practice the skills needed to play a sport or musical instrument, or to learn to dance. Create a card that illustrates how you used the LIFESKILL of Effort. Present the card to your coach or teacher. Share with your learning club two examples of how you used the LIFESKILL of Effort to improve your personal performance at something in the past two weeks.

- Pursue a "make and take it" hobby (e.g., model making, woodworking, knitting, photography, sculpting, or weaving) that requires effort. Obtain the needed materials and practice working on new skills. Stick with your practice until you've created three or more products. Choose two products to share in class and demonstrate two new skills you needed to make them.

- Begin a "collecting" hobby, such as rocks, shells, coins, stamps, autographs, or postcards. Collect and catalog 25 or more items. Include each item's name or classification, when you acquired it, any cost involved, and something special about it. Display your collection in the class library. Explain to a partner the LIFESKILL of Effort you needed to assemble your collection.

- Select a "doing" hobby, such as playing a sport or an instrument, singing in a choir, gardening, cooking, or birding. Practice your "doing" hobby for a month or more. Choose a tune you know, such as "Happy Birthday To You," and write three or more verses to teach your classmates strategies for using the LIFESKILL of Effort in your particular hobby. Print the verses on an overhead transparency and teach the class your song.

- Develop a plan to organize your school belongings (both in your desk and cubby/locker). Write a personal procedure for organizing materials for your daily lessons/assignments. Write end-of-the-day procedures for putting away any materials and preparing for the next morning. Make a "mini" two-week calendar. Choose two symbols, one for marking completion of the morning procedures and another for marking completion of the end-of-the-day procedures. Stamp the symbols on your calendar to indicate completion of procedures for each day. Share the calendar and the results of your effort with an adult.

- Design an award (trophy, flag, certificate) that recognizes individuals who are practicing the LIFESKILL of Effort on a day-to-day basis. Include a dedication and two or more symbols. Make a life-size model. Explain to your learning club why you chose this design.

- Read a biography about Thomas Edison, Rachel Carson, Jim Thorpe, Wolfgang Amadeus Mozart, or Walt Disney. Design a poster illustrating at least four of his/her most significant contributions to society.

- Observe athletes in training. List the attributes of putting forth effort for their sport and discuss your list with a partner. Describe 10 ways that your school would be different if such effort was applied to your school.

- Invite a motivational speaker to share the positive effects of the LIFESKILL of Effort with your class. Write a thank-you letter to him/her; share how you'll use one of the strategies he/she mentioned in order to encourage yourself to use the LIFESKILL of Effort.

- Create a role-playing scenario for six everyday situations; write each on a separate piece of note paper. Invite each learning club to pick one and role play that situation with two different solutions—one that requires the use of the LIFESKILL of Effort and one that doesn't. Discuss the consequences of each choice.

- Read a book, such as *Stone Fox* by John Reynolds Gardiner, and list examples of the main character using the LIFESKILL of Effort to solve problems. Share your list with your learning club.

SIGNS OF SUCCESS

Congratulations! Students are showing signs of Effort when they

- Practice mastering a new skill until they can do it with ease
- Offer to do something over because it isn't their personal best
- Ask others if they need help with a project
- Go out of their way to do something extra, something that is not required or expected of them
- Ask to learn something difficult
- Try and try again
- Never give up until they succeed

Keep trying! Students need more practice when they

- Don't care to improve themselves

- Refuse to complete work or redo work containing errors

- Pretend to work at learning a skill

- Give up after one or two tries

- Blame others for their poor results

- Ignore opportunities to improve

- Insist work is their personal best when they know that it isn't

- Act plain lazy

- Lack diligence

- Believe that everyone else has it "easy"

Literature Link ~ Effort

Primary Grades

Ant and the Grasshopper, The	Piper, Wally
Brave Irene	Steig, William
Dragon Wings	Yep, Lawrence
Going Home	Bunting, Eve
Maggie and the Monster	Winthrop, Elizabeth
Mike Mulligan and His Steam Shovel	Burton, Virginia Lee
More Than Anything Else	Bradby, Marie
New Coat for Anna, A	Ziefert, Harriet
Seeds of Peace, The	Berkley, Laura
Stellaluna	Cannon, Janell

Intermediate Grades

Day No Pigs Would Die, A	Peck, Robert Newton
Ditch Digger's Daughters: A Black Family's Astonishing Success Story	Thornton, Y. and J. Coudert
Gift for Tia Rosa, A	Taha, Karen T.
Iditarod Dream	Wood, Ted
Jip: His Story	Patterson, Katherine
Mother Jones: One Woman's Fight for Labor	Kraft, Betsy Harvey
Orphan Train Rider: One Boy's True Story	Warren, Andrea
Rosie, the Riveter	Coleman, Penny
Sadako and the Thousand Paper Cranes	Coeer, Eleanor
Snowbound	Mazer, Harry
Taking Flight: My Story	Van Meter, Vicki and Can Gutman

Middle School and High School

Daily Reflections for Highly Effective Teens	Covey, Sean
Herstory: Women Who Changed the World	Ashby, Ruth (ed.) and Deborah Gore Ohrn (ed.)
Kidstories: Biographies of 20 Young People You'd Like to Know	Delisle, James R. and Pamela Espeland
Within Reach: My Everest Story	Pfetzer, Mark and Jack Galvin

Teacher's Resource

100 Ways to Enhance Self-Concept in the Classroom	Canfield, J. and H. Wells

Date _____

Dear Family,

    As the students learn more about the various skills that will help them travel through life, they will explore the LIFESKILL of

~EFFORT~

    Effort is a crucial ingredient; it may be the determining factor between success and failure. While effort alone doesn't create achievement, it keeps us moving toward that goal. Therefore, any way we can nurture the development of this behavior in children will surely increase their quality of living.

    Students will learn to:

- Develop individual short- and long-term goals; each will evaluate his/her own progress

- Identify the attributes of personal effort by reading a biography

- Identify and observe citizens who are models of the LIFESKILL of Effort in our community

Ways you can help at home to emphasize the LIFESKILL of Effort include:

- Share personal examples of times when you, as parents, have used the LIFESKILL of Effort

- Teach your child how to create a timetable for short- and long-term projects

- Discuss with your family examples of the LIFESKILL of Effort on the evening news

- Identify ways that the LIFESKILL of Effort is needed in the world of work and to raise a family

    By working in partnership, schools and parents can stress the importance of effort for a successful life.

Sincerely,

_____

Your child's teacher

Chapter 16

Flexibility

"BE OPEN MINDED."

flexibility *n* **1:** capable of being flexed: pliant **2:** yielding to influence; tractable
3: characterized by a ready capability to adapt to new, different, or changing requirements

FLEXIBILITY: To be willing to alter plans when necessary

WHAT IS FLEXIBILITY?

Are you a person who easily adapts to change or do you become frustrated and upset if plans are altered? Since nothing in this world is certain except death and taxes, mastering the LIFESKILL of Flexibility allows us to adapt to changes, problems, and unexpected situations without undue emotional strain and unpleasantness for ourselves and those around us.

Flexibility indicates our willingness to alter specific plans and ideas to serve our needs or satisfy the needs of others.

What Flexibility Is Not

To be flexible is not to be rudderless, wishy-washy, or lacking opinions. It doesn't mean giving up our values, following the crowd, or caving in to peer pressure. It's the ability to dance through life, flexing with the moment when needed, altering our path for the moment, then returning to our goals and tasks as originally planned or recently revised based on experience.

Possible Pitfalls

Powerful emotional and personal beliefs can prevent us from embracing opportunities to change our plans or methods. Such intense feelings can produce negative character traits such as stubbornness and rigidity which often destroy, rather than nurture, productivity, relationships, and reputations.

WHY PRACTICE FLEXIBILITY?

Flexibility is a key ingredient in our ability to flex and flow with others in a give and take environment. Without such flexibility, succeeding socially—with friends, co-workers and even family—is all but impossible. Furthermore, being flexible often exposes us to new and better options because it enables us to "hang loose" while additional possibilities become available.

Just completing a task often requires flexibility. Things seldom go as expected. Refusal to be flexible often leads to impossibly long hours to complete a task or to quitting altogether.

Increase In Knowledge

Due to the increasing volume of knowledge in this Age of Information, our minds are continually exposed to new and invigorating ideas. Keeping an open mind to information that is inconsistent with our world view and opinions allows us to consider new ideas, update information, and to sometimes realize that what we had considered conjecture has become fact. Flexibility empowers us to change our minds and know that this is acceptable. If we aren't flexible enough to study new ideas and philosophies thoroughly, then we quickly become "out of touch" and not as effective in the work place, while parenting, or with friends.

Because we can't predict what life will bring, it is imperative that we always are ready to alter plans when necessary.

Unpredictable Environment

Change is hard to accept. It is much easier, and far more comfortable, to follow a set routine and hope everything will happen as anticipated. However, when people, events, and situations interact, their whole becomes bigger—and often unpredictably different—than the sum of the parts. This, in turn, affects our plans, thoughts, and actions. If we can bend a little,* adjust our plans or think in diverse ways, life usually becomes easier and our chances for succeeding often increase. Give students many different experiences with choice and change in order to give them practice in developing the LIFESKILL of Flexibility.

HOW DO YOU PRACTICE IT?

To no surprise, practicing the LIFESKILL of Flexibility requires both personal and professional work. The desire to control people and circumstances cuts across both areas. Personally, staying flexible is easy for those whom the Myers-Briggs/Keirsey-Bates personality inventory place on

---

* This does not mean bending one's sense of right and wrong, moral and immoral but rather taking a different approach to a problem or situation.

the perceiving end of the lifestyle scale.* These are the open, spontaneous, flexible folks. At the other end of the scale, judging (as in by decree, not in judgment of good or bad), people are organized, methodical, insist on closure, and work persistently from stated goals and priorities. A majority of those of us who become teachers are on the judging end of the scale. Being flexible is an act of will, a conscious and not very comfortable choice. Keeping our eye on the outcomes of our efforts rather than near-sighted focus on the processes we carry out helps.

Flexibility Is a State of Mind

Flexibility is a state of mind that requires giving up control, letting go attachment to our ideas so we can be open to the ideas of others, and accepting that our way isn't the only way.

Giving Up Control. We must be willing to give up controlling things, people, and events. If students are to learn to take ownership of and direct their learning, we must learn to share control of the classroom in meaningful and responsible ways. If we want colleagues to share the challenges and hard work of creating and maintaining a school known for its excellence, we must learn to share leadership, power, and control. If we want to enjoy life with family and friends, we must learn to not only go with the flow but to enjoy the journey as well. We must begin to trust that two heads are better then one, that group wisdom will emerge however messy and inelegant the process. "My way or the highway" is not the motto of a flexible person.

Letting Go. We must put aside emotional allegiance or attachment to our own preferred choices. We must be willing to take a second look and change our own minds. And, we must be willing to allow others to contribute to the idea pool. This doesn't mean "anything goes" or that we shouldn't have guidelines and standards but within these guidelines and standards we are open.

Accepting That Our Way Isn't the Only Way. We must fully understand and accept that every brain is different and thus every student and adult learns and does things differently. Rule of thumb: We tend to teach the way we ourselves learn, operating the way we prefer for our comfort zone rather than in ways that would most enhance learning for each and every student.** The LIFESKILL of Flexibility requires that we teach and interact with students in multiple ways, accepting and anticipating their different ways of learning.

For example, when appraising students' work, be flexible—look at the whole child's progress. Also, be aware that local and state curricula need to be adaptable for a wide variety of students, all of whom are at varying stages of learning. As we teach, we must use many different teaching methods, develop curriculum that is conceptual and grounded in a variety of "being there" experiences and hands-on materials, and provide personalized activities for all students in ways that help them understand the main ideas and grasp the "big picture." Imagine an enormous teacher's bag filled to the brim with strategies; if one technique doesn't work, just reach in and pull out another. Remember, each brain is unique and therefore each student will think and go about things differently.

---

* For an entertaining as well as enlightening exploration of personality preferences, see Chapter 7, *Making Bodybrain-Compatible Education a Reality: Coaching for the ITI Model* by Karen D. Olsen. (Kent, Washington: Books for Educators, 1999.) Lifestyle is defined here as how we want our life to unfold, not as in living high on the hog.

** For user-friendly discussions of important concepts from recent brain research, see Chapter 1 of the ITI book appropriate for your grade level. See also *Human Brain and Human Learning* by Leslie Hart.

We give lip service to tolerance of differences of others, teaching it, for the most part, as a philosophical stance. To us, it is merely a recognition of brain research findings: Each brain is unique and therefore each person will think and do differently. Teach students that differences are a function of unique brain wiring and that there is no one right way to think or do something.

Flexibility Is Not Merely Going with the Flow

Being flexible requires more of us than merely going with the flow—"Whatever you want is fine with me," "You choose . . . whatever," or the bureaucratic versions, "We do it this way because it's how we've always done it," and "We must do it this way because 'they' said we had to."

Flexibility requires that we own the new decision or choice—not blindly or mindlessly but because our common sense convinces us it's the better way.

Flexibility also requires that we implement the decision reached with the same vigor and commitment as when implementing our own decisions.

Helping Students Shift from "Me First" to "Us"

By focusing on the LIFESKILL of Flexibility, we help teach our students the concept of "us" rather than "me first" in ways they understand. For example, they can see how to make their learning club work better, how to make their class into a "Class Family" rather than a loose collection of strangers, and how to make their micro-society work. This LIFESKILL also helps students distinguish between being flexible and agreeable versus slavish adherence to the group norms of cliques and gangs and other forms of peer pressure.

Opportunities to practice the LIFESKILL of Flexibility are everywhere. In addition to formally planned inquiries such as those on pages 6-7 of this chapter, be sure to take advantage of teachable moments that pop up throughout the day.

WHAT DOES FLEXIBILITY LOOK LIKE IN REAL LIFE?

We

- Change schedules as necessary
- Keep an open mind and listen to both sides of a case when friends argue
- Take other roads to work when the regular route is under construction
- Purchase a different product when our favorite brand is unavailable
- Stretch a paycheck to ensure that all payments are made

- Go out of our way to pick up a neighbor's children from soccer practice when her car is disabled

- Offer to cook different foods for our in-laws who have special dietary needs

WHAT DOES FLEXIBILITY LOOK LIKE IN SCHOOL?

Staff

- Relinquish a high-prestige position on a committee to another teacher who wishes to participate

- Offer help in another class because their teacher will be late

- Change scheduling for special classes (P.E., music, art, technology) to accommodate schedule needs of another classroom

- Meet with parents at nontraditional times because of their work schedules

- Create choices for students through partners, learning clubs, inquiries (projects), co-curricular activities, after school activities, and the like

- Provide before- and after-school care that allows for various arrival and dismissal times

- Exude a positive attitude about unexpected schedule changes

- Change teaching assignments—grade level and/or subject areas—as needed

Students

- Ask another student for assistance when the teacher is temporarily unavailable

- Show a positive attitude when a special activity is canceled or postponed

- Work with a variety of classmates

- Choose many kinds of projects and inquiries

- Offer alternative ideas during class discussions

- Solve a problem using a new and creative technique

- Choose alternative materials when their first choice isn't available

- Work with other people when their best friends are occupied

- Play a different position on a sports team to fill in a gap

INQUIRIES TO DEVELOP FLEXIBILITY

Whole Group Inquiries

- At the end of the day, identify any situations during the day when the class used the LIFESKILL of Flexibility. For each situation, record in your journal at least two choices the class had for demonstrating the LIFESKILL of Flexibility plus the choice the group made. In one sentence, explain your personal feelings about these examples. Share your journal entry with your learning club.

- Read several fables written by Aesop. Develop a fable of your own that teaches about the LIFESKILL of Flexibility. Print your fable on the computer. Add graphics or illustrations. Dramatize your fable for another learning club. Ask them to predict the moral of the story. Share your moral and compare the two for similarities.

Small Group/Individual Inquiries

- Create a list of four or more activities you can do on the playground during recess or play time. Draw a star next to your favorite choice and then choose one of the others to do for the rest of the week. Share one reason that explains why having choices is good and one reason why having choices is not good. Share your ideas during a class discussion.

- Volunteer for three different classroom jobs, one week at a time. Decide which job requires the most flexibility and which one needs the least amount of flexibility. Share your thoughts with the class the next time classroom jobs are chosen.

- Listen to/Read a book about one of the following people: Ben Franklin, Leonardo da Vinci, Thomas Edison, Betsy Ross, Eleanor Roosevelt, or Rosa Parks. Illustrate one example of how he/she was flexible in his/her actions. Take the drawing home and explain your thoughts to your family.

- Listen to the same song recorded by three different jazz musicians. Study the variations of each group. Interview a musician to determine the importance of flexibility in a jam session. Write a rap, chant, or poem that teaches two or more ways of being flexible when playing music. Design a bookmark that shares these strategies and give it to a classmate who is taking instrumental music lessons.

- Investigate flexibility in the human body (such as in muscles, tendons, joints). Design two charts (with assistance from a physical therapist or physical education teacher) illustrating one exercise on each that will increase body flexibility. Share the information on the charts with a partner. Demonstrate the two flexibility exercises for your classmates.

- Read three or more newspaper stories about sentences handed down to criminals. Interview a lawyer or judge. Ask about flexibility in guidelines for determining appropriate sentences. Write to the lawyer/judge you interviewed and share one new idea you had as a result of the interview and how you feel about the use of flexibility in sentencing criminals.

- Choose a tune you know, such as "Row, Row, Row Your Boat," and write new lyrics that teach two advantages of using the LIFESKILL of Flexibility. Use the same lyrics in an alternative form (rap, chant, or poetry). Perform both for the class. Explain which is your favorite way and why.

- Learn about Howard Gardner's theory of multiple intelligences. Design a visual representation (such as a poster, brochure, video, or overhead transparency) of the "8 Kinds of Smart." Using music and movement, teach your classmates about the intelligences and how use of the intelligences invite using the LIFESKILL of Flexibility.

- Choose a location in your community that you would like to visit. Use a map to plan the most direct route from your home to the site and highlight that route in one color. Pretend that route is closed. Use the LIFESKILL of Flexibility to determine three or more other routes. Use three other colors to highlight each of these alternate plans. Ask an adult to check these plans for accuracy.

- Interview an architect, builder, carpenter, engineer, mason, or construction worker. Ask him/her how to determine what materials are to be used to build various structures. Create a visual aid that will demonstrate to your classmates two or more reasons for using flexible building materials on some structures. Explain these reasons to your learning club.

- Design three bridges to test the flexibility and strength of these materials: toothpicks, paper, and clay. Make the bridges and test them by using objects of different known weights.

SIGNS OF SUCCESS

Congratulations! Students are showing signs of Flexibility when they

- Openly listen to others' ideas and change their opinions accordingly

- Volunteer to change seats or rearrange a schedule to help a classmate

- Work freely with a variety of staff members and students

- Practice new strategies and skills in many different ways until mastery is reached

- Help negotiate settlements for disagreements

- Embrace change as exciting rather than frightening

- Attempt a new activity, hobby, or sport

- Willingly change their schedule for special classes to help another class

Keep trying! Students need more practice when they

- Refuse to try a new experience

- Reject other opinions before even hearing them

- Decline an opportunity to negotiate; won't settle differences amicably

- Rebuff an opportunity to apologize; refuse to accept an apology

- Are upset by small changes in daily schedules and activities

- Do not want to accommodate other people just because it would inconvenience them

- Are rigid in their decisions and actions

- Automatically dispute grades or directions

LITERATURE LINK ~ FLEXIBILITY

Primary Grades

Alexander and the Terrible, Horrible, No-Good, Very Bad Day	Viorst, Judith
Baby Sister for Frances, A	Hoban, Lillian
Bea and Mr. Jones	Schwartz, Amy
Cloudy with a Chance of Meatballs	Barret, Judy
Evening at Alfie's, An	Hughes, Shirley
Huge Harold	Peet, Bill
Imogene's Antlers	Small, David
Jalapeno Bagels	Wing, Natasha
Little Painter of Sabana Grande, The	Markum, Patricia Maloney
Make Way for Ducklings	McCloskey, Robert
Stellaluna	Canon, Janell

Intermediate Grades

Door in the Wall, The	de Angeli, Marguerite
Family Under the Bridge, The	Carlson, Natalie Savage
Farolitas of Christmas	Anaya, Rudolfo
Girl Called Al, A	Greene, Constance
Henry Huggins	Cleary, Beverly
Julie of the Wolves	George, Jean Craighead
Look Through My Window	Little, Jean
My Side of the Mountain	George, Jean Craighead
Rifles for Watie	Keith, Harold
Stone-Faced Boy, The	Fox, Paula
Tales of a Fourth Grade Nothing	Blume, Judy

MIddle School and High School

Crazy Horse Electric Game, The	Crutcher, Chris
How the Garcia Girls Lost Their Accents	Alvarez, Julia
100 Men Who Shaped the World	Yenne, Bill
100 Women Who Shaped the World	Rolka, Gail Meyer

Teacher's Resource

Multiple Intelligences In the Classroom	Armstrong, Thomas

Date _____

Dear Family,

I'm sure you'll agree that our newest LIFESKILL is necessary for managing our daily schedules as adults or students. Today's rapid pace of living creates an endless number of changes in our plans every day. The boss calls an unexpected meeting, an appointment changes, a neighbor can't carpool because of illness, or our car breaks down. This LIFESKILL is

~FLEXIBILITY~

Here are some strategies and activities that will assist your child in developing flexibility as a skill for life. We will:

- Observe and list classroom experiences that require flexibility

- Invite a guest speaker to discuss flexibility in the workplace

- Role play situations requiring change and demonstrating positive responses

- Study the importance of flexibility in various occupations

- Examine science and health principles that relate to flexibility

In the home setting, your child's understanding of the LIFESKILL of Flexibility will be enhanced by:

- Observing family members react positively to change

- Learning to make age-appropriate choices

- Practicing peaceful resolutions to disagreements

- Understanding that change can be exciting rather than frightening

- Planning for emergency situations in the home, such as fire, intruder, bad weather situations

Life is always changing. Teach your child the strategies that will help him/her to be successful.

Sincerely,

_____

Your child's teacher

Chapter 17

Friendship

"FRIENDSHIPS IMPROVE LIFE."

friendship *n* **1:** the state of being friends **2:** the quality or state of being friendly: friendliness
friend *n* a person whom one knows well and is fond of; an ally, supporter, or sympathizer

FRIENDSHIP: To make and keep a friend through mutual trust and caring

WHAT IS FRIENDSHIP?

Friendship describes the caring, affectionate, playful, and usually strong emotional bond we experience with an assortment of companions during various stages of our lives. It is a relationship in which we share who we are and who we want to become, our hopes and our fears.

Friendships Are Like Rainbows

Friendships, like rainbows, come in a wide spectrum. Some friendships are intimate and can have enormous impact on our lives. Some are more limited, even if long-standing, when we chat about the weather and less consequential things. Some are new with people we know little about but with whom we feel a kindred spirit.

Friendships can command our complete trust and affection; over time they can evolve into an intimate relationship. Unlike family ties, we choose these relationships and we must continue to earn them.

Some friends know us inside and out—our private self and our public persona. Their impact in our lives is huge because they know our roles in life and how we carry them out; they can give us accurate, honest feedback. Other friendships are limited to specific contexts such as work, a party, church, parent participation preschool, the neighborhood home owner's association, political organizer, or hobbies or sports.

Whatever the degree of intimacy, friendships are not static, made one day and forever the same thereafter. Making a friend is one thing, but continuing to earn his/her respect and trust is another. Friendships are dynamic, ever changing. They are gifts we give ourselves.

Choice of Close Friends

Because of their power to influence and nurture us, we should choose our close friends with deliberation and care rather than wait for accidental meetings, e.g., who moves in next door, who belongs to the country club, who sits next to us in a high school class, or who agrees with us when we whine.

Every parent's worst nightmare is that his/her child will "fall in with bad company," that an acquaintance will prove to be "a bad influence." And well they should worry because friendship is a two-way street, mutually self-sculpturing. Our friendships virtually change the course of our lives, for better or for worse.

Be clear, the friends we make and keep are the result of choices we make day by day, by default or by deliberate decision.

Friendships and Developmental Stages

Like other LIFESKILLS, the capacity to make and keep friends is developmental. With maturity and experience, most of us add the personal and social skills that make richer friendships possible.

In the Beginning. The art of friendship develops slowly. Young children tend to be egocentric. They don't share toys unless an adult is there to prod them. Before the ages of four or five, children generally play side by side, not necessarily together. Adults determine many of these early experiences, choosing the who (participants), where (location), when (time schedule), why (occasion), and how (transportation).

Growing Up. Gradually, children begin to reach out to others and tenuous relationships form. Think back. There is nothing like that first best friend. Who was yours? Do you know where he/she is now? Do you keep in touch? What drew you to each other? While in the elementary grades, friendships are usually drawn from classmates at school or from peers sharing sports, neighborhood playgrounds, scouts, hobbies, and so forth.

This early practice often involves play more than the skill of friendship but as children grow older and become more interested in others, they interact consciously with others in ways that encourage them to want to be a friend. As children become more independent, their friends come from ever-widening circles. Common interests, proximity, and age are common factors that influence friendships.

Initially, lacking experience and judgment, children often make errors in determining who they want for a friend and who they don't. Hurt feelings often result when the friendship is terminated by one and not understood by the other. Only after many experiences can we finally conclude who is a likely candidate to become a trustworthy friend and who is not.

Moving On. During teen and young adult years, a young person's peer group is the most important source of friends. At this stage of life, he/she is highly mobile—riding bikes, taking buses, and driving to local hang-outs. Groups of teen friends may walk, talk, and dress alike just to point out that they are different! Status within the peer group is all-important.

The teenager's highly charged emotional state generally carries over into friendships, making them extremely volatile—often, best friends one day and worst enemies the next. As social skills lag behind a keen desire to have friends, relationships sometimes unfold in hurtful ways (e.g., using put-downs, embarrassing comments, and rude noises) as the young person attempts to connect with others. Extremely close, tight-knit friendships often form in this emotional atmosphere and often last a lifetime. Even if we haven't seen our friend in years, we pick up the conversation as if we had never been apart.

Adult Friendships. Fortunately, most of us continue to grow in our ability to reach out beyond ourselves to enter into adult friendships, linking with neighbors, co-workers, church members, club or interest group members, and companions. Many of the same components that were present in our childhood friendships form the core of adult skills to make and keep friends such as the Lifelong Guidelines and the LIFESKILLS of Caring, Cooperation, Flexibility, Integrity, Responsibility, and Sense of Humor, to mention but a few. Happily, however, previous experience with forming and keeping friendships makes it easier and more comfortable. Adult judgment, tempered by years of experience, helps us make wiser decisions about who to choose for a friend and what degree of friendship is appropriate to seek with that person. More refined personal and social skills make it easier to carry out our decisions.

WHY PRACTICE FRIENDSHIP?

We humans are social animals. If isolated at any time in our lives, but particularly when young, we become estranged from ourselves as well as others, out of kilter, less than we are and can be.

Friendship: A Personal and Social Imperative

Being with others is a personal and social imperative. Mastering the LIFESKILL of Friendship is a necessity, not a luxury. In the long run, our success at forming friendships shapes our lives more powerfully than our grasp of the 3 R's. In 1991, the U.S. Department of Labor listed in its report, *What Work Requires of Schools*, the personal quality of sociability that young people must have upon entering the work force. The Department defines "sociability" as the ability to demonstrate understanding, friendliness, adaptability, empathy, and politeness in group settings.*

The skills for making and keeping a friend are the same skills for making and keeping the long-term relationships of marriage and parenting. Whether at home or work, within the family or in the community, making and keeping friends is critical to our success and personal well-being. As teachers, we need to invest considerable time and effort in helping students practice and master this LIFESKILL.

---

* Quoted in *TRIBES A New Way of Learning and Being Together* by Jeanne Gibbs, p. 33.

Friends As Mentors

A good friend has our best interests at heart and, having earned our trust and respect, is well-positioned to help us find our way through life. For most of us, our professional as well as personal lives would be very different were it not for the mentoring/peer coaching of our close friends. Through them, we develop areas of expertise and interests we would not otherwise have and go on adventures full of life-enriching experiences we would not have planned for ourselves. (For a discussion of mentoring and coaching in the context of the ITI model, see *Making Bodybrain-Compatible Education a Reality: Coaching for the ITI Model* by Karen D. Olsen, available through Books For Educators, Inc.)

Friends As Mirrors

Friends are a kind of mirror of who we are (our values and our dreams), who we want to be (and be known for), and, too often, who we are afraid we are. Friends with dreams help us get past yesterday, see today more clearly, and look beyond today to prepare for our future. They help us clarify who we want to be and to test our dreams against reality. Their accurate feedback helps us see our lives more objectively.

As we develop the LIFESKILL of Friendship, our circle of friends grows wider and more diverse. This diversity in friends helps us to know about the world beyond people like us. Conversely, consistency of values among our friends tells us how truly we hold to our values.

Friends As a Source of Nurturing and Support

However tough-skinned, worldly, and self-sufficient we may think we have become, everyone needs a hug, a long heart-to-heart talk, and some outside opinions from time to time. Support from an informed source, one who knows us well, is much more comforting than a blanket, "Gosh, what a tough break" rejoinder. Sometimes knowing we have a "3:00 A.M. friend" is all it takes to get us over the hump. Just knowing that we have options based on the support of our friends (a loan or a work team over the weekend) helps us get through our difficulties.

Friends who have dreams and work to make them a reality help us plan our own dream-inspired courses of action to get us where we want to go, by a path consistent with our goals. Good friends are the most important gift we can give ourselves.

HOW DO YOU PRACTICE FRIENDSHIP?

Making and keeping friends is not automatic or an act of luck; it requires intention and effort. All the Lifelong Guidelines are needed plus the LIFESKILLS of Caring, Cooperation, Flexibility, Integrity, Responsibility, and Sense of Humor. Lucky are the children who learn early in life to use these skills consciously.

Success at friendship is a two-step affair: We must carefully select and cultivate a friend; then, we must continue to earn his/her friendship.

Making a Friend

The skills needed to make a friend come from the very core of who we are. Here are some pointers to keep in mind. As you adapt this list and brainstorm other ideas with your students, keep their developmental levels in mind.

The "Gift of Gab" with People We Have Yet to Meet. We can't make a friend of someone we don't know. Therefore, we must work on our capacity to chat comfortably with people we don't know so that we can begin to uncover areas of common interest and common values. This ability immediately widens our potential circle of friends. Even introverts, to their surprise, find that such chance encounters have greatly enriched their circle of friends.

Go for Quality, Not Quantity. Making friends is not a competition. More is not necessarily better. "Better" comes from depth and richness. It is useful to make a clear distinction between "an acquaintance," "a friend," and "a close friend." Because maintaining a friendship takes time and attention, it is unrealistic to think that everyone we meet and like will become and remain a friend. How big our circle of friends can become depends heavily upon the nature of our responsibilities to self and others, job and community. Being a party animal and friend to one and all may not balance well with our responsibilities to our employer and our family or even our responsibility to ourselves to become our own person. Be realistic. To "have" a friend, one must "be" a friend.

Acting on the belief that we must belong at all costs is always—*always*—detrimental in the long run. Go for quality, not quantity.

Know Thyself. Life puts many people in our path. Some are great candidates to be a friend; most— yes, most—are not. We must know ourselves well enough—who we are now and who we want to become—to choose people who will bring out the best in us, not our worst; people who will complement us, not necessarily copy us; people who will challenge us, not stagnate with us.

Friendship is not a "search and rescue" operation. Getting into relationships "because he/she needs me" is dangerous territory. Such a relationship is not friendship, it is co-dependency. The difference is huge.

Conquer Your Ego. No emotionally healthy, well-balanced person wants to be around a self-centered, egocentric person or one who is needy and clings to others. And that cuts both ways. If we want to succeed at having friends, we must get beyond ourself and be someone that others want to be with. Getting beyond self requires doing daily homework on ourselves to ensure that we continue to grow. It's a bore to be around someone who isn't growing, who isn't in the process of becoming, who is stuck in his/her current point of view, and whose conversations stay centered on the same topics.

Keeping a Friend

To keep a friend, we need all of the Lifelong Guidelines and LIFESKILLS plus the common courtesies. In addition, keep in mind the following:

Be Caring and Show It. If you care, show it in tangible, unmistakable ways. If you feel too reserved or too quiet to do so, make a commitment to move beyond your sense of limitations and comfort zone. Friendship is as much about the other person as it is about you. To keep a friend, make sure that person knows you value them, care about them, are there for them. Friendship is about the other person. Plus, what goes around comes around. In a good friendship, that person lets you know they value you, care about you, are there for you.

Don't Take a Friend for Granted. Too often, we treat relatives and close friends with less regard and fewer courtesies than we treat more distant friends and acquaintances. As the old saying predicts: "Familiarity breeds contempt." We exhibit less civility and a double standard. For example, we yell at our siblings in ways we would never yell at a classmate or we "dress down" a spouse in ways we would never criticize an employee or colleague. Just because someone is a close friend doesn't mean that they don't deserve our best social graces and genuine care. Send them thank-you cards when they've done something especially helpful and nice. Remember their birthdays with cards and presents. Be as punctual with friends as you would with business clients. Diamonds might be forever; friends are not. We must continue to earn their respect and regard and we must continue to value them and show them that we do.

Friends Aren't Crutches. A mark of maturity is that we know where our friends end and we begin. We don't "need" our friends to make our life work; nor do we assume that they will always be there supporting us. We are a whole and complete person but we do appreciate and value each friend for the contribution they make to our lives.

Give and Take. Good friendships are well balanced and work to the benefit of both. Expect to follow as well as lead, support as well as be supported. The goal of a good friendship is accelerated growth and well-being of both.

Get—and Stay—Beyond Yourself. Life is about making a difference, making a contribution. View your close friendships as opportunities to make a difference—to them directly and, in partnership with them, performing acts that enrich your community and the world.

Most accomplishments in life are team efforts; learn to be a good team player and expect your friends to be your accomplices. Time with friends should further you on your life's path, not distract you.

WHAT DOES FRIENDSHIP LOOK LIKE IN REAL LIFE?

We

- Welcome new families to the neighborhood and make them feel included
- Guide a new employee around the company and teach him/her the ropes
- Ignore rumors and seek out the truth
- Write cards, letters, and e-mail to relatives and friends in times of celebration, joy, sympathy, and stress
- Listen when a friend is in need
- Offer positive feedback and don't use put-downs
- Spend quality time with our friends
- Visit during times of stress or illness
- Share materials, toys, and belongings
- Help our friends learn new concepts and information
- Tell friends the truth but do so tactfully
- Understand when friends make mistakes
- Offer compassion when needed

WHAT DOES FRIENDSHIP LOOK LIKE IN SCHOOL?

Staff

- Greet people pleasantly on or off school grounds
- Assist parents in locating information that will help improve their child's education
- Share personal materials with other teachers
- Keep in touch with staff members after their reassignment
- Confront rumormongers
- Observe the emotions and feelings of others and offer help when needed
- Welcome new staff members and other employees
- Include everyone in school social activities; avoid cliques

Students

- Offer to help classmates when needed in any way they can

- Ignore or confront classmates who spread hurtful rumors

- Learn more about classmates' lives and interests in order to be a friend

- Tell the truth in tactful ways

- Keep secrets unless someone is endangered

- Are friendly to all classmates

- Share materials

INQUIRIES TO DEVELOP FRIENDSHIP

Whole Group Inquiries

- Brainstorm the attributes of the "perfect friend." Create a T-Chart (Looks Like, Sounds Like, and Feels Like and Doesn't Look Like, Doesn't Sound Like, and Doesn't Feel Like) listing the characteristics of a good friend. Write a paragraph, short story, poem, song, or essay using some of the phrases from the chart to honor this person.

- Brainstorm and write your own story of friends or friendship. Check it for spelling, grammar, and punctuation. Process and print it out on the computer. Compile all of the individual class stories to create a "Chicken Soup for Friends" book. Add illustrations/ graphics as desired. Bind and display in a prominent place in your classroom.

- Choose a pen pal from a list provided by your teacher. Write an introductory rough draft of a letter sharing your personal interests (e.g., favorite books, hobbies, sports, organization memberships). Ask a classmate or the teacher to edit your letter for any errors. Design special "pen pal" note paper and copy the letter in your best handwriting. Address and mail the letter and respond to any answers you receive.

- Designate a "National Friendship Day" to celebrate in your classroom and school. Before selecting a day, check the school calendar for an open date. Invite a poet or card designer (graphic artist) to visit the class and set up a few patterns for expressing appreciation. As you near the actual date, draw another student's name from a jar and design a friendship card for that person. Hand out the cards and offer "thank yous." Include the larger school community by creating posters advertising this special event and suggesting ways to show appreciation, such as cards, songs, poems, notes, posters, essays. Organize an assembly with skits sharing ways to strengthen friendships. Perform for the school audience.

Small Group/Individual Inquiries

- Design a poster/collage that illustrates a way that you are a friend to "Mother Nature."Put this title at the top of a sheet of 12"x18" paper: MY BEST FRIEND ~ NATURE! Include a drawing or photos of yourself being a good friend to some plants and/or animals from the natural world. Share this with your best friend in class.

- Read the poem, *The New Kid on the Block* Brainstorm two or more things that would worry you if you were going to a new school. Introduce yourself to someone who is new to your class. Help him/her learn the procedures for: lining up, visiting the bathroom, getting food in the cafeteria, and recess.

- Choose two nursery rhymes that teach about friendship. Recite the rhymes for your class; add actions that show friendship.

- Read a story about friendship (see the "Literature Link" at the end of this chapter). Create two lists. On one, identify actions that "Help Friendships" to develop and on the other identify actions that "Hurt Friendships." Share the lists with a classmate or another learning club.

- Prepare a statement of appreciation for the friendship of at least one classmate at the weekly class meeting. Use the format for giving a compliment. Offer a paper copy for the person to keep.

- Interview an adult in your family about one special childhood friendship. Ask questions such as: How did you meet? How old were you when you met and how long did the friendship last? What common interests did you share? Where is the friend today? How is your best friend today different from that friend? Share the interview in a brief presentation to the class (five minute or less).

- Invite a conflict resolution expert to speak to your class. Ask him/her to share four or more ways that friends can resolve/express differences in feelings and opinions. Create a chart/banner/poster reinforcing those methods and hang it in the classroom. Create a conflict resolution center/peace table. Provide a table, two or three chairs, a tape recorder with calming music, and written procedures for resolving problems. Ask learning-club members to help role playing three or more situations that might necessitate a trip to the center. Act them out for your classmates.

- Create a classified advertisement that identifies four or more personal qualities you look for in a friend. Remember that ads are short, to the point, and may use capital letters/graphic symbols to attract the attention of readers. Share this ad with a partner and then with your learning club. Post your finished product on a bulletin board titled "WANTED: FRIENDS."

- Design a handmade or computer-generated "Get Well" card for a classmate who is absent because of extended illnesses or a "sympathy" card for someone who has recently lost a family member or close friend. Include appropriate expressions for a speedy recovery or condolences over his/her loss. Mail the card to that person when you feel you have done your personal best to express your thoughts and feelings.

- Read through some of the inclusion activities in *Tribes: A New Way of Learning and Being Together* by Jeanne Gibbs and choose one that is appropriate for your class (age and grade level). Collect any materials that are needed and practice the activity (giving directions, asking reflection questions, and offering follow-up suggestions) with your learning club three or more times. Present the activity to your classmates. After the inclusion activity is completed, reflect on the participation and responses of the group. Discuss with your learning club two things that you learned from this inquiry that will help make you more skillful in making and keeping friends in the future.

- Create a friendship bracelet by using embroidery yarn and fancy knots, or design beads by rolling strips of colored advertisements from magazines or colored paper to form beads. String the beads onto fishing line and knot; use an 8" piece for a bracelet or 17" piece for a necklace. Present this friendship jewelry to a special person.

- Study a pair of famous friends from any time period. Design a poster about how the pair achieved their fame because of their friendship. Describe five or more characteristics that strengthened their friendship and two other interesting facts. Share the information with a partner or your learning club.

- Research one of the following people: Henry David Thoreau, Jane Goodall, Jacques Cousteau, Rachel Carson, or someone else approved by your teacher. Learn how this person was a friend to animals or nature. Prepare and present a five-minute skit (remember C.U.E.—Creative, Useful and creates an Emotional Bridge) that conveys this special kind of friendship to your classmates in an entertaining and informative way.

- Identify and research a way you can express friendship toward animals. Write to three or more community support organizations requesting additional information that teaches about the cause. Create your own three-sided, colored pamphlet teaching about the need to participate in groups that protect wildlife. Share this with another interested student or adult.

SIGNS OF SUCCESS

Congratulations! Students are showing signs of Friendship when they

- Greet people in a friendly manner every day

- Offer to share something special

- Provide support for a friend who is nervous, scared, or sad

- Include a variety of classmates in daily school and after-school activities

- Talk with a new or lonely classmate, especially during lunch and recess—prime social times

- Create a handmade gift for a friend

- Help a fellow student who has been absent a few days to catch up with assignments

- Ensure that everyone on their team has a fair chance to participate in the game

- Honor a promise to a friend

- Respect the ways a person is different from themselves

- Participate in organizations such as scouts, YMCA, 4-H, and neighborhood clubs

- Remain loyal to a friend even if other friends don't seem to appreciate this person

- Design get-well cards for sick friends

- Give to the relationship as much as they take

- Don't take their friendships for granted

Keep trying! Children need more practice when they

- Can't seem to keep friends over a period of time

- Act silly to get their classmate's attention

- Lie to exaggerate their personal qualities

- Hit, bite, or kick people when they are angry

- Call people names or use put-downs as part of their daily language

- Harass or tease someone because of his/her general appearance, race, religious, or ethnic background

- Spread lies about people

- Refuse to share a friend with others

- Deliberately ignore some classmates

- Bribe someone to be their friend with toys or money

- Are mean to animals

- Steal classmates' property

- Abuse the environment

- Form cliques and contribute to a sense of, "If you're in, you're someone, but if you're out, you're nobody."

LITERATURE LINK ~ FRIENDSHIP

Primary Grades

Berenstain Bear's Trouble with Friends	Berenstain, J and S
Best Friends	Kellog, Steven
Chester's Way	Henkes, Kevin
Everette Anderson's Friend	Clifton, Lucille
Julius	Johnson, Angela
Miss Viola and Uncle Ed Lee	Duncan, Alice Faye
My Friend Jacob	Clifton, Lucille
Play It Again, Rosie	Brooks, Ruth
Secret Friend, A	Sachs, Marilyn
We Are the Best of Friends	Aliki
You're Not My Best Friend Anymore	Pomerantz, Charlotte

Intermediate Grades

Cat's Meow, The	Soto, Gary
Ernestine and Amanda	Belton, Sandra
Faithful Friend, The	San Souci, Robert
Fly, Homer, Fly	Peet, Bill
Friendship, The	Taylor, Mildred D.
Jennifer and Josephine	Peet, Bill
Lily's Crossing	Giff, Patricia Reilly
Number the Stars	Lowery, Lois
Roll of Thunder, Hear My Cry	Taylor, Mildred
Shoeshine Girl	Bulla, Clyde Robert
Sign of the Beaver, The	Speare, Elizabeth
Taste of Blackberries, A	Smith, Doris B.
Wall, The	Stine, William

Middle School and High School

Cay, The	Taylor, Theodore
Holes	Sachar, Louis
Last Days of Summer	Kluger, Steve
Outsiders, The	Hinton, S.E.

Teacher's Resources

Beyond Discipline: From Compliance to Community	Kohn, Alfie
What Kids Need to Succeed	Benson, Peter L., Judy Galbraith and Pamela Espeland

Date _____

Dear Family,

As we begin another LIFESKILL experience, I invite you to think of those relationships that have been important in your life because our class is moving on to the LIFESKILL of

~ FRIENDSHIP ~

Children want friends but do not always understand the processes needed to develop friendship—how to make and keep a friend. It is important for them to understand that each experience acts as a stepping stone to reach the next level of trust. Our class will:

- Create a variety of projects based on the concept of friendship

- Compare positive and negative friendship practices

- Participate in community circle or class meetings

- Research famous friends (fiction and nonfiction)

Here are some ways you can provide LIFESKILL support at home:

- Allow your child to invite friends over to play on a regular basis; help him/her plan for their arrival in ways that will help build friendship

- Involve your child in activities outside of the school community so that he/she can cultivate friends with a variety of interests

- Support your child through difficult relationships; help them learn from such experiences how to be and keep a friend

- Model how to be a friend with your friends; label what you are doing so your child can understand and translate it to his/her world

- Share how you have cultivated and nourished a friendship that began in elementary school

There is an old song that perhaps says it best:
"Make new friends but keep the old.
Some are silver and the others are gold."

Don't forget! Many children consider family to be their best friends.

Sincerely,

_____

Your child's teacher

Chapter 18

Initiative

"Do it now."

initiative *n* 1: an introductory act or step 2: energy or aptitude to initiate action: enterprise

INITIATIVE: To do something because it needs to be done

WHAT IS INITIATIVE?

Of all the Lifelong Guidelines and LIFESKILLS, Initiative and Integrity are the most inner-driven. They can't be forced from outside; they must be formulated, nurtured, and put into action from within. Initiative and Integrity are twin LIFESKILLS. Initiative without Integrity becomes bossiness or bullying; Integrity without Initiative becomes guilt or cowardice.

Initiative is sparked by an inner voice that propels us not only to pay attention but to act. It can be as simple as picking up a towel left on the floor or as complex as whistle blowing on corporate fraud or government malfeasance. It fires our actions, inventions, and creative endeavors. It runs on high octane—an inner motivation fueled by success with past challenges and our deep commitment to live up to our values and beliefs. It compels us to do something because it needs to be done and to re-do something until it meets our internal standards for quality and correctness.

Initiative differs from responsibility. Initiative is prompted by an internal, rather than an external, source. Responsibility asks us to respond to situations moment by moment while initiative prompts us to anticipate situations and create—or play a significant role in creating—them.

WHY PRACTICE INITIATIVE?

Initiative is important on many levels. Quite simply, if we don't practice the LIFESKILL of Initiative, how will anything get done? Who will be the inventors, the "doers," and the volunteers in our family, community, state, nation, and world? Who will start the work that needs to be done? Who will further science, technology, and the arts? Who will carry the work of a democratic society? Who will further civilization?

Initiative and Citizenship

The LIFESKILL of Initiative is an essential quality of citizens of a democratic society. As Edmund Burke put it, "The only thing necessary for the triumph of evil is for enough good men to do nothing."* As participating citizens in a government "by the people," we must practice initiative. When we see something that needs to be done, we must do it. We must inform ourselves and push the wheels of government to solve problems and ensure a just society. We can't wait to be told what to do; we must act. The ITI model recommends frequent social/political action projects to give students practice in taking initiative to solve problems using our democratic processes. (Such projects also provide opportunities for applying the knowledge and skills students are studying in order to reach mastery and create long-term memory.)

When working in groups, such as a school community, the LIFESKILL of Initiative is the difference between wishing for more effective learning environments and outcomes versus making them a reality.

Life abounds with adventure as we challenge ourselves to take chances while other people are still calculating the risks and puzzling over decisions. Initiators step out boldly and blaze a trail for the hesitant to follow.

Initiative and Personal Well-Being

On a personal level, taking action—taking the initiative—is fundamental to our expression of self. Without it, our personalities would be beige, flat, unremarkable. Without it, we can't reach out to form relationships with family, friends, or co-workers. Taken to the extreme, lack of initiative contributes to powerlessness, hopelessness, isolation, and, eventually, death of the self.

The LIFESKILL of Initiative is essential to our well-being.

HOW DO I PRACTICE INITIATIVE?

Because LIFESKILLS of Initiative and Integrity are so closely connected and because both are so at the core of who we are, surface applications or "seatwork" practice of initiative are worthless, even counterproductive. We must model the LIFESKILL of Initiative from the beginning, day in and day out. We must help students create a foundation which they can build on.

Building a Foundation

To practice the LIFESKILL of Initiative, we must have well-defined, clearly articulated values, standards for behavior and workmanship, and goals. In short, we must know who we are and what we stand for. And, we must have the courage of our convictions—the willingness to act on them.

---

* Edmund Burke, letter to Sheriffs of Bristol, dated April 3, 1777.

To help our students develop the LIFESKILL of Initiative, we must help them clarify their values, establish high expectations and standards for themselves, and set short- and long-term personal and academic goals they are passionate about. These are the foundations of the LIFESKILL of Initiative.

Using Curriculum Content

As with the other LIFESKILLS, Initiative is developed and strengthened through its use. Give students meaningful problems, dilemmas, and issues to wrestle with. Many such opportunities can be teased out of curriculum content as the year unfolds. Still others pop up in the daily news. When watershed events occur, such as the fall of the Berlin Wall, the Columbine High School shootings, or a presidential election, encourage students to discuss how their lives will be affected in the future; encourage them to take the initiative to examine the issues in terms of how they will affect their personal plans for the future, however tentative such plans may be.

Using Daily Classroom Management/Leadership Strategies

Make the LIFESKILL of Initiative a daily focus of your classroom management and leadership strategies. The development of the values, standards, and goals necessary for taking initiative can easily be incorporated into the following ongoing activities. For example:

Collaborative Work. Collaborative work requires enormous amounts of initiative, individually and as a group. To focus on the LIFESKILL of Initiative in collaborative work, teach students to use pre-planning, mid-way analysis, and post-assignment discussion. It is easy to add a question or two to help students focus on the LIFESKILL of Initiative. For example:

- Pre-planning: What are our group goals for this assignment? What do we hope to accomplish personally? What Lifelong Guidelines or LIFESKILLS will we most need to succeed at this task? How will this assignment help each of us achieve our academic and/or personal goals?

- Mid-way analysis: How are we doing so far? Are we on track? Will we reach our goals? Are we proceeding as we had planned? If not, why not? Are our methods working? Are they consistent with our values and standards or are we taking unwarranted shortcuts or questionable paths? What do we need to change in order to succeed? Does each member freely volunteer ideas and effort to ensure success? If we're stuck, how can we get ourselves moving again?

- Post-assignment discussion or "processing the process"—What worked? How well did we work together as a group, providing both leadership and support of the group? What did we learn about ourselves as group members and about ourselves personally? Did we avoid perfectionism, yet complete the task on time and meet expected standards? How can we improve our process and product next time?

Class Meetings. Encourage students to bring issues to class meetings. Support them in speaking their minds fully, accurately, confidently. Teach them to initiate conversations to resolve interpersonal issues, an invaluable skill throughout life. Help them see that how the class operates is as much their concern as it is yours as teacher.

Provide Leadership Opportunities. Create opportunities for all students to be in leadership roles on a daily basis. Serving successfully as a leader is one of the most powerful ways* to practice the LIFESKILL of Initiative. It is also the quickest and surest way to elevate self-esteem and confidence, prerequisites for living the LIFESKILL of Initiative.

Provide Genuine Choice. Of all the areas to demonstrate the LIFESKILL of Initiative, one of the most important is initiative in directing one's own learning. Structure your curriculum so that students have genuine choices about how they study. After direct instruction and guided practice, allow students to choose their inquiries. You as teacher set out the options, any one of which will accomplish what you want to have happen. Also encourage students to write their own inquiries which can then become one or more of the options you offer them. Encourage them to explore, to discover lifelong interests, hobbies, and vocations.

WHAT DOES INITIATIVE LOOK LIKE IN THE REAL WORLD?

We

- See a job that has to be done and do it (e.g., raise money for schools and churches or run for political office)

- Create organizations to help solve community problems

- Tackle the hard problems of the community as pro-active citizens

- Invent new machines to make work easier

- Research scientific ideas for better health

- Recycle materials to protect limited resources

- Organize a Neighborhood Watch group

- Help family members, neighbors, and friends during a crisis

- Want change and work toward finding positive answers

- Act in spite of others' possible negative reactions

- Make things happen, sometimes against great odds

---

* For a fascinating, research-based discussion of the power of leadership roles to change social status and self-perception, see *Designing Groupwork: Strategies for the Heterogeneous Classroom, Second Edition* by Elizabeth Cohen (New York: Teachers College Press, 1994), Chapters 6 and 8.

WHAT DOES INITIATIVE LOOK LIKE IN SCHOOL?

Staff

- Recognize a problem and lead efforts to resolve the situation

- Develop problem-solving skills and offer possible solutions

- Offer to serve as chairperson or committee members

- Endorse innovative ideas that support learning

- Reach out to staff, parents, and children when they are hurting or need assistance

- Offer to coach/mentor fellow teachers

- Take courses to continually update knowledge of strategies, curriculum, and skill development that strengthen learning

- Volunteer to be faculty advisors for student groups such as student council, clubs, sports, and interest groups

- Initiate a schoolwide recycling program

- Provide parents with information about different ways of learning

Students

- Offer to show a new student around the school; start new clubs and interest activities

- Initiate a project without prompting or nagging

- Bring in materials about topics currently being studied; do research in the library

- Raise "hard" questions about social issues

- Stand up for students who are being put down

- Ask for extra help to understand curriculum and learn skills

- Contribute suggestions on small group projects

- Volunteer to do tasks that are important to be done but uninteresting to do

INQUIRIES TO DEVELOP INITIATIVE

Whole Group Inquiries

- Listen as your teacher reads *The Hole in the Dike* by Norma Green (or another story about initiative the teacher chooses). Brainstorm five or more ways the hole in the dike could have been repaired. Rate them from "most practical" to "least practical." Ask ten other students which solution seems best to them. Distribute this information to your learning club.

- Organize a food collection from your school. Ask the director of a food bank what kinds of food (fresh, canned, preserved, dried) they most need. Create posters, advertisements, and flyers to educate the school community and encourage them to donate. Divide the products into categories, such as fruit, vegetables, food staples, as they are brought to school; record the number of items in each category. As soon as the collection date is set, arrange for adult drivers to deliver the items directly to the food bank.

- Investigate the lives and experiences of three or more contemporary entrepreneurs who are different from one another in age, background, and the products/services their business provides. Write an article, create a collage, or design a poster exhibiting at least two differences and similarities in their personalities, experiences, and achievements. Share your product with the class.

- Volunteer to be a helper for the class bottle drive. Choose one of the following activities:

    — Design a poster on 12"x18" paper that tells the date(s), the place, and the time(s) of the bottle drive.
    — Count and record the family name and number of bottles as they come to the room.
    — Sort the bottles into the correct plastic bags or containers for recycling.
    — Deliver the bottles (with an adult) to the recycle center.
    —Design a thank-you note from the class to be printed and given to each family that donated bottles.

Small Group/Individual Inquiries

- Ask an adult in your home for two or more examples of how he/she uses initiative at the workplace. Take notes or draw some pictures to help you remember his/her words. Discuss with this adult what you could learn from these examples to help you use initiative at school. Share your information with other members of your learning club.

- Brainstorm with your learning-club members any situations you all feel need to be discussed at a class meeting or during community circle time. Add the item(s) to the agenda or share the club's concerns with the teacher. Practice explaining your situation so that others will understand during the meeting.

- Show you are prepared to make informed decisions by demonstrating or explaining how to do five of the following:

    — Report a fire and report a prowler

    — Operate a fire extinguisher, explain how to extinguish different kinds of small household fires, and ways to check a smoke detector

    — Read a timetable for your local bus or subway system and identify three alternate routes to school

    — Order a meal from a menu and compute the total cost and the tip

    — Turn off the water under a sink and for your entire home

    — Prepare a list of emergency numbers to be posted in your home

    — Call 911 to report an emergency. Be prepared to include your name, address, phone number, and the nature of the emergency

- Create a time capsule that contains items and information representing you and your classmates. Include a class picture with students' names, key newspaper articles that chronicle the times, and one personal item per student. Also include a list of class events and special projects. Place the capsule in a special place with directions for its opening, including the date, time, and place.

- Learn to "sign" at least ten phrases that would help you communicate with a deaf person in distress. Practice these signs until you can make them with ease. Teach them to a partner.

- Attend a baby-sitters' training course to prepare you to take care of babies/young children. Demonstrate three of the following: feeding and burping a baby, changing a diaper, dressing the baby for a cold/hot day, entertaining a toddler, choosing and reading a story to a three-year old, or three of the most important danger signals to watch for. Prepare and share this demonstration for other interested students in your class. Upon completion of the course, design business cards that emphasize your training and advertise your services.

- Start a collection of interesting items such as seashells, baseball cards, rocks/minerals. Begin a log about your collection. Include an acquisition form for each item; write a description of the item, where it was found or purchased, cost (if applicable), the date acquired, and any personal memories. Assign each item a catalog number. Research your collectibles; list in your log at least two interesting facts you learned about each item. Prepare a five-minute talk on this collection. Identify two careers that are related to your collection. Present the information to your class or learning club.

- Practice a sport (team or individual) that is new to you. Research its history and learn the rules. Watch a few professional/college games in person or on television. Create an overhead transparency that illustrates the main goals of the game and two or more important strategies for success. Determine if the same rules are followed at your level of participation. Share this information with some younger students who have shown an interest in participating in this activity.

- Inform yourself about a global issue that also affects people in your community, such as pollution, human rights, hunger, health issues, or housing. Determine one or more local organizations that are working to make a difference there. Interview the organization's leader and identify three major efforts currently under way. Decide two or more actions that you can take to assist in the cause. Tell a partner and your teacher what you plan to do.

- Compose a song with lyrics that expresses your feelings about having and using the LIFESKILL of Initiative in the field of science and research. Create three verses, two of which should be about the experiences of famous scientists such as Albert Einstein and what they accomplished by using the LIFESKILL of Initiative.

- Invent a tool, machine, or aid that will provide a solution for a problem currently affecting your life. Draw plans to scale, list the materials you need, and create a prototype. Demonstrate your invention for the class.

- Take photographs of 10 or more people in your community who are using the LIFESKILL of Initiative, such as food bank volunteers, disaster clean-up crew, meeting of civic leaders and citizens to solve problems. Create a photo essay that expresses the message, "I am taking the first step to help solve a problem." Share this collection with three adults in your school.

- Investigate five or more major corporations or local businesses. Write the CEO for information about how the company encourages development and use of the LIFESKILL of Initiative. Carefully examine procedures that enable employees to share ideas, be creative, and develop new products. Locate statistics on the effectiveness of any company policies that encourage the LIFESKILL of Initiative. Write one procedure of your own that you feel would encourage enterprise and ingenuity. Present your findings to the class.

SIGNS OF SUCCESS

Congratulations! Students are showing signs of Initiative when they

- Suggest divergent ideas

- Speak up against injustices

- Demonstrate signs of leadership

- Organize a group to solve a problem

- See work that has to be done and do it

- Tackle a job that no one else is willing to try

- Speak their minds even though others may not agree

- Develop interests in various areas

- Welcome new students and their families to the school

Keep trying! Students need more practice when they

- Avoid sharing ideas because of what others might think

- Follow others most of the time and rarely voice or implement their own ideas or solutions

- Give up trying to think creatively

- Respond to problem-solving opportunities with apathy and listlessness

- Always wait for someone else to take on a job

- Allow other people to think for them

- Cling to methods that don't work just because that's the way it's always been done

LITERATURE LINK ~ INITIATIVE

Primary Grades

Bears on Hemlock Mountain	Dalgliesh, Alice
Doctor DeSoto	Steig, William
Elves and the Shoemaker, The	Brothers Grimm
Flossie and the Fox	McKissack, Patricia
Hole in the Dike, The	Green, Norma
Jamaica's Blue Marker	Havill, Juanita
Little Toot	Gramatky, Hardie
Lyle Crocodile	Waber, Bernard
Sweet Clara and the Freedom Quilt	Hopkinson, Deborah
Wings	Lionni, Leo

Intermediate Grades

All for the Better: The Story of El Barrio	Mohr, Nicholasa
Caddie Woodlawn	Brink, Carol R.
Child of the Silent Night: The Story of Laura Bridgman	Hunter, Edith Fisher
Flight of the Fox, The	Murphy, Shirley Rousseau
It's a Mile from Here to Glory	Lee, Robert C.
Lone Hunt, The	Steele, William O.
Long Journey, The	Corcoran, Barbara
Lupita Mañana	Beatty, Patricia
Maldonado Miracle, The	Taylor, Theodore
Martin Luther King, Jr.	Bray, Rosemary L.
Song of the Trees	Taylor, Mildred
Wagon Wheels	Brenner, Barbara

Middle School and High School

Backwater	Bauer, Joan
Boy and the Otter, The	Lloyd, A.R.
Girls Who Rocked the World: *Heroines from Sacajawea to Sheryl Swoopes*	Weldon, Amelie

Tall Mexican: The Life of Hank Aguirre,
    All-Star Pitcher, Businessman,
    Humanitarian
	Copley, Robert E.

Teacher's Resources

Brain Gym (Teacher's Edition, Revised)	Dennison, Paul and Gail
Directory of American Youth Organizations	Erickson, Judith B.
Smart Moves: Why Learning Is Not *All In Your Head*	Hannaford, Carla

Date _____

Dear Family,

Our next LIFESKILL is Initiative. To quote Henry Ford, "If you think you can, or if you think you can't, you're right." These commanding words provide guidance to parents, teachers, and other adults playing a part in children's lives because our reactions and feedback help to shape their self-image. Our words help paint the picture of

~INITIATIVE~

We will be investigating the LIFESKILL of Initiative and searching for ways to incorporate this LIFESKILL into our daily lives by:

- Reading biographies of famous inventors, artists, and scientists

- Researching ways companies appreciate and encourage enterprise

- Volunteering to work on a school or neighborhood project (for example, collecting food items for a food bank)

- Welcoming any newcomers to our classroom and school

- Understanding the place initiative occupies in the business world

Your family can support the LIFESKILL of Initiative by encouraging your child to:

- Create, start, and finish projects

- Be an original thinker, a new-idea person

- Think for himself or herself and not blindly follow any group

- Welcome new children in the neighborhood

Please share with your child some of your experiences with the LIFESKILL of Initiative, both while growing up and as an adult. Together, our school and your home are shaping the thinkers and doers of the 21st Century.

Sincerely,

_____

Your child's teacher

Chapter 19

Integrity

"ALWAYS BE TRUE TO ONESELF AND OTHERS."

integrity *n* **1:** honesty, incorruptible
2: firm adherence to a code, especially of moral or artistic values: incorruptibility
3: the quality or state of being complete or undivided: completeness; unimpaired, soundness

INTEGRITY: To act according to a sense of what's right and wrong

WHAT IS INTEGRITY?

Of all the Lifelong Guidelines and LIFESKILLS, Initiative and Integrity are the most inner-driven. They can't be forced from outside; they must be formulated, nurtured, and put into action from within. Integrity and Initiative are twin LIFESKILLS. Integrity without Initiative becomes guilt, cowardice, or the worst mix of self-righteousness and I-told-you-so. Initiative without Integrity becomes bossiness or bullying.

Integrity is our inner voice of wisdom, a voice that speaks the truth about whether there is resonance or discord between our words and actions and our sense of what's right and wrong. Like a tuning fork, it tells us if we are in harmony with our beliefs or living in life-sapping discord. This LIFESKILL lies at the core of who we are, what we believe, and what we stand for. It is the touchstone for all other LIFESKILLS and Lifelong Guidelines.

WHY PRACTICE INTEGRITY?

In a society whose teens and 20- and 30-year-old males wear T-shirts sporting the slogan, "Don't get mad, just get even" and cars sport bumper stickers that say "My kid beat up your honor student," integrity is sometimes seen as old-fashioned. Getting even, striking back, putting a hurt on someone, seeking retribution, saving face, protecting ego—even if you are the person who is wrong or at fault—are all championed by movies and prime time sit-coms and dramas. Image and status are everything.

What Goes Around Comes Around

So why not go with the flow and forget about the LIFESKILL of Integrity? There are selfish reasons for living a life of integrity as well as selfless ones—practical reasons as well as philosophical and moral reasons. Besides being concerned about how our life impacts others, the sanity and stability of our own lives depend upon a measure of predictability and stability in others; without it, we can't make our own life work. Integrity is a two-way street—what goes around comes around.

This dependability and predictability in relationships comes largely from integrity. When the people around us lead their lives with integrity, we know how they will interact with us and others, in situations and with ideas. They are steadfast; they don't waiver depending on who or what or circumstances or whim. Who they are today is who they will be next week and the month after. We know where we stand with them. We trust them. We respect them. We value being in their presence.

If we want integrity in others, we must deserve it by having integrity ourselves.

Integrity As a Source of Personal Power

Of all the LIFESKILLS, Integrity generates the most personal power. People with integrity are in high demand as trusted counselors, dependable politicians, effective business partners, treasured spouses, and valued friends. We listen to what they have to say and consider it carefully. We can depend on their word; we trust who they are and what they stand for. In our lives, we willingly give them our respect and we honor their power.

Integrity Opens Doors. Because first impressions are often misleading, reputations built up over a lifetime are much more reliable. One of the centerpieces of a person's reputation is integrity. If someone is known for his/her integrity, doors open; if integrity is questionable, many doors close. The number and kinds of doors that open to us often make the difference between success or failure in life. They make the difference between satisfaction or discontent, dreams realized or fantasies that float beyond our reach. Integrity plus opportunity is a powerful mix.

Integrity Is Fragile. As the boy who cried wolf too many times discovered, once your reputation is lost, it's extremely hard to rebuild it. As Susan Kovalik's father often warned his young daughter: "It takes a thousand acts to build a good reputation but only one lapse in integrity to lose it." Integrity is not an on-again, off-again quality. It is a lifetime endeavor, a lifetime work of art.

Integrity As Basis for Society and Government

Democratic societies cry out for leadership based on integrity—a government with effective leaders of strong character, immune to corruption, opportunism, or moral decay. They also cry out for citizens of integrity who in turn demand integrity in those they elect and in those who serve on juries, vote in elections, pay just taxes, and stand up for the less fortunate and less powerful members of society. When integrity wanes, nations fall.

HOW DO YOU PRACTICE IT?

We develop integrity primarily by seeing it in action—modeled by those we admire and respect. If we model taking the high road, children will learn to make decisions based on principles rather than expediency. If we model sticking to standards rather than giving in to short cuts, children will commit to doing their personal best. If we model doing a job from beginning to end and taking pride in our accomplishments, children will willingly adhere to codes of excellence. If our behaviors consistently match the words we speak, children see integrity. What we do always out teaches what we say we do.

Start Early

Parents are the first and most powerful models of the LIFESKILL of Integrity. They teach through their day-to-day interactions with their child and others—from their insistence on sharing and fairness with playmates to issues of respect of ownership and self-restraint and from their reactions to their law-based government to how they make their religion's teaching relevant to their lives.

Building integrity starts in the cradle and proceeds throughout life. Many of life's lessons come from making mistakes, using bad judgment, and then agonizing over the results. From these errors, we determine which actions do not correspond to our sense of right and wrong and the person we want to be. Some decisions make us feel bad while other choices make our heart sing. Initially we look to the responses of families, friends, and coworkers; eventually our sense of right and wrong becomes sufficiently internalized that we make our own judgments.

Teaching the LIFESKILL of Integrity must be central to how each classroom operates. In a democratic society, integrity of its citizenry is a necessity, not an option; it is a requirement.

Use the Teachable Moment

The goal of character development is to educate the conscience in such a way that a person does what is right without being told and without being watched. This can't be done through a series of worksheets; it can only be done through modeling and use of the teachable moment.* Helping children solve a real dilemma at the moment it occurs is one of the most effective learning experiences. For example, students enter the classroom all abuzz about a pushing-shoving incident in the hallway; discussion ensues about what act of integrity could have stopped the incident before it escalated out of control. Or, a student points out similarities between organized crime during Prohibition and the rule of gangs in their neighborhood today; this prompts a discussion of loyalty versus integrity. The teacher nurtures and guides such discussions rather than simply cutting them off as a bird walk from the "real" curriculum.

---

* The "teachable moment" is a deliberate instructional strategy in the ITI model. Teachers are encouraged to stay focused in the present and use what comes up at the moment as a teaching opportunity to connect curriculum content and the Lifelong Guidelines and LIFESKILLS to real-world situations.

Help Students Build an Inner Foundation

Help students develop their sense of what's right and wrong by framing dilemmas for discussion that are important to students. Pull from classroom and campus issues, current news, and curriculum. Insist that students continually examine who they are and what they stand for through journal writing and discussion during class meetings. Help them clarify their values, establish high expectations and standards, and set personal and academic goals. Don't let a day go by without giving students opportunities to make the LIFESKILL of Integrity relevant to their lives and their perspective of what's right and what's wrong. The LIFESKILL of Integrity is developed by degrees and inches over time. If it were an easy task, the percentage of our citizenry considered to be people of integrity would be sharply higher.

Use Curriculum Content

Dig deeper into curriculum content. Plumb for meaningful problems, dilemmas, and issues as a focus for student dialog. Bring in current news about oil spills, illegal dumping, or the death penalty, watershed events such as the fall of the Berlin Wall, the Columbine High School shootings, or attacks on Family Planning Clinics, plus local community issues and schoolwide concerns. Have students examine these real-world events through the lens of the concepts being studied in their subject area content. Avoid factoids and focus on how concepts can be generalized and used to inform us about situations new to us. Show them that academic rigor is, in fact, an extension of integrity—an awareness of when we know (understanding at a high level of expertise) and when we don't know (surface knowledge only).

Use Daily Classroom Management/Leadership Strategies

Using daily classroom management and leadership strategies to focus on integrity makes the LIFESKILL of Integrity come alive through modeling and discussion. See the discussion of collaborative work, class meetings, and providing leadership opportunities and genuine choice on pages 18.3 and 18.4.

WHAT DOES INTEGRITY LOOK LIKE IN THE REAL WORLD?

We

- Remain true to our goals by continuing to work on them without selling out to shortcuts
- Keep promises made to ourselves and others
- Tell the truth even when it gets us into trouble
- Try to locate the owners of found objects

- Point out an error to cashiers even when the error is in our favor

- Use accurate figures when computing income taxes

- Follow through on projects to completion

- Remain loyal to family and friends yet help them own up to their problems and misdeeds

- Live within our means

- Honor others by showing up on time for appointments with them

WHAT DOES INTEGRITY LOOK LIKE IN SCHOOL?

Staff

- Go above and beyond what the job description requires in order to complete important tasks

- Insist that gossip and put-downs be eliminated

- Provide honest appraisals of student accomplishments

- Keep their word to other students, parents, and fellow staff

- Model honesty, strength, and firmness of character

- Insist that religious, ethnic, and cultural identities be respected

- Demonstrate fairness in all areas

Students

- Resist peer pressure and speak and act from their own values and beliefs

- Do what they say they will

- Earn the money they spend and only spend what they earn

- Readily own up to mistakes of omission and commission (even when known only to them)

- Can sift through cultural, neighborhood, and family values and beliefs to extract universal principles; abandon any values and beliefs that are inconsistent with these universal principles

- Respect fellow students and staff even if they disagree with what they say

- Take charge of their own learning and commit themselves to excellence

INQUIRIES TO DEVELOP INTEGRITY

Whole Class Inquiries

- Learn to play five or more games, such as checkers, Monopoly, chess, solitaire, Scrabble, or dominoes, that require integrity by the players. Play each game at least once with someone in your class. Discuss why integrity is an important aspect of each game and share your feelings about the results after you have finished playing the game.

- Choose a situation from the following list: finding a lost object, being undercharged for an item at the store, witness a friend being put-down, witness a stranger being put-down, breaking a school rule, fighting on the playground, or being wrongfully accused. Enlist the support and assistance of your learning club to create a five-minute skit that demonstrates two ways to approach the problem. Have one approach show a lack of integrity and the other present a strong example of the LIFESKILL of Integrity. Perform the skit for the class and lead the discussion about questions raised.

- Collect five or more newspaper articles about citizens exhibiting integrity. Create a mindmap of observable behaviors and characteristics. Conversely, locate five or more articles about people lacking integrity. Create a "Consequence Chart" for each article. List the positive and negative outcomes for each. For each negative consequence, brainstorm other courses of action that employ integrity. Discuss this information with your class.

Small Group/Individual Inquiries

- Design a "thank-you" card for a child in your class/school who has shown that he/she knows how to act according to a sense of what is right and fair. Draw a picture on the front that shows the actions this child followed. On the inside, write "Thank you" and one other sentence sharing your feelings. Deliver the card to this schoolmate.

- Listen to the story *The Emperor's New Clothes*. Decide whether or not you would have told the emperor about his missing clothes. Share your thoughts about this with a classmate.

- Write a rhyme or chant of four or more lines that teaches other children the "right" thing to do if they find something that doesn't belong to them. Add motions to help teach the lesson. Invite your learning club to present this to another class.

- Play the game of "Telephone." Line up with your classmates. Ask the teacher to whisper a message in the first person's ear who then whispers the same message to the next person in line. Continue in that manner. Ask the last person in line to repeat the message he/she received out loud for the group to hear. Discuss the difference in messages and how the LIFESKILL of Integrity could be used to prevent mistaken messages and rumors.

- Create a T-chart with the following title: "Ways to Lose Integrity and Ways to Gain Integrity." List five or more possibilities for each category to show some of the many ways integrity is gained or lost. Post the chart in the classroom and explain the material to a friend.

- Create a class pledge based on the following LIFESKILLS: Integrity, Initiative, Friendship, and Caring. Make the final copy on the computer using a fancy font, color, and graphics. Teach the pledge to your learning club and invite the class to recite it along with your group. Develop a way to check on your growth in matching your behavior to the words of the pledge.

- Dramatize four different skits for the class, each illustrating integrity. Act out each situation two ways: one using integrity and one without using integrity. Provide each student with a piece of 8" by 11" paper folded into quarters. Ask the students to number each rectangle from one through four to match the skit presentation numbers. Invite them to draw the solution they would choose for each of the skits. Lead a discussion about their various reasons for making the choices they did.

- Design a lost and found box for your classroom. Choose a box large enough to hold many items and decorate it with your favorite colors. Write the title "LOST AND FOUND" in large, easy-to-read capital letters. Create an inventory sheet; include object, location of object when found, date, name of person who found the item, other information useful for finding the owner, and information the owner might need to write a thank-you note. Complete the form when something is placed in the box. Introduce your box to the class and ask them where to place it for easy access. If more than one box is created, offer them to other classes or to teachers of special subjects.

- Design a class problem-solving box. Choose a carton at least as large as a shoe box. Decorate it with wallpaper or wrapping paper and add a slit in the top. Place a label on the box that states, "What's Your Dilemma?" Place some index cards and a pencil next to the box. Invite fellow classmates to write any problems on a card and drop it in the box. During class meetings, choose one card a day to brainstorm possible solutions. Discuss how the LIFESKILL of Integrity affected your brainstorming and choice of solutions.

- Identify one of the major areas of environmental concern in our community, such as water pollution, preservation of natural or historical landmarks, lack of public transportation, or trash disposal. Research your topic to determine how local, state, and federal laws affect the environmental quality in our area. Determine who is responsible for enforcing these laws. Invite one or more local political or legal representatives to your class to explain the relationship between following the laws and the LIFESKILL of Integrity. Explore a career linked to environmental law and develop a pamphlet that explains the connection. Pass the pamphlet out to other interested students.

- Research the correct way to footnote material from sources (books, encyclopedias, songs, movies, speeches, and the Internet) that you are using to support your own work. Give one example for each of the above categories. Teach a partner how to correctly identify ideas belonging to others.

- Visit a store during a major sale. Take your calculator along and compute the sale price of ten or more items to determine if the store has priced the merchandise accurately. If the prices are correct, create an "Integrity Award" that includes the name of the store, the date you visited, the prices checked, and your signature as a satisfied consumer. If the sale prices are not accurate, write a letter to the general manager expressing your concerns about the inaccurate pricing. Suggest that the prices be corrected to earn back customer trust and respect. Mail either the award or the letter of concern to the store's general manager. Explain to your learning club the steps you have taken to ensure accuracy in pricing.

- Research shoplifting in three or more local stores. Determine how much is taken in a week, month, and year. Compute the average age of the accused shoplifters and the cost to the nonshoplifting customer. Find out what punishment is given for a shoplifting conviction. Share two ways stores are protecting themselves from this kind of theft. Role play three or more ways you could use the LIFESKILL of Integrity to prevent a friend from shoplifting.

- Research local laws about juvenile delinquent behavior. Interview two or more people who work in the juvenile justice system, including police, court, and rehabilitation. Use the information to write a play, skit, story, or produce a short video (5-10 minutes) for an audience your age. Discuss with your learning club how a juvenile could use the LIFESKILL of Integrity to avoid breaking the law by shoplifting or driving while under the influence of alcohol or drugs.

SIGNS OF SUCCESS

Congratulations! Students are showing signs of Integrity when they

- Know the difference between right and wrong and choose to do right even if no one is watching

- Recognize when they have made an unwise choice and do all in their power to correct it

- Fulfill a promise or contract and keep their "word"

- Accept responsibility for their actions

- Tell the truth even though there may be unpleasant consequences

- Walk away from peer group pressures to do negative things

Keep trying! Students need more practice when they

- Lie to get out of trouble

- Keep items they have found and don't try to locate the owners; steal things

- Break a promise; say one thing but do another

- Are constantly late for work or school

- Violate school commitments

- Understand the difference between right and wrong and deliberately choose "wrong"

- Emulate substandard behavior from TV, movies, books, videos and "real-life" situations

- Believe that "If it doesn't hurt anybody, what's the harm?"

- Believe that it is all right to remove materials from their school because "teachers expect a certain amount of stuff to disappear"

- Refuse to accept responsibility for their actions; make excuses for their behavior

Literature Link ~ Integrity

Primary Grades

Day's Work, A	Bunting, Eve
Emperor's New Clothes, The	Anderson, Hans Christian
Frederick's Alligator	Peterson, Esther A.
I Have a Dream	King, Dr. Martin Luther Jr.
I'll Tell on You	Lexau, Joan
Jamaica's Find	Havill, Juanita
Jimmy Lee Did It	Cummings, Pat
Legend of the Bluebonnet, The	dePaola, Tomie
Little Seven Colored Horse: A Spanish-American Folktale, The	San Souci, Robert
Molly's Lies	Chorao, Kay
Molly's Pilgrim	Cohen, Miriam
Sam, Bangs, and Moonshine	Ness, Evelyn
Samantha Learns a Lesson	Adler, Susan

Intermediate Grades

Adventures of Pinocchio, The	Colladi, Carlo
Best Christmas Pageant Ever, The	Robinson, Barbara
Frightful's Mountain	George, Jean Craighead
Hundred Dresses, The	Estes, Eleanor
Jacob Two-Two Meets the Hooded Fang	Richler, Mordecai
Pistachio Prescription, The	Danziger, Paula
Rosa Parks, My Story	Parks, Rosa
Story of Thurgood Marshall, The	Arthur, Joe
Thief, The	Turner, Megan W.
Twenty and Ten	Bishop, Claire H.
Wringer	Spinelli, Jerry

Middle School and High School

Call of the Wild	London, Jack
Chocolate War, The	Cormier, Robert
Finding My Voice	Lee, Marie G.
Legend of Jesse Owens, The	Nuwer, Hank

Teacher's Resource

Family Virtues Guide, The	Popov, Linda Kavelin

Date _____

Dear Family,

The next LIFESKILL is perhaps the most important of all. It is the LIFESKILL of

～ INTEGRITY ～

Most of us, at sometime in our lives, have had to deal with the pain and destruction that takes place when people around us lack integrity. We have also enjoyed the company of people with high integrity. Over the years we have collected pictures of the qualities we would like our children to have.

We define the LIFESKILL of Integrity as "To act according to a sense of what's right and wrong." To support students' development of this LIFESKILL, we will:

- Role play situations that require integrity and discuss possible choices

- Continue to focus on problem-solving strategies

- Brainstorm the attributes of people with integrity

- Find and examine examples of integrity in our community

As parents raising your children in an ever more complex world, there are things you can do to support character development at home. Here are a few ideas:

- Read and share favorite family stories that explore what's right and wrong

- Insist that your child return borrowed items to their original owner

- Teach your child to make promises only when he/she can carry them out

- Teach your child to walk away from peer group pressures to do negative things

Given what our children will experience in the course of their lives, much rides on their knowing right from wrong and having the courage to do what's right. We, as educators, are here to support you in your quest to raise a respectful, caring, and trustworthy child, a person of integrity.

Sincerely,

_____

Your child's teacher

Organization

Chapter 20

"CLUTTER CAUSES CONFUSION."

organization *n* **1:** the act or process of organizing or being organized
2: arranging or forming into a coherent unity or functioning whole
3: arranging by systematic planning and united effort

ORGANIZATION: To plan, arrange, and implement in an orderly way, to keep things orderly and ready to use

WHAT IS ORGANIZATION?

Organization is a state of mind, an insistence that everything have a place and everything be in its place—in working order and ready to go. It's an internal standard that demands that we not leave projects unfinished or tools and leftover materials lying about.

In this busy world with its competing demands, it has become increasingly difficult to complete responsibilities, satisfied that we've done our "personal best." Many of us have good intentions but lack either the skills for the task or the short- and long-term planning methods to see a job through from its inception to completion. This inevitably leads to crisis planning, frustration, and, often, a deep sense of failure.

The organized mind looks for clear purpose. It ties vision to the task at hand and to ways to accomplish a task.

WHY PRACTICE ORGANIZATION?

Have you ever failed to even begin a project because you knew that it would take forever to gather what you needed? Have you ever blown a commitment because it took you so long to get organized you missed the deadline? Do you feel as if you're doing less than you know you're capable of because your desk is disorganized and you can't find what you need when you need it? Have you ever been passed over for a promotion even though you knew more about the business than the person who won the job? But his tidy appearance and work space made him look as if he knew much more than he did?

If you've answered yes to any of those questions, you already know why it's important to practice organization. Strong organizational skills are a pathway to greater productivity, effectiveness, and spontaneity. They help us release our creativity and vitality. They bring peace to our lives.

Being organized is important: It saves us time because we don't have to search for things (everything is readily at hand); it improves the quality of our work (we have the right tools, information, materials, and resources when they're needed); and it increases our motivation to move on to the next task (there aren't 10 things left over from previous tasks that must be done before we can get started on the next).

Time Is Money and Sanity

The LIFESKILL of Organization is reflected in the book title, *If You Haven't Got the Time to Do It Right, When Will You Find the Time to Do It Over?* by Jeffrey J. Mayer. It drives home the importance of staying organized so that we have time to do the job right the first time.

It appears that the Holy Grail of the 21st century will be *time*—how to find it, where to get more of it. Today, more than ever, saving time by being organized is a personal imperative. Life without timesaving organization would be a nightmare. Effectiveness and efficiency depend upon it, as does our sanity.

Organization makes the difference between success and failure in our work and the difference between a life of all work with no time to play or a balanced life of work and personal time.

Improving the Quality of Our Work

Quality work is impossible without the right tools, information, and resources—all available as we need them, not in helter-skelter fashion. Whether in a blue-collar trade or in a white-collar position, our professionalism hinges on our ability to get and stay organized. No matter how gifted, how well financed, how experienced we may be, how superior our idea or approach . . . all is for naught if we're not organized to fully do the job.

Increasing Our Motivation to Move On

In *Human Brain and Human Learning,* brain-compatible learning pioneer Leslie Hart points out that the biochemicals produced when a mental program doesn't work and must therefore be aborted make us feel upset, uncomfortable. In evolutionary terms, it could be threatening, even life-threatening.* In an unorganized environment, disruption in mental programs and plans is common and frequent. Such negative emotions make us less adventurous and more conservative

* See *Human Brain and Human Learning* by Leslie Hart. (Kent, Washington: Books for Educators, Inc., 1998), p. 160-161.

in order to avoid failure. We're less motivated to move forward to new things and more ill at ease throughout the project.

Improving Our Ability to Think

It's a little-known fact, and quite unbelievable for some, that tidiness and simplicity in our working environment improve our ability to think. Lack of clutter, the orderly availability of tools and resources, calming colors (not more than two coordinating colors plus accent color), live plants, full-spectrum lighting, music (soft, instrumental, 60-beats a minute) all help create an environment that enhances thinking. The research on this is clear and commanding.*

Our old pictures of the "enriched environment"—a blast of bright colors, profusion of things covering every wall and hanging from the ceiling, materials and resources from previous and future projects—are simply not supported by current brain research. Visit a five-star hotel and tune into your visceral experience; you'll undergo firsthand what brain research is telling us.

The physical, emotional, mental, and spiritual dimensions of being human are all connected; thus, attaining harmony with our physical environment contributes to greater wholeness in our lives. It is, therefore, essential that we plan our environment (along with actions and emotions) to enhance our quality of life. Our task is to create a mind- and soul-enriching environment in which to live, work, and play.

Likewise at school, we can increase the probability that our students will also become adept at organizing their own time—and lives—if we fully develop and model the LIFESKILL of Organization.

What Organization Is Not

Being organized does not mean being inflexible, nor uncreative, nor compulsive about cleanliness and tidiness. For most things in life, knowing where you're going and how you'll get there improve the likelihood that you will reach your goals.

Being organized is not slavish adherence to tried and true processes. It's insisting that we select processes that will help us achieve our goals. It's a way to approach life and manage situations.

HOW DO YOU PRACTICE IT?

For some of us, the urge to be organized is innate, a part of our personality preferences or temperament** since birth. For others, the yen to be organized is a low priority.

---

* For more information, see the ITI model text for your grade level and *Healing Environments* by Carol Venolia (Berkeley, California: Celestial Arts, 1988).

** For a fascinating and highly useable description of temperament/personality preferences, see Chapter 7 in *Making Bodybrain-Compatible Education a Reality: Coaching for the ITI Model* by Karen Olsen (Kent, Washington: Books for Educators, 1999) or, go to the source: *Please Understand Me II: Temperament, Character, Intelligence* by David Keirsey (Del Mar, California: Prometheus Nemesis Book Company, 1998).

For those who can depend on inner cravings to be organized and tidy, perhaps this chapter can help you further strengthen and refine your skills.

For those who feel no inner urge to be organized, reread why we should practice organization. For you (and I am among your ranks!), being organized is an intellectual choice rather than an instinct or inner urge—a decision to be made moment by moment, over and over and over again, day after day. First, choose to become organized! Then, use the following tips to help you strengthen your organization skills.

Start with Your Physical Environment

Start with mastering your physical environment. Don't just clean your house, organize it as you clean. To reduce clutter and competition for storage space, ask yourself "Does this support me now?" If you haven't used an item or worn it within the past 12 months, donate it to Goodwill or a recycling agency of your choice. Are you a pack rat? Then limit yourself to two keepsakes per year. (Just the process of determining value among your treasures will enrich your memory bank as well as help cut down on clutter.)

Are the tools/materials you use most frequently readily at hand? Are those for emergencies kept handy where you and others in your household can readily find them? If not, put labels on the shelves where things go and create an inventory list showing location of items. If you clear out and reorganize all in the same day, your labeling will fit the amount of stuff you have in each category. Then, stick with it and follow the labels. Remember the old adage, "A place for everything and everything in its place."

Do you have children six-years old and up at home? If so, try the labeling process with them in their room. Teaching children how to organize—and stay organized—prevents a lifetime of friction over messy rooms, half-completed jobs, and endless nagging over any number of issues. Learning at an early age to be organized is a gift.*

Next, take on your classroom. The same questions apply. Students in third grade and up can help with the organizing process and are quite good at it. Everyone would like the opportunity to live in a five-star hotel environment. That's what your classroom can be!

Daily Living Is A Management Tool

Why is starting with the physical environment so important? Because, as every architect knows, form dictates function in obvious and subtle ways. The best way to practice the LIFESKILL of Organization is to design and use your environment as an effective management tool—a tool to keep yourself organized. Let me emphasize this: Create an environment that helps shape your behavior, one that helps you be organized every minute of the day . . . at home and at school.

---

* Maria Montessori intuitively understood the power of organization and its link to development of the brain almost 100 years ago. Her emphasis on organization, on things having a beginning, middle, and end, and on working at a task at increasing levels of difficulty is seamlessly interwoven into her program. This is one of the reasons her preschool program is so powerful and so popular throughout the world.

Doesn't this make common sense? Yes. Remember, being organized isn't just another task, another thing to do. It is *the* most important thing to do! It shapes the moment and the day, your mood and your effectiveness. It saves time that we can spend on things other than work—family time, hobbies, recreation, time to grow, and so forth. Looked at from this perspective, organizing becomes an intriguing, worthwhile challenge.

However, for those of us who aren't organizers by nature, how do we proceed? One way is to look at the "whole picture," then break it down into smaller, more manageable pieces. For instance, we can divide the search for organization into three main topics: personal time management starting with personal items (such as our own laundry, toiletries, hobbies, personal spaces), our work space (desk/office organization), and room organization. For each topic, identify the patterns that create confusion, disarray, and clutter. Then identify orderly management procedures that will increase productivity—for us and for our students.

Find A Mentor

For many of us, identifying what should be better organized and how to do it is easy. For others, it is more difficult. We might know what's "wrong" but, no matter how hard we have tried, we can't seem to *fix* it! Even harder is keeping the fix going! But you know what? Every school has at least one ready-made, super-duper, handy-dandy, natural-born organizer who is willing to share secrets for getting and staying organized—those little tips that allow one to meet deadlines, find any paper within one minute, and rid the room of unused "teacher stuff."

Ask for advice and then try following it in incremental steps. Remember, many small successes lead to major accomplishments.

To begin, ask your organization mentor to "do" your classroom with you. As you move to each area, ask for tips on how he/she organizes similar areas. Practice asking yourself the following questions and acting on your answers:

- Does this item support me now? If not, how do I make myself throw it out or recycle it?

- What are the most common activities that occur here? What common procedures, tools, and resources should be readily available? How can I create a place for everything and have everything in its place?

- What is the most appropriate organizational system for filing and keeping track of important items/information of this kind? What activities take place in this area and what is needed for them?

- How do I keep my organizational processes alive and well? How much time do I need and how often? How often should I check that the organizational system is working and up-to-date?

Time Management Strategies

Handling the same piece of paper twice is a time management no-no. And yet, on a once clear desk and work space, my papers never seem to go anywhere; even worse, they seem to multiply overnight like rabbits.

To get things moving, we must be decisive, acting quickly on questions such as those above. Don't waffle. Decide within 30 seconds of asking yourself the question, and act on it immediately. Don't allow yourself to even entertain the "later" word. Later never comes and paper never goes.

To practice time management strategies, I recommend forming a Time Wasters Anonymous Club on campus. Find a colleague or colleagues who want to raise their professional and personal skills in this area. Meet daily at first to share successes and support. Half the battle is remaining conscious of the intention to use time well. Then, follow the time management tips below in a small area of your life, such as handling homework, team planning work, house cleaning, responsibilities for the children or nurturing your relationship with loved ones.

Once you have mastered one area, expand to a second, still rather small area. With each success, take on another part of your life while simultaneously keeping the earlier plates spinning. Stop expanding when your successes stop. Then, re-examine the areas you've chosen; we weren't all born to be master jugglers. Ask yourself if the areas you are working on are the most important; if not, refocus your energies.

Recommendations for improving time management:

1. Set priorities, with the most important tasks first and the least important last

2. Break the tasks into smaller pieces if necessary

3. Make a list with important "To Dos" at the top

4. Limit the list to tasks you can complete in the time you have allotted

5. Take one task at a time and follow it through to completion

6. Cross out each task on the list as it is completed

7. At the end of each day, ask yourself what you have learned about "doing" organization. Is it becoming more automatic? Are you developing a habit of mind for it?

WHAT DOES ORGANIZATION LOOK LIKE IN THE REAL WORLD?

- The staff at the doctor's office can find our medical records when we arrive for our check-up

- Bar codes provide a universal system for coding pricing and other information

- Bank records accurately reflect the activity in our accounts

- We complete and submit assignments on time

- The Little League sign-up representative notes the check number for our payment and provides a receipt

- Airlines run on time

- Jobs get completed as agreed; productivity is high, quality of product/service is high

WHAT DOES ORGANIZATION LOOK LIKE IN SCHOOL?

Staff

- Maintain a clutter-free classroom that reflects a feeling of open space

- Return homework, tests, and projects with grades and comments in a timely fashion

- Record and file on-going assessments for each student

- Locate materials and books with ease

- Provide clear, concise lesson plans for guest teachers (substitutes)

- Organize desk and teacher materials in an orderly fashion

- Can respond quickly and easily to administrative and parental requests for information

- Find paperwork when needed

- Turn in work on or before due date

Students

- Turn in homework, class work, tests, and projects on or before the due date

- Maintain clutter-free desks

- Show up for special activity practices according to schedule

- Bring materials that are necessary for projects

- Give notes from their teacher to their parents and bring responses back to class

- Remember gym clothes, art smocks, and musical instruments on scheduled days

INQUIRIES TO DEVELOP ORGANIZATION

Whole Group Inquiries

- Create a diagram that shows how all of your personal materials will be placed in your cubby or locker to keep it neat and orderly. Label all of the items on the picture. Practice placing everything on the shelf until you know how to do it by heart. Share your plan with a partner.

- Memorize your student number assigned by the teacher and place it in the upper right-hand corner of every paper you do for class. When the papers are passed back, select those you want included in your portfolio. Put them in your portfolio file. Be prepared to share and explain some of your work with your parents at our annual conference.

- Brainstorm the steps your learning club should follow at the end of the day to leave your group area organized and neat. Write the procedures in a positive way. Add visuals to help jog the memory. Slip the "End of the Day" procedures into a plastic sleeve and place in your learning club's procedure binder. Review with your table mates as needed.

- Keep a homework notebook or calendar. Write down all of your assignments. Note the date when each was assigned and when it is due. Use two different colors if that will help. Also list any materials, notes, or permission slips you should bring to school. Share this organizer with your family at least once a week.

Small Group/Individual Inquiries

- Learn how to create a mindmap* of important information by using webs, graphics, and various colored markers or pens. To practice, create a mindmap of your life. Make a circle in the middle of the page and smaller circles around the center circle, like the sun and its planets. Write your name in the center circle and the following in the outer circles: family, school, friends, hobbies, sports, clubs, and pets. Add additional information in an organized way by drawing branches off each circle and from each line that links the center oval to each outer circle. Record important information, one fact to a branch. Share your personal web with a partner. Compare and contrast your answers with his/her answers.

- Create a partner plan for packing your book bag or backpack at the end of the school day. You and your partner will each pack homework materials, parent notes, lunch boxes, and personal items in each of your own book bags. Do a buddy check to make sure that your partner has packed each item. Give each other a "high five" when you remember to include everything you need for that night.

- Learn to hang your jacket, coat, sweatshirt or sweater on a hanger or hook so it doesn't fall off. Practice with each item as you wear it to school. Decide which garment is the

---

* For an easy-to-use guide to graphic organizing, or mindmapping, for note taking and studying, see *Mapping Inner Space* by Nancy Margulies (Zephyr Press: Tucson, Arizona, 1991). For an example, see page 4.3.

hardest to keep on the hangar. Discover a trick that will help you to keep the clothing where it belongs. Share the trick with a classmate.

- Create a picture schedule for your notebook that shows the schedule for special classes such as art, music, physical education, or computer.

This is one way to make the chart:

SPECIAL CLASSES				
M	T	W	Th	F

or

SPECIAL CLASSES				
Monday	Tuesday	Wednesday	Thursday	Friday

Choose a symbol for each class: sneaker or ball for physical education, paintbrush for art, music note for music, disk or mouse for computer. Draw the symbol on the day you go to that class. Bring this schedule home so you will know when to bring special supplies, materials, and clothing.

- Plan a meal for your family; include salad, main course with two vegetables, bread, dessert, and beverage. List all the items you would need to buy to create this meal. Using weekly newspaper supermarket ads, compute the total cost. Then compute the cost per person. Offer to prepare this special treat for your family.

- Investigate the field of time management. Invite a specialist to visit your classroom and share five or more organizational strategies with the students. Create a poster as a visual reminder of these strategies after the presenter is gone. Place it in a prime location in the classroom so that others can easily refer to it as needed.

- Interview an adult in your family or school about how they plan their daily schedule. Identify four or more strategies they use to coordinate the day's events so they flow from one to the next. List these strategies in your homework notebook for future reference.

- Learn how to create a Venn diagram, a graphic organizer that compares and contrasts information about two topics. With a partner practice making two circles with an over-lapping space in the center. Put your name above one circle and the partner's name above the other circle. List attributes that the two of you share in the central overlap area (for example, we both like dogs and cats). In the part of the circle under each name, iden-tify the ways in which you are different (for example, Tommy likes to play basketball versus I like to swim). Share your Venn diagram with two other classroom partners.

- Create a "Homework Procedure Book" that includes the following topics: time, place, materials, and packing and unpacking my book bag. Try the procedures for one or more weeks and adjust as needed. Explain them to your teacher.

- Write new lyrics for "Twinkle, Twinkle, Little Star" (or a song of your choice) that compare a day in the life of an unorganized versus an organized person. Write three or more verses and include at least one strategy that will help other students in your class become more organized. Add movements and motions to enhance the message of your lyrics. Teach the song to your classmates.

- Plan a campaign to run for a class or school office. Determine what issues are important to discuss. Design posters and write a speech to share your ideas about important topics. Introduce yourself in a friendly way. Congratulate your opponent on a good campaign (whether you win or lose). Reflect on your campaign with a friend or the class advisor. Could your campaign have been more effectively organized? How? Would this have changed the outcome of the election?

- Dramatize a story (such as *The Seven Chinese Brothers*) with your learning club members, one that teaches a lesson about organization. Present it for the students in a lower grade. Ask them to draw and explain any lessons they learned from the skit. Ask them to share their answers with your teacher and evaluate how well they understood the skit's message.

- Research the recipe for one of your favorite meals or desserts. Ask for permission to make the dish at home. Organize all of the materials and ingredients. Follow the steps in the recipe. While you are waiting for the treat to bake, cook, or set, wash your dishes and utensils and clean up spills on the counter and floor. Analyze how you could have been better organized and more efficient. Share your self-evaluation (rating) with a friend.

SIGNS OF SUCCESS

Congratulations! Students are showing signs of Organization when they

- Can find any specific paper within a minute when requested to do so

- Meet all deadlines for at least a month

- Have a relatively clean desk top with a few necessary items showing

- Remove something from their desks without a pile of other materials tumbling out

- Move about the classroom without dropping materials or losing items

- Keep important papers neatly arranged in a binder

- Return library books and other borrowed materials on time

- Manage a project from beginning to end with minimal prodding from the teacher

Keep trying! Students need more practice when they

- Discover Halloween cupcakes still in their desks on Valentine's Day

- Stash old beverage cups, snack wrappers, and lunch remnants (that would make good material for mold experiments) in their desks

- Avoid their cubby/locker because it is jammed with things that are ready to fall out when the door opens

- Find mittens in their lockers in May

- Are consistently late for meetings or practices

- Never have the materials they need for school

- Can't find items they are sure they "put somewhere"

- Miss gym more than once a month because they keep forgetting to bring sneakers to school

- Receive so many overdue notices from the librarian that the fine is larger than their allowance or your paycheck

- Return a signed parent permission form one month after the class has taken the trip

Literature Link ~ Organization

Primary Grades

Anthony Who Used to Be Rich Last Sunday	Viorst, Judith
Caring for My Things	Moncure, Jane Belk
Corduroy	Freeman, Don
Curious George	Rey, Margaret
Franklin Is Messy	Bourgeois, Paulette
If You Give A Mouse A Cookie	Numeroff, Laura
Jamal's Busy Day	Hudson, Wade
Matchlock Gun, The	Edmonds, Walter D.
Saturday Market	Grossman, Patricia
Seven Chinese Brothers, The	Mahy, Margaret
Tortoise Solves A Problem	Katz, Avner
What Happened to Patrick's Dinosaur?	Carrick, Donald and Carol

Intermediate Grades

All Upon a Sidewalk	George, Jean Craighead
Be a Perfect Person in Just Three Days	Manes, Stephen
Cat Ate My Gymsuit, The	Danziger, Paula
Cesar Chavez: A Real-Life Biography	Zannos, Susan
Dear Mr. Henshaw	Cleary, Beverly
From the Mixed-Up Files of Mrs. Basil E. Frankweiler	Konigsburg, E. L.
Jane Adams: Pioneer for Social Justice	Meigs, Cornelia L.
Muir of the Mountains	Douglas, William O.
Otherwise Known As Sheila the Great	Blume, Judy

Middle School and High School

Absolutely Normal Chaos	Creech, Sharon
Black Hands, White Sails	McKissak, Patricia and Frederick L. McKissak
Buried Onions	Soto, Gary

Teacher's Resource

Simply Organized: How to Simplify Your Complicated Life	Cox, Connie and C. Evatt

Date _____

Dear Family,

"Mom, where are my sneakers?" "I can't find that paper the teacher said *you* had to sign!" "Where did you put my backpack?" "I can't find my homework!" "What did you do with my baseball glove?"

Sound familiar? Life has become more hectic than ever. To help develop effective coping techniques, our LIFESKILL emphasis for the next two weeks is

~ORGANIZATION~

As a class, we will determine the characteristics of the LIFESKILL of Organization as we:

- Create an orderly plan for doing class work and homework

- Arrange the classroom for maximum use

- Remove excess materials from the classroom

- Brainstorm ways to problem solve using orderly steps

There are numerous opportunities at home to reinforce the LIFESKILL of Organization. Your child can:

- Organize his/her own room as often as necessary to provide a safe and healthy environment, one in which work and play can readily and easily occur

- Work with other family members to create an escape route from the house in case of fire or other emergencies

- Pack his/her own backpack and be responsible for the contents

- Pick up play things and put them back where they belong

- Plan, prepare, and serve a family meal

- Create a homework/recreation schedule

If your child creates other projects using the LIFESKILL of Organization, please let us know so we can share them with other families in our next newsletter.

Sincerely,

_____

Your child's teacher

Patience

Chapter 21

"PATIENCE SMOOTHES THE ROAD OF LIFE."

patience *n* **1:** the capacity, habit, or fact of being patient
patient *adj* **1:** bearing pains or trials calmly or without complaint
2: manifesting forbearance under provocation or strain **3:** not hasty or impetuous
4: steadfast despite opposition, difficulty, or adversity

PATIENCE: To wait calmly for someone or something

WHAT IS PATIENCE?

With technology, transportation systems, fast-food restaurants, and life moving along at an ever-increasing rate, we feel as though we are not accomplishing much *unless* we also move at an increasingly fast pace. This interest and fascination with going faster and faster does not bode well for patience which requires calmness, tranquillity, and tolerance. With adrenaline swirling throughout our bodies, patience often seems a distant goal.

Patience involves learning to wait . . . and wait . . . and wait . . . and wait . . . until it is our turn to pay at the checkout counter, order ice cream at the stand, explain our version of the story, listen to ideas before sharing our own, persevere to learn a skill, or allow the emerging butterfly to dry out its wings on its own time schedule. It means waiting in a quiet and calm manner, not with our eyes rolling, arms folded, and foot tapping. Patience requires us to appreciate that things done well take time, that expertise doesn't come overnight, that much of our sense of satisfaction about something is because we earned it, through patience and persistence, over time.

Patience requires that we give up wanting to control everything and be willing to wait until something runs its course or someone completes what they're doing before they join us. Patience is being able to enjoy the spring without yearning to rush to the swimming pool for summer.

Patience is a vital component of eight other LIFESKILLS: Curiosity, Effort, Flexibility, Friendship, Organization, Perseverance, Problem solving, and Resourcefulness.

WHY PRACTICE PATIENCE?

Can you imagine life and everyday occasions if no one used the LIFESKILL of Patience? The noise level would surely increase as people demanded what they wanted when they wanted it and how they wanted it. Traffic lights and other instructions would be ignored. Road rage would be the norm, not the exception. Tagamet, Zantac 75, and other indigestion soothers would be the "candy" of choice at every party and business meeting. Examples of frustration gone awry would be everywhere. Not a pretty prospect.

Why practice the LIFESKILL of Patience? There are many reasons—personal and societal.

Personal Benefits from Practicing Patience

Because the people who will benefit from our patience are often those who admonish us to use the LIFESKILL of Patience, we often disregard their advice. After all, our being patient benefits them . . . what's in it for us? It's important that all of us, and especially students, understand that the primary beneficiaries of patience are they themselves. Here's why.

Patience Is a Lifesaver. Patience—truly felt inside, not just restraining the body language that would reveal we are about to blow our top—is our best defense against most stress-related illnesses and premature aging. Overdoses of adrenaline, harmful cortisols, high blood pressure, and most heart disease are significantly reduced when we respond to circumstances with patience instead of frustration. As we are often admonished, we cannot control events but we can control our response to them.

Patience also saves energy. Anger and frustration eat us up inside. Just mellow out!

Patience Creates More Minutes in the Day. More minutes in the day! Now there's a thought-provoking idea! Falling into frustration or losing our temper is time wasted. Remaining calm and thoughtful gives us more minutes in the day to use as **we** choose. Patience gives us adequate time to think about situations, ideas, and responses in an analytical way which in turn improves our decision making.

Being Patient Improves Learning and Performance. As we know from brain research, when emotional override occurs,* thinking is significantly impaired and learning and performance levels nose-dive. If we want to be at our best, now and in the future, mastering the LIFESKILL of Patience is a necessity for us, not a luxury for those around us.

Societal Benefits from Patience

Life would be very different if patience were practiced in our homes, on our streets, and in our governmental agencies. The benefits of patience to society are numerous. They include issues of safety, higher academic achievement, stronger families, and active citizenship.

---

* For a discussion of the powerful effect of emotion on learning and performance, see *ITI: The Model* by Susan Kovalik, Chapter 2 (Kent, Washington: Susan Kovalik & Associates, 1997).

Physical and Psychological Safety. Patience on our roadways would significantly reduce auto accidents. Patience about becoming rich would significantly reduce crime—on the streets and the white-collar variety such as the Savings and Loan scandal of the 1980s. Patience on Capitol Hill to work on solutions that benefit the greatest number of people would significantly reduce "pork barrel" spending. Patience in stock market investing would make the system seem more secure and less risky. Patience on the street would translate into less racial, ethnic, religious, and class tensions.

Higher Academic Achievement Levels. Imagine the effect of greater patience in schools—better planning and instruction by teachers and better, more thorough learning by students. We believe our embarrassingly low literacy rates and appalling drop-out statistics would improve significantly.

Stronger Families. Patience in the home—spouse to spouse, parent to child, sibling to sibling—would strengthen family bonds. Less frustration, less child and spousal abuse. Less tension and better communication, less drug and alcohol abuse. The more patience with differences and mis-understandings, the lower the divorce rate. Does this sound like pie in the sky? We don't think so. Over and again we hear parents complaining about not having enough time, of feeling harried and rushed.

Being Patient Increases Likelihood of Change Occurring. Two important ingredients for making change happen are trust in leadership and overcoming resistance to change. According to J. Edwin Dietal,* patience is key to both. "Being patient is a major element in earning trust." Dietal also goes on to say that "Most people resist change. A combination of patience and persistence is needed for change to occur—patience enough for the change to occur and persistence enough so that the status quo does not overwhelm and kill the proposed change."

Citizenship Would Come Alive. If citizens were willing to work at the process of guiding their government instead of impatiently throwing up their hands and saying they're powerless to change things, we would have much more accountability from politicians and better solutions for our pressing problems.

HOW DO YOU PRACTICE IT?

If patience is to become a habit, it must first be consistently modeled for children. As parents and educators we must give our children every opportunity to experience situations, both in school and the real world, that require patience, forbearance, and moral stamina.

Modeling Patience

As parents and educators, we know that "Do as I do" is much more powerful than "Do as I say." Thus, we have no choice but to model a high degree of patience. This is especially impor-tant, and not easy, when dealing with students who may not have acquired the skill of waiting

---

* "Exceptional Leadership: Leading Through Patience and Persistence" by J. Edwin Dietal. Practice Development Website. http://www.abenet.org/lpm/newsletters/skills/w98Dietel.html

in a quiet, calm manner before they come to us. Patience is learned slowly, through a variety of experiences, over an extended period of time, and absorbed primarily in an atmosphere where it is consistently modeled.

Patience Develops Gradually

Patience takes time. Period. It is a LIFESKILL that exists only when internalized. Externally, it can be coached but not coerced.

Parents Start the Process. Parents start the process by gradually extending the amount of time before they respond to their child's request for their attention. For example, the parents first finish their sentence in a conversation with someone on the phone before responding to the child, then later their paragraph, then finally their entire conversation. Parents also encourage patience in the form of manners: "Wait your turn for the slide, swing, toy, etc." When toddlers visit the store or the doctor's office, parents teach them that they must wait their turn to pay or before entering the examining room.

Very young children may have all the patience in the world for a favorite toy but may erupt into a temper tantrum when a snack or mother's attention is not immediately forthcoming. Gradually, as a conceptual idea of time emerges, it becomes easier to wait; they learn to endure and to understand that delay doesn't necessarily mean denial. As children develop confidence in the procedures for waiting, they learn to trust that what they need or want will, in the end, be responded to.

In the Classroom. In the classroom, teachers slowly extend the time students calmly wait using techniques such as wait time and having groups frequently discuss their use of the LIFESKILL of Patience when working together. Other ways to practice patience include multi-age classrooms and buddy systems, discussing the benefits of patience, and, above all, consistently modeling patience day in and day out.

WHAT DOES PATIENCE LOOK LIKE IN THE REAL WORLD?

We

- Wait at the intersection while other drivers take their turns

- Repeat a question or comment for someone who did not hear it

- Understand if the doctor is called away on an emergency while we're in the office for our scheduled appointment

- Practice a meaningful skill over and over until it is mastered (bike riding, roller skating, keyboarding, painting, etc.)

- Use active listening skills while someone is talking

- Stand in line at the store, bank, or supermarket

- Remain "on hold" on the telephone

- Search for employment

- Teach someone to tie shoelaces

- Learn how to use/program the VCR, computer, scanner, printer, and fax machine

WHAT DOES PATIENCE LOOK LIKE IN SCHOOL?

Staff

- Listen as students explain about their behavior

- Teach a skill and provide adequate time for students to identify and understand the patterns and acquire the program(s) for using what they understand

- Wait for a parent who is late for a conference

- Submit a grant proposal and await the results

- Prune the materials budget again and again

- Give new strategies a fair chance to work by trying them more than once

Students

- Take adequate time to become proficient at a skill

- Wait for other people to finish talking before they speak

- Stay in line to go to special classes and lessons

- Wait to use materials that someone else is using

- Share by taking turns in community circle or during class meetings

- Wait for others to get organized before class starts

- Hold onto their ideas until asked to share

INQUIRIES TO DEVELOP PATIENCE

Whole Class Inquiries

- Brainstorm ways to pass the time (e.g., practice the times tables, spelling words, addition facts) while waiting in line or expecting something to happen. Design an individual poster identifying ten quiet, personal activities that will help you spend waiting time in an educational way. Use color and graphics to create a strong visual reminder of these activities. Share yours with a partner and practice active listening while he/she shares with you.

- Learn Brain Gym strategies* as your teacher presents them to the class. Choose two that will help you to develop patience; practice them at least 10 times in the next week. Keep track of when you use them and reflect on whether or not the exercises are helping you to develop patience. Share your thoughts with your learning club.

- Invite a research scientist to visit your classroom and share his/her research strategies. Specifically ask about the LIFESKILL of Patience in that field of study. Request examples of situations when patience is needed and used. Create individual thank-you notes; include some new idea that you heard relating to the research or to developing patience. Send the card to the scientist and share your reflections with your learning-club members.

- Work as a class family to create an "Australia," or island of refuge, within the room. Include a chair (bean bag, rocker, overstuffed), small table with a lamp and plant, a reassuring book (*Alexander and the Terrible, Horrible, No-Good, Very Bad Day* by Judith Viorst) and a headset with relaxing classical music. Write classroom procedures for using this space in an appropriate way. You and other students may visit there to quietly reflect, remove yourself from distractions, wait patiently for some activity to begin, or to take a "cooling off" time. After the first three visits you make to Australia, include your reflections in your journal and share them with an adult.

- Interview a parent/guardian for examples of how adults need to use the LIFESKILL of Patience with children in their care. Ask about age and personality differences that affect a child's ability to be patient. Brainstorm two or more ways children can practice patience with busy adults and compile the information for the class to use. Bring these ideas back to the adult you interviewed as helpful strategies.

Small Group/Individual Inquiries

- Practice counting by 1's, 2's, 5's and 10's when you have to wait in line somewhere during the day. Count quietly in your head. Notice whether or not this strategy makes waiting easier for you.

---

* See either *Brain Gym* by Paul and Gail Dennison (Edu-Kinesthetics, Inc.: Ventura, California,1989) or *Smart Moves: Why Learning is Not All in Your Head* by Carla Hannaford (Great Ocean Publishers: Arlington, Virginia, 1995).

- Observe one of your teachers. Find three or more ways he/she shows patience when working with children. Choose one of those ways and practice it at home and in school. Explain to your teacher what you are doing and how he/she helps you get new ideas.

- Make a list that explains why your age is the very best age anyone can be. Include three or more reasons why you think that. Compare your ideas with a friend to see if you have any that are the same on both lists.

- Interview an adult about his/her employment. Ask permission to take notes or record the interview. Request five or more examples of times when the LIFESKILL of Patience has been an important part of his/her workday. Identify any of these examples that might offer tips for students using the LIFESKILL of Patience at school. Create bookmarks that illustrate these examples and hand them out to classmates.

- Interview the manager of a local fast-food restaurant. Request background information about his/her company's entry into the fast-food market. Listen for company policy that provides insight into their production philosophy. For example, McDonald's "a serving a second." Ask about their research on time management, food preparation, and how they deal with unhappy patrons who have little or no patience. Then interview the manager from one of the best, most expensive restaurants in town. Ask the same questions. Compare and contrast the information. Write thank-you notes to both managers sharing what you have learned about the LIFESKILL of Patience in relation to the restaurant business.

- Develop a savings plan so you can purchase a special item such as a bicycle, roller blades, or a gift. Brainstorm at least three ways to earn money. Determine a minimum amount that you will save weekly. Plan your jobs and keep a journal of the work you have done, the date completed, the amount of money earned, and the amount still needed. When you have reached your goal, share the strategies and skills you used with your learning-club members.

- Read one of the stories from the "Literature Link" list. Divide a piece of drawing paper in half. On the top or left half, illustrate one story scene in which the LIFESKILL of Patience was not practiced and on the bottom of the right half, one drawing to share a part of the story in which the LIFESKILL of Patience was practiced. Explain to a partner which part helped the story character to solve problems.

- Learn to play a new board game (e.g., Monopoly, checkers, chess, Life, Candyland, Scrabble). Ask a friend to help you learn the rules. Play the game four or more times during the next two weeks. Test your patience level as you learn new rules and strategies. Share your feelings and insights with your game partner.

- Create a system for a teacher to use when students must wait to meet with him/her. Make a 4" x 6" blank index card for each student in class; number the cards starting with number one. Punch a hole in the top of each card, put them in numerical order, and place on a stand with a hook. Write procedures giving students directions for removing a card and waiting for their turn with the teacher. Have another hook where used cards can be hung until they are needed again. Give this project to a teacher and invite him/her to try the plan for two weeks; ask for feedback on how the system is working.

- Research a new hobby or craft, such as knitting, carving, sewing, collecting, painting, photography, sculpting, that you want to learn. Find someone in your school who is proficient in this skill and is willing to teach you the basic steps. Practice the beginning steps until they feel automatic. Design and create a finished product. As you share the piece with your learning club, explain how the LIFESKILL of Patience supported you.

- Create your own personal T-Chart (poster, transparency, pamphlet) for the LIFESKILL of Patience. Write four or more phrases for each of the following categories: Looks Like, Sounds Like, and Feels Like (and Doesn't Look Like, Doesn't Sound Like, and Doesn't Feel Like). Add graphic reminders. Volunteer to share your project with students in a lower grade. Invite those students to add more phrases that are age-appropriate for them. Create a second visual using their phrases and present it to the class to keep.

- Plant a flower or tree seed in a small pot. Record your observations daily as the seed sprouts and begins to grow. Include height, amount of food/water provided, amount of growth, and other observable changes each day for a month. Note in your journal three or more examples of the LIFESKILL of Patience you needed. Share your research with a fellow classmate.

- Dramatize the following real-life situations with your learning club:

  ~ You're waiting in line to speak with the teacher.
  ~ Your group is lining up to go to P. E.
  ~ You need a color marker that another student is using.
  ~ Someone is pushing ahead of you.
  ~ A new skill is very hard to understand.

For each predicament, show two responses, one not using the LIFESKILL of Patience and one using it. Practice each skit three or more times until each person understands his/her responsibilities. Present the skits for your classmates and let them determine which solution exemplifies the use of patience.

SIGNS OF SUCCESS

Congratulations! Students are showing signs of Patience when they

- Wait quietly for their turn and don't become angry or verbally abusive while in line
- Offer to help other students/staff members who need to complete a task
- Talk politely even when they are feeling upset
- Wait patiently on the phone through music and recorded voices
- Listen while others complete what they're saying before beginning to inject their own ideas
- Save money to buy something special (bike, book, toy)
- Teach a skill to someone who is having a hard time learning it
- Wait politely for others to get their food before starting to eat

Keep trying! Students need more practice when they

- Lose their tempers because they don't get what they want
- Speak rudely to someone who is trying to help
- Ride their bikes too fast and dart in front of walkers
- Hang up the phone on someone trying to explain something they don't want to hear
- Push or shove people out of the way
- Refuse to share materials
- Grab items from others' hands
- Refuse to wait their turn to use some object/toy/materials
- Give up too easily; don't spend adequate time practicing an important skill
- Demand the teacher's immediate attention for nonemergency matters

LITERATURE LINK ~ PATIENCE

Primary Grades

Alexander Who Used to Be Rich Last Sunday	Viorst, Judith
Art Lesson, The	dePaola, Tomie
Babushka's Doll	Polacco, Patricia
Bicycle for Rosaura, A	Barbot, Daniel
Carousel	Cummings, Pat
Keep the Lights Burning, Abbie	Roop, Peter and Connie
Leo, the Late Bloomer	Kraus, Robert
Molly and the Slow Teeth	Ross, Pat
Not Yet, Yvette	Ketterman, Helen
Today Is the Day	Riecken, Nancy
What's the Hurry, Harry?	Steiner, Charlotte

Intermediate Grades

Helen Keller: From Tragedy to Triumph	Wilkie, Katharine
Henry David Thoreau: Walden	Lowe, Steve
Hole in the Dike, The	Green, Norma
King of the Wind	Henry, Marguerite
Phoebe, the Spy	Griffin, Judith B.
Snow Treasure	McSwigan, Marie
Twenty and Ten	Bishop, Claire H.
Verano de Los Cisnes, El	Byers, Betsy
Where the Red Fern Grows	Rawls, Wilson

Middle School and High School

California Blues	Klass, David
160 Ways to Help the World: Community Service Projects for Young People	Duper, Linda Leeb
Summer of My German Soldier	Greene, Bette

Teacher's Resources

Brain Gym	Dennison, Paul and Gail
Small Miracles: Extraordinary Coincidences from Everyday Life	Halberstam, Yitta and Judith Leventhal
The Tao of Teaching	Nagel, Greta

Date _____

Dear Family,

Remember the saying, "Patience is a virtue"? *Webster's Dictionary* defines patience as waiting calmly without complaint; steadfast; faithful; dependable—all excellent character traits in a family member, friend, and an employee. The next LIFESKILL topic for our class is

~ PATIENCE ~

As family members, you understand how demanding one child or a few children can be. In the classroom, where we have many more students, the LIFESKILL of Patience is an extremely important skill for both the teacher and the students to use. Some of the ways we will develop a deeper understanding of the LIFESKILL of Patience include:

- Brainstorming constructive activities that can be done while waiting in a line

- Interviewing parents/guardians about ways to use patience when parenting

- Role playing situations that show impatience and then patience

- Listing many situations in which we might need to be patient

At home, you can further continue our study of patience by:

- Insisting that children take turns

- Reading chapter books—one chapter per night

- Encouraging your child to set some long-term goals, such as saving for a pair of roller blades, a bike, or a movie ticket

Family members are their children's best role models. Help your child to become a better learner by modeling a sense of perseverance, patience, and inner strength.

Sincerely,

_____

Your child's teacher

Chapter 22

Perseverance

"STICK WITH IT!"

perseverance *n* the act or condition or an instance of persevering: steadfastness

PERSEVERANCE: To keep at it

WHAT IS PERSEVERANCE?

Perseverance can be the crucial difference between success and failure in most aspects of life. We might define it as "stubbornness under control."

Think back to a time when you learned to tie your shoelaces. Did you master the skill the first time you were shown how to do it? No! How about the second time? No! You may not remember the exact number of tries it took before you could make the "x," slip the end under, pull it tight, make a loop, circle the other tie around it, slip the middle of the tie in under the loop, pull, and finally end up with a bow. It required much practice and resolve.

Perseverance grows in the face of a challenge. It's the ability to stay with a chore or a goal despite inexperience and problems. It's a crucial ingredient in the development of inner strength and stamina, in the ability to pursue goals, and in the determination to "hang in there" through all sorts of highs and lows in childhood and adulthood.

Fortunately, we are born with perseverance. Babies don't give up! Infants begin to understand this notion as they experiment with mobiles, teething rings, and rattles during their first months. Throughout their first year of life, they continuously persevere as they conquer tremendous physical challenges, such as learning to turn over, sit, crawl, stand, walk, and run. They fall, they get up, they fall again, they get up again.

Perseverance is a concept children learn naturally through their own discovery processes. However, it is easily squashed if the tasks presented are age-inappropriate (and therefore impossible) or meaningless (why bother). Furthermore, if family or school pressures seem to demand perfection, we are forever disappointed in our performance because it doesn't measure up to the expectations of others and/or ourselves. These are all killers of perseverance.

"Stick to It" Attitude

Perseverance is a combination of endurance, doggedness, and determination. It is believing in yourself, your ideas, and goals—sometimes in the face of criticism and others' lack of faith in who you are and what you are accomplishing. Perseverance is a commitment to yourself to follow through with your plans, a responsibility to yourself to stick with it until you reach your goals.

Motivation Is Crucial

Motivation plays a huge part in our ability to presevere: If we lack motivation, our level of perseverance falls; conversely, if we are highly motivated, our level of perseverance rises. When it comes to the LIFESKILL of Perseverance, motivation must be internal. We persevere because we say so. During a crisis or challenge, the most basic jobs can become remarkably difficult. At these times, it is important to acknowledge our perseverance in order to give ourselves a boost and the energy to stay with our plans. At other times, we may take our actions for granted and not recognize our perseverance; this weakens our motivation to keep going.

WHY PRACTICE PERSEVERANCE?

Expert-level skill and knowledge does not grow on sugar plum bushes ready to be plucked by wandering passers-by. Expertise, regardless of the level of God-given talent underneath it, is the result of lots of hard work driven by lots of perseverance. As Calvin Coolidge said: "Nothing in this world can take the place of persistence. Talent will not; nothing is more common than unsuccessful men with talent. Genius will not; unrewarded genius is almost a proverb. Education will not; the world is full of educated derelicts. Persistence and determination alone are omnipotent. The slogan "press on" has solved and always will solve the problems of the human race."*

Strong Effort Is Helpful

Effort counts! We always remember to appreciate success but often forget to acknowledge the hard work that led to it. Perseverance leads to continuing progress. It's not only the initial effort a child puts forth in conquering a challenge that matters but the staying power as well.

Perseverance is an important trait at all stages of life. It is vital that students learn it as early as possible because it supports many of the other crucial experiences of childhood—exploring and making sense of the world. The LIFESKILL of Perseverance is the engine that drives success.

---

* Calvin Coolidge Memorial Foundation. http://www.calvin-coolidge.org/

HOW DO YOU PRACTICE IT?

Conscious practice of perseverance requires several factors.

There Must Be a Clear Goal in Mind. Students must have a vision of what they are pursuing that is strong enough to feed their efforts and fire their internal motivation. The goal must be valued by students, too; what the board of education thinks is terrific or what politicians think will look "foxy" to the voters is of little consequence here. To persevere, students must understand and value what they're pursuing.

Modeling Is Key. Students must have opportunities to watch others and to visualize what is possible. The one-room schoolhouse and multi-age settings are ideal because older students model what is possible. If you find yourself in the traditional same-age classroom, use cross-age tutoring to bring students together. Also, remember that you are an important source of modeling as well.

Processing the Process. "Processing the process" is a phrase that recurs throughout this book. It is a key instructional strategy to help students internalize Lifelong Guidelines and LIFESKILLS because it gives them immediate feedback on their behavior and performance. The phrase refers to discussions that immediately follow completion of a group task, the focusing on how the group performed as a collaborative unit. It is an excellent vehicle for getting students to reflect on how well they used a Lifelong Guideline or LIFESKILL.*

Self-Talk. "Processing the process" is a group structure for internalizing the Lifelong Guidelines and LIFESKILLS; self-talk is a private, individual way. Through self-talk, we are our own teacher and mentor. Teaching students strategies for processing the process, brainstorming, and problem-solving teaches them "self-talk," the internal dialogue needed to analyze what we do and how and why.

Flexibility. The LIFESKILL of Flexibility is indispensable when persevering. As we continue to work at something, we often must change what we are doing and how we are doing it. Unwillingness to make such changes, lack of flexibility, usually dooms us. Perseverance is not compulsive persistence, working over and over at an approach that doesn't work; it is working smart until we succeed.

Resiliency. Resiliency is the ability to take failure on the chin and bounce right back, to learn from the experience but not be destroyed by it or forever run by it. If we can't roll with the punches life throws our way, we can't persevere. Teach students that failure is their teacher, not their enemy. Teach them by example how to learn from failure without succumbing to disappointment, frustration, or humiliation.

---

* For a discussion on "processing the process," see *Tribes: A New Way of Learning and Being Together* by Jeanne Gibbs, Sausalito, CA: CenterSource Publications, 1995, pp. 100, 114-116.

Teacher As "Guide-on-the-Side"

It's natural to want to "save" or "rescue" children when things go wrong. However, the only lesson learned then is that someone else will fix it for them. To persevere is to go through the challenges, the roller coaster emotions, and the alternating successes and failures, to emerge on the other side with the motivation to carry on that must come from within. There are no short cuts on this one—no save-the-pain or labor-saving devices. When it comes to developing and using the LIFESKILL of Perseverance, we must do it for ourselves.

The teacher as a "guide-on-the-side" rather than the "sage on the stage" can make the task easier. Here are several strategies:

- Provide daily conversation about and practice in problem solving and identifying goals (both short- and long-term)

- Model an optimistic outlook and describe your own tussles with the LIFESKILL of Perseverance

- Encourage effort

- Provide stress relief; when times get tense, encourage students to take short breaks and talk about their work ("self-talk")

- Allow students to set their own pace whenever possible

- Help students identify group behaviors that hinder perseverance and those that facilitate it

- Celebrate genuine accomplishments, not just for reaching goals but also for "staying with it"

A Word About Choice

Too often we expect, even demand, that students persevere at tasks even we would have a hard time completing, such as dull worksheets, assignments that repeat what they already know, or concepts that are beyond their experience and ability to understand. In truth, much of our traditional curriculum is inexcusably inappropriate—worksheets are meaningless and repetitive; concepts aren't given a real-life context we can understand or relate to. When we ask our students to persevere, let's make sure that the content and the process of the task are kid-friendly and that there is an element of choice.

When choices are present, the learner can express preferences about why, what, and how he/she is learning. Choice provides students a feeling of control over their learning environment, offers a variety of ways to engage the senses, and causes them to constantly re-evaluate decisions. When using the LIFESKILL of Perseverance, choice is a constant. Do I continue? Do I stop? Do I give up?

Evaluating and judging are ways to decide if their efforts are worth it. Students ask questions such as: Am I willing to settle for second best? If I don't achieve the desired results, will the struggle have been worth it? Will persevering now help me later in life when I face a variety of tough challenges?

Re-examine the Curriculum and Time-Honored Processes

Many aspects of traditional education chip away at student willingness to persevere with their assignments. The biggest culprits are curriculum that is meaningless to students and age-inappropriate plus the negative effects of competitive grading.

Meaningless Curriculum.
For the most part, the curriculum we study today is unchanged from 100 years ago. If you want to scare yourself to death, go to a secondhand bookstore and search for old textbooks. The 60-year old elementary science text and the 100-year old middle school civics book I found were startlingly like today's. And, the course of study for today's high schools is very similar to that of the comprehensive high school created and set in cement from 1890 to 1920.* The few changes over the years are a result of adding more, not selectively paring away. Such *backward* looking content does a poor job of preparing students for the 21st Century and it also does a poor job of engaging students and stimulating the desire to persevere in their studies.

Because our curriculum was created prior to knowledge of how the brain learns, it shouldn't surprise us that much of it is age-inappropriate,** calling for mental processes that students don't yet have. Unable to understand what they are studying they lose motivation to persevere and are forced into memorization. Application, and long-term memory, are thus impossible.

A third contributor to meaninglessness is the change in students. At the dawn of the 20th Century, students were very much engaged in the family enterprise—farming, their parents' store, sons joining the occupation of their father at an early age. These students knew a lot about the world from firsthand experiences as they accompanied their parents through the day. In contrast, today's students have but a vague notion what their parents do and typically have limited experience with the family's economics, their community, government, and so on. Yesterday's students brought their experiences with them to the classroom; today's students are starved for real-world experiences. The secondhand sensory input of books works if knowledge about the topic being read is already understood from firsthand experience.

Bringing Meaning to Curriculum.
To pare away curriculum that is age-inappropriate, use the process of "selective abandonment." Selective abandonment starts with acceptance that there is far too much content in the typical curriculum to handle in the year. So, rather than letting the clock determine where we leave off (for example, never getting through WWII in your history course), we, the teacher, deliberately select the most important things to be left behind.

As you do so, select those items that are student-killers—concepts so beyond students' developmental abilities that students will feel like failures plus factoids that seem meaningless to students and make paying attention so difficult.

---

* For a fascinating discussion of our curricular roots, see *Synergy: Transforming America's High Schools Through Integrated Thematic Instruction* by Karen D. Olsen (Kent, Washington: Books for Educators, Inc., 1998), Chapter 1.

** See *Thinking And Learning: Matching Developmental Stages with Curriculum and Instruction* by Larry Lowery (Kent, Washington: Books for Educators, Inc., 1989)

WHAT DOES PERSEVERANCE LOOK LIKE IN THE REAL WORLD?

We

- Follow through on ideas

- Complete projects (building a house, making a gift, cooking dinner)

- Keep trying until we succeed (driving a car, graduating from high school, finding a job)

- Refine an invention or product until it is marketable

- Finish jigsaw and crossword puzzles

- Read a book from beginning to end

- Resubmit claims for medical insurance after they have been rejected

- Get a second, or even third, medical opinion in cases of serious or mysterious illnesses

- Weed and weed and weed our garden and yard

- Master a sport or game

- Learn to program the VCR

- Insist that a company abide by its guarantees and customer satisfaction policies

- Work out personal relationship problems and misunderstandings

WHAT DOES PERSEVERANCE LOOK LIKE IN SCHOOL?

Staff

- Search for the best prices for supplies and materials

- Provide adequate time for pattern recognition and mental program development

- Follow up on student test results by planning specific lessons/work for students

- Maintain our classrooms as a clutter-free environment

- Reschedule parents who have missed a conference

- Change an existing environment to one that is more bodybrain-compatible

- Videotape themselves teaching a lesson, watch it with a mentor/colleague, listen to feedback, and set goals for improvement

- Insist on support from "the system" for students with special learning abilities

- Complete reports, orders, and paperwork in a timely fashion

Students

- Stick with a project from beginning to end

- Pre-write, write, and re-write a story until they are satisfied with the results

- Read a book from cover to cover

- Invest time in developing friendships

- Practice computation facts until mastered

- Create reasonable timetables for assignments and work until each project is completed

- Work to reach personal, educational, and social goals

- Learn to spell complicated words

- Complete a jigsaw puzzle

- Invest practice time to learn skills needed to succeed in games and sports

- Remember previous lessons learned and use that knowledge to solve present-day problems

- Join the Scouts, 4-H, YWCA, or other such groups or volunteer for Habitat for Humanity, Homeless Shelters, etc., and remain a member for at least two or three years

- If they want to quit, analyze why, then stick with it until they've gleaned value from the experience

INQUIRIES TO DEVELOP PERSEVERANCE

Whole Group Inquiries

- Research, share, and discuss famous quotations about the LIFESKILL of Perseverance (see examples below). Choose one and design a "mock up" business card for the author. Include the quotation, the person's name, and an illustration or graphic that explains the words. Make 10 of these cards and hand them out to five or more special people in your life. Ask them to share their interpretation of the quotation. Create your own quotation teaching about the LIFESKILL of Perseverance and share it with one person.

  —"Whether you think you can, or think you can't, you're right." Henry Ford
  —"Courage and perseverance have a magic talisman before which difficulties disappear and obstacles vanish into thin air." John Quincy Adams
  —"Few things are impossible to diligence and skill. Great works are performed not by strength, but perseverance." Samuel Johnson

- Plan a "perseverance quilt" of 5" x 5" squares (fabric or construction paper) with your classmates and teacher(s). Invite each student to draw a symbol/illustration representing some time when he/she had to use the LIFESKILL of Perseverance. Intersperse appropriate quotations with solid colors. Sew or glue the squares together and present the gift to your school or local library to display.

Small Group/Individual Inquiries

- Read/Listen to the story of *The Little Engine That Could* by Watty Piper. Practice saying, "I think I can, I think I can, I KNOW I can!" Say this to yourself each time you feel like you can't finish something. Draw a picture of the little engine and keep it in your notebook as a reminder of the lesson.

- With your learning club, brainstorm two or more solutions for each of the following situations:

    — In physical education class, everyone except you has thrown the basket through the hoop.
    — There are three spelling words that you just can't seem to learn.
    — Your best friend has learned to ride a bicycle without training wheels but you still need to have them on for balance.

- Learn how to zip, tie, button, and velcro any clothing that you wear to school. Practice each skill at home with some help from an adult until you can dress and undress by yourself.

- For one week keep a log that documents the amount of time you spend on each of the following activities: sleeping, eating, attending school, watching television, playing video games, using a computer, and physical exercise such as sports, aerobics, dance, hiking, weight lifting. For the second week, create a revised play/recreation schedule that supports a healthy lifestyle on a daily basis by increasing the amount of movement time in your life (outdoor and indoor). Choose specific exercises, games, or movement that you plan to do each day. Keep a journal for at least one month that reflects your use of the LIFESKILL of Perseverance to help you stick to this new plan. Share these reflections with someone whose opinion you respect.

- Learn how to use a computer program, e.g., Inspiration, PrintShop, Hyperstudio. Create one finished product, such as a poster, card, bookmark, award, or web page that teaches four or more perseverance strategies. Share this material with your learning club.

- Play a board game, such as Monopoly, Scrabble, Mah Jong, checkers, or chess, in "tournament" style. Intentionally keep the game going and keep score. Make a graph to represent the players' scores for two weeks. Share any patterns that appear with your game partners and discuss perseverance strategies that supported your tournament.

- Investigate your school's recycling plan for cans, paper, and other reusable items. Volunteer to record and track the amount of materials recycled and any income made. Write a song with three or more verses that reinforces the concept of perseverance in re-using materials for another purpose. Negotiate a plan to use the money to help less fortunate people in the community.

- Research the Women's Movement in the Unites States. Choose your own state if you would like to focus on a special interest area. Discover any advances that have been made in women's rights since 1900. Narrow your information down to one of the following topics: voting, family issues, employment, obtaining credit, or owning property. Identify one woman who has shown leadership and persistence in helping to change the status quo and laws affecting women's rights. Present the information using visual materials such as transparencies, video, photographs, charts, drawings.

- Choose an inventor/scientist who had a difficult time convincing people to produce/use his invention, discovery, or product. List three or more strategies that didn't work in catching the interest of business people. Then identify three or more strategies that did. Create a "Perseverance Award" for your inventor. Include his/her name, accomplishment, and successful strategies. Include graphics and color for an attractive presentation. Explain your reasoning to the class.

- Research one of the following leaders known for his/her leadership in the Civil Rights movement or peace movements using nonviolent strategies: Dr. Martin Luther King, Jr., Mahatma Gandhi, Rosa Parks, or President Jimmy Carter. Chronicle three setbacks and three achievements. Reflect on any current events that further advance your leader's beliefs. Design a United States postage stamp honoring this leader for his/her LIFESKILLS of Perseverance and Effort.

- Read at least three books on household pets and their care. Choose one of the pets and create a "Pet Care Chart" detailing the following: 1) eating/feeding habits, 2) exercise required, 3) interests/play, 4) peculiarities, 5) training, and 6) life span. Determine four or more examples of occasions when LIFESKILL of Perseverance will be required during the pet's lifetime. Share your information with a veterinarian, trainer, breeder, or pet store owner for accuracy. Design a pamphlet that prepares people to care for your particular pet and will encourage them when times are tough. Use graphics or photographs for added visual appeal.

- Choose a skill (such as oral reading, paragraph writing, computational math, reading comprehension, physical strength) in which you would like greater proficiency. Devise a skill improvement schedule with adequate time for you to practice and experience using the skill. Locate a mentor to help you master this skill; ask for any additional advice. Locate a quotation to help you persevere and remain focused. Keep daily records in your journal of your beginning and ending times, of your work alone or with assistance, your rate of improvement in mastering the skill and any reflections about your ability to stick to your goal. Share progress notes with your parents, a friend, the teacher, or your learning-club members.

- Define the following terms: threatened, endangered, and extinct wildlife. Research an animal listed in one of these categories for your state or region. Determine the conditions of the animal's location, needs, enemies, and any additional factors that hinder its perseverance to survive. Educate your classmates with a visual presentation (such as a video, computer program, photographic essay, or transparencies) on this animal's fight for continued existence. Provide addresses of organizations that support your cause and invite interested students to write letters requesting additional information on ways they can help.

SIGNS OF SUCCESS

Congratulations! Students are showing signs of Perseverance when they

- Join a school club or team and work hard to improve their skills

- Complete short- and long-term goals on time

- Identify injustices and work to rectify them

- Keep working to find alternative solutions to real-life problems

- Master bike riding without wobbling or falling; challenge themselves to master an obstacle course

- Save money for many weeks to buy a special gift for someone

- Ask questions about work, ideas, and concepts until they understand the content

- Learn academic skills through determination

- Stick with a difficult task until it is completed

- Ask for help mastering difficult tasks

Keep trying! Students need more practice when they

- Never seem to complete projects, inquiries, and homework by the due date

- Give up learning something after one or two weak attempts

- Begin to assemble a kit/model but neglect to complete it because they run into problems

- Accept the first idea they hear without investigating choices; insist their way is the only one way to do something and forget/refuse to look for other options

- Accept failure as normal

- Keep saying "I'm bored!" and give up easily

- Shy away from new challenges

LITERATURE LINK ～ PERSEVERANCE

Primary Grades

Akiak	Blake, Robert J.
Allie's Basketball Dream	Barber, Barbara E.
Anthony Reynoso Born to Rope	Cooper, Martha and G. Gordon
Flute Player, The	Eversole, Robyn
Little Engine That Could, The	Piper, Watty
Martin Luther King Day: Let's Meet Martin Luther King, Jr.	De Rubertis, Barbara
Miss Rumphius	Cooney, Barbara
Uncle Jed's Barbershop	Mitchell, Marjaree King
Where the Buffaloes Begin	Baker, Olaf

Intermediate Grades

Blind Colt, The	Rounds, Glen
Boundless Grace	Hoffman, Mary
Dancing Flea, The	Landa, Mariasun
Darius, the Lonely Gargoyle	Estlack, Micha
Dear Mrs. Parks: A Dialogue with Today's Youth	Reed, Gregory
Eleanor Roosevelt: A Passion to Improve	Spangenburg, Ray and Diane Moser
Incredible Journey	Burnford, Sheila
Isabella: A Wish for Miguel	Newman, Shirley P.
May'naise Sandwiches & Sunshine and Tea	Belton, Sandra
T.J.'s Secret Pitch	Bowen, Fred
Tuck Triumphant	Taylor, Theodore
Wizard's Hall	Yolen, Jane

Middle School and High School

*Chinese Cinderella: The True Story
of an Unwanted Daughter*   Yen Mah, Adeline

Juan Gonzalez   Tuttle, Dennis

*Quilted Landscapes: Conversations
with Young Immigrants*   Strom, Yale

Teacher's Resource

The 7 Habits of Highly Effective People   Covey, Stephen R.

Date _____

Dear Family,

We have begun to study the LIFESKILL of Perseverance. Children are analyzing those skills which will be useful in adulthood as spouse, parent, employer, employee, friend, and neighbor. The development of the LIFESKILL of Perseverance in childhood is critical because it is the basis for curiosity, determination, stamina, steadfastness, and academic achievement. Some ways that we will learn about this LIFESKILL include:

- Reading biographies of famous people who were known for using the LIFESKILL of Perseverance

- Setting short- and long-term goals

- Developing a class project that requires the LIFESKILL of Perseverance

As this study begins, would you please take a few minutes to review some stories with your child about when he/she was a baby—stories that show how he/she persevered then to master an important skill plus some examples of ways your child perseveres now. Also share times in your life that this LIFESKILL has supported what you were doing. During our class meetings, the students will have an opportunity to share some of those positive experiences with their classmates.

Some suggestions for the home connection include:

- Starting a family scrapbook including photographs and stories identifying use of the LIFESKILL of Perseverance

- Pointing out news articles that contain true-life examples of perseverance

- Brainstorming ideas for problem solving when your child seems "stumped" about what to do next

As John Quincy Adams stated, "Courage and perseverance have a magic talisman before which difficulties disappear and obstacles vanish into thin air."

Sincerely,

_____

Your child's teacher

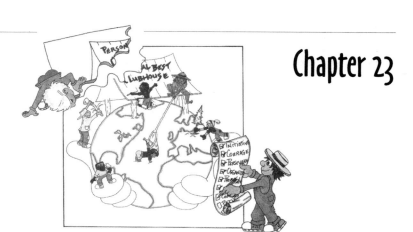

Chapter 23

Pride

"CELEBRATE YOUR PERSONAL BEST."

pride *n* the quality or state of being proud as **a:** a reasonable or justifiable self-respect **b:** delight or elation arising from some act, possession, or relationship **c:** proud behavior

Pride: Satisfaction from doing your personal best

WHAT IS PRIDE?

Pride is not a set of skills or a bank of knowledge. We don't *do* pride, we experience pride. It is a gift from our molecules of emotion.* It is the thrill of reaching the top of a mountain and looking out over a fabulous vista. The other Lifelong Guidelines and LIFESKILLS are what get us to the mountain top. But the anticipation of the exhilaration of being on the mountain top is a big part of what motivates us to acquire the necessary skills and knowledge to get there. Pride is a combination of feelings that drives us to do our personal best and feeds our sense of self-worth in a respectful, rather than arrogant, way. It is accompanied by a deep sense of satisfaction, well-being, and joy—a natural "high." Pride is the inner engine of motivation and the desire to do well.

Pride is readily recognizable—the individual stands tall, shoulders back, eyes clear and focused, and the walk confident.

Avoiding False Pride

In America, the word pride often conjures up images of someone who has a haughty, disdainful attitude or one who gets to the top by stepping on others. For example, the neighborhood bully who takes "pride" in the way people fear him, his reputation as a tough guy. Or, a teenager who has built a reputation around being an intellectual outcast, or a drug king, or Mr. Cool. A sense of pride built upon self-destructive or antisocial behavior is false pride—a feeling of importance that is misguided and fleeting and that masks the gut feeling that things really aren't all that great.

---

* See *Molecules of Emotion: Why You Feel the Way You Feel* by Candace Pert.

False pride also occurs when someone is praised for inferior work and behavior. This kind of false pride is all too often the outcome of programs designed to build self-confidence by asserting that a person's doing great whether they are or not. Or, even worse, that they're great just because they exist and are "unique," all separate from their performance, behavior, character, and attitudes. However, as Madeline Hunter once said, when her buttons had been pushed by someone asking how her program built positive self-image, "Teach students to be successful readers, writers, and mathematicians. Then they will have something to feel good about." As paraphrased by a very wise one-room schoolhouse teacher, "If a kid is a pain in the neck and he and everybody else knows he is, telling him he's a wonderful person is a lie and he knows it. Teach him how to be successful in his studies and with his peers. A positive self-concept will follow."* Self-respect, positive self-concept, and self-confidence in life are earned, not conferred upon us by others.

WHY PRACTICE PRIDE?

For most of us, there are many day-to-day tasks, such as washing dishes, that bore us while others, such as cleaning the toilet, we abhor. We do them not because we enjoy the process but because we know the job needs to be done and that we'll feel good when the job is done and done well, that we'll experience the dance of those molecules of emotion** which produce the sense of pride.

Pursuing pride ensures that we will expend enormous effort, have legitimate interest in the results, and tap into our potential. It helps to perpetuate a self-fulfilling prophesy: "Because I worked hard, I did my personal best, and I succeeded; I can repeat this experience another time."

Without developing the LIFESKILL of Pride, our self-esteem, self-image, and self-confidence dwindle and our motivation and productivity decrease.

HOW DO YOU PRACTICE IT?

Again, pride is not something you do, it is something you experience. But we can help students take the prerequisite actions to make experiencing pride possible and even likely. These actions include consciously practicing the other Lifelong Guidelines and LIFESKILLS, applying oneself to mastering academic skills, learning to accept acknowledgement graciously, being aware of the difference between personal best and perfectionism, and observing others as models.

Consciously Practice the Other Lifelong Guidelines and LIFESKILLS. Pride must be earned. Mastering the Lifelong Guidelines and LIFESKILLS opens doors to new opportunities and new areas of support. Becoming someone others want to be around attracts friends who support the best you can become. Most importantly, learning how to be a friend helps you become a friend to yourself, directing the voice inside your head—your self-talk—to provide useful, positive feedback and direction.

* A conversation with Dulcie Brown, a highly effective teacher who spent the first half of her 30-year career teaching in one-room, K-8 schools, 1977.

** The "molecules of emotion," a term coined by Candace Pert, are ligands, peptides, hormones, and steroids produced by various organs in the body which carry information/instructions to cells throughout the body. These proteins are literally the physical origins of emotion. See her book, *Molecules of Emotion: Why You Feel the Way You Feel.*

Apply Oneself to Mastering Academic Studies. Skills and knowledge expand our opportunities—throwing open new doors, opening up new possibilities in our personal lives and on the job. Teach students to love to learn so that learning something new is a source of joy and pride rather than drudgery. Also, help them develop a sense of "knowing when you know and when you don't know" to avoid deluding themselves that a little knowledge is all there is about a subject or all that they need. Allow their learning to unfold naturally rather than force it to fit the regiment of the classroom and your convenience as teacher.

Learn to Accept Acknowledgement Graciously. Although we all yearn for acknowledgement, we typically do a poor job of receiving it. We say, for example, "Oh, this old thing? Oh, it's nothing; I picked it up last week at Goodwill." Learn to respond first with, "Thank you," and mean it. Then, if you feel anything else should be said, add something like, "I appreciate your noticing." Allow the acknowledgement to sink in.

Be Aware of the Difference Between Personal Best and Perfectionism. Most of us would like what we do to be perfect, the best, but life is a busy affair. We don't always have the resources, time, and energy we need to reach perfection on every task. If we get caught up in perfectionism, we will be forever disappointed in ourselves. Happiness in life is coming to terms with the reality that personal best is just that—the best we could do given resources, skill and knowledge, and the circumstances of the moment. The mark of maturity is allowing ourselves to feel pride for both process and product when we deserve it while refusing to indulge in false pride when our work may look good to others but we know we didn't give it our personal best.

Observe Others. For children from highly dysfunctional situations, experiencing pride may be rare. Therefore, the LIFESKILL of Pride must be modeled at school and built into the curriculum as deliberately as history and mathematics. To take pride in their own accomplishments, such students may need prompting, a series of questions that help them conclude that they have, in fact, done their personal best. Yessssss! Then join them; take pride in your role in helping them learn this vital LIFESKILL. Pride shared is infectious.

WHAT DOES PRIDE LOOK LIKE IN THE REAL WORLD?

We

- Start businesses and name them after our families

- Accept compliments and acknowledgements with grace

- Sponsor awards acknowledgements, e.g., Employee of the Week, Realtor of the Year, Outstanding Teacher of the Year, Most Improved Softball Player, Volunteer of the Week

- Join organizations and actively participate in activities that support the organizations' goals, e.g., Lions Club, Optimists, Girl Scouts, Boy Scouts, 4-H, sports teams, choirs, church groups, booster clubs, and professional organizations

- Vote in local, state, and national elections

- Give handshakes, hugs, pats on the back, kisses, and smiles to friends and colleagues who have assisted in accomplishing something worthwhile

- Guarantee any services you perform

- Vote in every election and march in the Memorial Day and Fourth of July parades

WHAT DOES PRIDE LOOK LIKE IN SCHOOL?

Staff

- Plan lessons and thematic connections with care

- Sponsor teams, clubs, and other extracurricular activities

- Attend school presentations after regular school hours, such as plays, musicals, games, concerts, academic competitions, and intramural sports

- Wear the school T-shirt, button, or jacket

- Acknowledge all cultures, races, and religions and share their pride in who they are

- Recognize students' "personal best"

- Take the necessary steps to ensure that the school is always ready for guests

- Teach students how to welcome guests

- Provide articles for the local newspapers that describe the classroom curriculum and projects

Students

- Participate actively in extracurricular activities

- Sing the school song, know the mascot's name, and understand the mission statement

- Turn in papers that are neat, on time, and accurate

- Acknowledge friends who are doing their Personal Best

- Wear school logo clothing

- Share the concepts and knowledge they are learning with other students, parents, and guests

- Share positive statements about their culture, heritage, and religion and that of others

- Feel good about a job well done

- Acknowledge the cooperative effort in group projects

INQUIRIES TO DEVELOP PRIDE

Whole Class Inquiries

- Design an "I am proud of you" card for someone special in your life. Write at least one way you feel this person is honorable and courageous. Present the card and share his/her reactions to receiving the card with your learning club.

- Create a "Community Pride" bulletin board in the classroom. Clip articles from the daily newspaper(s) that reflect self-respect or pride in individual or group projects. Highlight important phrases that reflect pride. Create a web or mind map organizing these phrases. Update the bulletin board weekly. At the end of one month, invite the class to vote on which individual/group most deserves a "Pride Award." With a group of classmates, create this award. Print out one each month and present it in person or by mail to the individual or group named in the chosen article.

Small Group/Individual Inquiries

- Show a "personal best" piece of work to a partner. Tell him/her why you feel proud of what you have done.

- Draw a picture for your teacher illustrating one reason why you are proud to be in his/her class.
  OPTION: Write a note to your teacher explaining one reason why you are proud to be in his/her class.

- Explain how you would feel in each of the following situations:

    ~ You are a new student in a school. When you enter the building you see writing on the walls, paper and trash on the floors, and gum stuck on the doors.
    ~ You are a new student in a school. When you enter the building you see children's artwork on the walls, clean, shiny floors, and clean surfaces everywhere.

- Record in your journal five or more of your personality characteristics that make you feel proud to be who you are. On another day, write on the topic "I am most proud of. . . ." Share your thoughts with a friend/learning club member.

- Learn the meaning of the word "pledge." Research the history of our country's pledge of allegiance and any customs or manners that are associated with saying it. Volunteer to share the information with the class and lead them in reciting the Pledge of Allegiance at the start of each school day. Learn two verses of a patriotic song and teach it to the class. Print the words on a transparency so that each student is able to see and read the words. Invite each student to share one action or idea that makes them proud to be living in America.

- Invite a representative from the VFW or a similar veterans' group to visit your class and teach flag etiquette, including holding, folding, and treating the flag with pride and respect. As a learning club, learn to handle the flag with respect and responsibility; practice using a desk-sized flag.

- Review the requirements that noncitizens must follow to become citizens of the United States of America. Obtain sample questions they must answer correctly before their citizenship is final. Ask for volunteers to take the test and learn if they have the necessary knowledge to become citizens. Contact federal representatives and arrange for your classmates to attend a naturalization ceremony and sing a patriotic song. Find out how many new citizens will be sworn in during the next ceremony in your area. Make a congratulatory card that comments on their pride in citizenship for each person. Attend the ceremony and present the cards. Write your feelings about participating in this event in your journal and discuss them with a partner.

- Design a folder to hold samples of your personal best work done at school or at home. Date each paper and organize them by subject, size, style, or date. Brainstorm standards or attributes to judge each paper before including it in the folder. Tape these standards to the inside cover of the work portfolio. Once a week, browse through the folder, remove any work that no longer meets your standards. Add any new paperwork, photos, or examples of personal best that make you feel pride as a student. Share the contents of the folder at a parent-teacher-student conference and explain why you are proud of each one as an example of your Personal Best. Also offer it to classroom guests who are interested in learning more about your personal growth and achievements.

- Create a banner for your learning club that includes the following information–group name, members' names, mascot, and a song, chant, or cheer. Use colored markers, crayons, and a piece of poster board. Practice the song, chant, or cheer quietly so that other learning clubs will be surprised when they hear it. Be prepared to share your product with the whole class.

- With your learning club, brainstorm the attributes or characteristics of a great group. Identify five that are most important to all of you. Create checklists for your learning club/study group to complete, after working together cooperatively. Include a way to evaluate such interpersonal skills as Active Listening, using No Put-Downs, Personal Best, and providing positive feedback. Share your individual observations and feelings. If necessary for the next time, set new goals.

- Brainstorm appropriate ways for an audience to behave and to show their appreciation for a high-quality performance. Prepare a skit about inappropriate ways of showing respect and pride. Then replay the skit showing appropriate behaviors. Offer to teach these skills through drama, music, and physical movement to younger children before they attend any shows or performances.

SIGNS OF SUCCESS

Congratulations! Students are showing signs of Pride when they

- Share "personal best" papers with their parents
- Research their cultural roots and share the information with their classmates
- Learn to speak their native language correctly and are open to learning other languages
- Play a musical instrument in the school's marching band
- Chant positive school cheers at sports events
- Compliment classmates on their knowledge of different cultures
- Introduce their class as "the best in the school"
- Enter a local/state/national competition in any curricular or extracurricular area
- Attend a class or school reunion

Keep trying! Students need more practice when they

- Boo or use derisive language during a school event
- Deface school property
- Use put-downs about someone's race, culture, religion, or economic status
- Turn in incomplete, messy, or inaccurate class work
- Condemn someone else's efforts and "personal best"
- Can't find a sport, club, or activity in which to participate
- Neglect to use the Lifelong Guidelines and LIFESKILLS in daily life
- Refuse to participate in class or school programs
- Mock students from other schools
- Keep a messy, sloppy desk and locker

LITERATURE LINK ~ PRIDE

Primary Grades

Amazing Grace	Hoffman, Mary
Best Bug to Be, The	Johnson, Dolores
Birthday Basket for Tia, A	Mora, Pat
Dandelion	Freeman, Don
Elephant's Wrestling Match, The	Sierra, Judy
It's Not Easy Being A Bunny	Sadler, Marilyn
King Bob's New Clothes	Deluise, Dom
Mirette On the High Wire	McGully, Emily
Nina, Nina, Ballerina	O'Connor, Jane
Patchwork Quilt, The	Flourney, Valerie

Intermediate Grades

African-American Inventors	McKissack, P. and F.
Baseball in April	Soto, Gary
Call Me Gretzky!	O'Connor, Jim
Elephants Never Forget	Sanderson, Jeannette
Otherwise Known As Sheila, the Great	Blume, Judy
Pride's Challenge	Campbell, Joanna
Pride of the Green Mountains: The Story of a Horse and the Girl Who Turns to Him for Help	Baker, Carin Greenberg
Pride of Puerto Rico: The Life of Roberto Clemente	Walker, Paul Robert
Samantha's Pride	Campbell, Joanna
Summer of the Swans, The	Byers, Betsy
Trumpet of the Swan, The	White, E. B.

Middle School and High School

Contender, The	Lipsyte, Robert
Lesson Before Dying, A	Gaines, Ernest J.
M.C. Higgins, the Great	Hamilton, Virginia
Runner, The	Voigt, Cynthia

Teacher's Resources

All Eyes Up Here	Carr, Tee
Winners and Losers	Harris, Sydney J.

Date _____

Dear Family,

Our class is continuing to define and study the attributes of the LIFESKILLS. We are moving on to

~ PRIDE ~

Many years ago, it wasn't considered to be in "good taste" to show pride; it was thought to be a sign of arrogance, conceit, and rudeness. However, we have since learned that pride can also have positive effects. Pride is that feeling you get when you believe that you have done something worthwhile that is part of a bigger picture, a bigger accomplishment.

As a class, we will:

- Take time to acknowledge ourselves and others for doing Personal Best

- Find ways to show our appreciation for a performance and join in the pride for a job well done

- Evaluate and acknowledge the Lifelong Guidelines and LIFESKILLS used while working together on learning-club projects

- Discover the pride of being a citizen in a democratic society

As a family, you can teach your child about pride by sharing your family's stories of success and "fighting the good fight" even if the end goal was lost

It is also helpful to:

- Include your child in family traditions by explaining their importance/significance

- Share stories of times when your family has felt pride

- Share your child's excitement about a great significant accomplishment

- Explain your personal work stories about jobs well done and the pride you felt

Pride is an important LIFESKILL since it is a vital source of motivation for much of what we do. Children want to do their personal best and experience well-deserved pride.

Sincerely,

_____

Your child's teacher

Problem Solving

"CHALLENGE YOURSELF TODAY"

problem *n* **1:** a question raised for inquiry, consideration, or solution **2 a:** an intricate, unsettled question **b:** a source of perplexity, distress, or vexation
solving *v* **1:** to find a solution

Problem Solving: To create solutions for difficult situations and everyday problems

WHAT IS PROBLEM SOLVING?

Problem solving isn't limited to the weighty and complex questions of life or the realm of rocket science. Problem solving is an everyday activity of each of us. When we pop out of bed on a workday and rush to the closet, one problem we face is, "What's not too dirty, not too wrinkled, and matches my slacks?" Then, "Let's see, what can I grab for breakfast that can be put together in the few minutes I have left?"

On a more academic level, none of you could read this book if you hadn't become problem solvers somewhere along the way. Readers must solve phonetic puzzles about the sounds letters make and the pronunciation of those sounds to form words (does this set of letters follow the rules or is it an exception). Readers need to solve the meaning of those words in context to understand the message being communicated. Also, how did you get a copy of this book? Did you order it through the mail? Via fax? By a phone call? Over the Internet? Each of these activities requires problem-solving* skills. All day, every day, our brains and bodies work together to decode a multitude of puzzles—some simple, others difficult. Then, we seek workable solutions. Problem solving is purposeful thinking focused on a particular topic.

The ability to solve problems is a prized commodity in the workplace and invaluable in our personal and family lives. Without it, our options in life are indeed limited.

---

* Note to the reader: Students may be confused by "problem solving" appearing sometimes with a hyphen and sometimes without. Help them learn the rules of hyphenating: No hyphen when the two words are used as a noun; a hyphen when they are used as an adjective, as in "problem-solving strategy."

Problem Solving from a Brain Research Perspective

Howard Gardner, professor of psychology at Harvard University, considers problem solving a key element in defining intelligence. For him, intelligence is not a number but something far more powerful and practical—"a problem-solving and/or product-producing capability . . . that is valued across cultures."* Gardner identifies eight intelligences: logical-mathematical, linguistic, spatial, musical, bodily-kinesthetic, naturalist, interpersonal, and intrapersonal. Very importantly, each of these intelligences operates from a different part of the brain and are typically used in varying combinations. Singular problem-solving or product-producing thinking from only one intelligence is not the norm.

While we are born with all eight intelligences, we develop some more than others due to personal preference and/or the encouragement and practice afforded by family and culture. This, along with the fact that no two brains are the same, results in very different problem-solving performances in our classrooms. We should provide students opportunities both to hone their strengths and to improve weaknesses. Life isn't choosy; there are no guarantees that where it drops us will be a good fit with our strengths. Thus, each student should be encouraged to develop his/her capacities in all eight areas to the fullest extent possible. The challenge to teachers, therefore, is to provide many problem-solving opportunities which call on as many intelligences as possible.

I strongly recommend that you acquaint yourself with Gardner's multiple intelligences. User-friendly sources include *Seven Kinds of Smarts* by Thomas Armstrong and *Teaching and Learning Through Multiple Intelligences (revised)* by Linda Campbell, Bruce Campbell, and Dee Dickinson plus the ITI book for your grade level (see bibliography at the back of this book).

What Problem Solving Is Not

The human brain does not have to be taught to solve problems—it's a built-in, automatic function as natural as breathing. It naturally seeks patterns in a powerful, meaning-making process that is propelled by both survival instinct and curiosity. Schemes to teach students critical thinking through contrived, step-by-step approaches to solve particular kinds of problems are not supported by brain research about how the brain works. What teachers can and should do, however, is to provide students with lots of opportunities to solve problems—problems meaningful to them, not the dry, who-cares worksheet variety.

Practice handling real problems is how we train our ourselves to be effective problem solvers. Every area of curriculum content should pose worthwhile problems for students to solve. Practice develops not only problem-solving capabilities but strengthens self-concept and increases the likelihood that learning will be stored in long-term memory.

WHY PRACTICE PROBLEM SOLVING?

Since life is composed of one problem-solving experience after another, trying to avoid problem solving is futile and foolish. Once a baby's eyes focus and a rattle is in view, problem solving

* *Frames of Mind: Theory of Multiple Intelligences* by Howard Gardner. (New York: Basic Books, Inc., 1985), p. xi.

begins. When a toddler can't reach the cookie in the jar, problem solving continues. Want to ride a bike like the big kids? Solve the problem by learning how! Don't know what career you want? Research, become an intern, work for a temporary employment company. Daughter's sick but you can't miss work? Call grandma, a friend, a "sick kid" sitter, take a personal day off. Wonder what to do about dinner? Look in the freezer, run to the store, make reservations at a local restaurant. Need money? Drive to the cash machine, borrow from the kids (your own personal ones, of course), raid the home emergency fund, or figure out how to solve the problem without money.

A Typical Day In The Life Of . . . (Insert Your Name Here)

Daily living, including what goes on at our workplaces, provides an unending parade of opportunities to analyze situations, generate alternative solutions, choose the most feasible solution, and then implement it. And, since every solution raises more problems, the need to solve problems is as unavoidable as breathing. Think about what's happened in your life today and the many questions you faced. Have you solved them all? If you're like most people, probably not; some inquiries take longer than others to solve. Do we always get to "like" our solutions? Not necessarily! If the old, overworked, over-repaired car breaks down again and our favorite choice is to buy a newer model but there's no money, then we may have to settle for another quick fix until we can save enough cash or float a loan to cover the purchase price of a new car. But, in the meantime, we have a short-term solution.

Practice problem solving? We can't live without it! But by consciously noticing the problems and their solutions, we can make future decisions faster and more confidently.

HOW DO YOU PRACTICE PROBLEM SOLVING?

As mentioned earlier, problem solving is an innate capability that we have been perfecting since infancy. When we were hungry, we developed a distinct cry that our parents recognized as a "feed me" signal; when wet, we developed a variation on the food cry that communicated our need; when we wanted attention, we learned to be coy and charming. We've been solving problems all our lives.

However, to further enhance students' problem-solving capacities, we as teachers must provide students lots of practice and help them become more conscious of their problem-solving processes.

Give Students Lots of Practice

Give students lots and lots of practice. Make your assignments and inquiries problem-solving tasks, not memorization drills or lowlevel recall tasks. Design activities around issues of genuine concern to students, thus worthy of their time. The problems should connect to the world beyond school. (See chapters on how to write inquiries in the ITI books for your grade level.)

Successful experience solving problems becomes a self-fulfilling prophecy: "I've done it before, I can do it again."

Make Problem-Solving Processes More Conscious

There are many ways to make problem-solving processes more conscious. Here are but a few. Once students get started, they will create their own.

Teach Students How to Use the Generic Steps in Problem Solving. Sometimes simply bringing to mind the generic steps* in problem solving can help. When students feel lost, it helps to ask themselves, "Where am I now? Am I still working to analyze the problem? Have I exhausted the possibilities; have I generated all the possible alternative solutions? Do I know enough to make an informed choice among the alternatives?" With these basic steps in mind, students can travel around their mental landscape, exploring their problem, moving and sorting the pieces until the problem is solved.

Teach Students About Multiple Intelligences. Give your students practice solving problems using all eight intelligences. Teach them to rewrite inquiries by substituting one intelligence for another so that they can tackle a problem using their strongest intelligence(s). In others words, help them realize that there is more than one way to analyze a problem, more than one useful perspective, more than one way to think about the problem.

Teach Students to Talk to Themselves. Teach students to become conscious of their inner voice—how to direct it and keep it positive and accurate. Self-talk such as, "I don't know what I'm doing; I'll never be able to get this," is not helpful. On the other hand, "Man, this is easy; I'll blitz this one, no worries," may not be accurate either and may lead to overlooking valuable information. Have them consciously ask themselves where they are in the generic problem-solving steps.

Useful self-talk might include: "Where have I seen this kind of thing before? What do I already know about this situation?" "I heard my dad talk about this once. Now, what did he say?" "Perhaps I'm not looking at the real issues here . . . just the most obvious ones. What else could be causing this problem?"

Teach Students How to Process the Process. In the TRIBES program,** teachers are encouraged to have students analyze the process of working together after each group assignment. The analysis can be about the content of the assignment, the way members of the group worked together, the quality of their product, or, for our purposes here, how their problem-solving processes worked. Was it the result of random guesswork, did they have a hunch or hypothesis that guided them, did prior experience help? Was it easy or difficult (if difficult, what did they learn from the process)? Was it helpful to repeat to themselves the generic steps in problem solving? And so forth.

Although "processing the process" with a group is similar to self-talk, it often produces greater feedback potential because it draws on the wider resources of two or more brains.

Allow Children to Make Mistakes and Experience the Consequences. Often, having trouble making decisions is due to lack of experience in making decisions. Parents and teachers too often wish for a mistake-free

---

* The generic steps in problem solving are: identify the problem, generate possible solutions, select the most feasible alternative, implement the chosen alternative.

** See *TRIBES: A New Way of Learning and Being Together* by Jeanne Gibbs (Sausalito, California: CenterSource Systems, 1995).

Chapter 24—Problem Solving

life for their students. Not possible! It wasn't and isn't for us, why should it be any different for our students? If the consequences aren't life threatening or likely to do long-term physical or psychological damage, allow students to experience the unworkability or dissatisfying results of ineffective problem-solving decisions. Inconvenience, disappointment, and even a little pain are great teachers. Allow the experience—things, events, or other people—to teach the students. The more adept they become at learning from the circumstances around them—without lectures from the adults in their lives—the better off they'll be.

Make Sure Students Can "See" a Problem and Alternatives. If students are hesitant to engage in problem solving, finding it consistently unsettling, and/or impulsively pick unworkable solutions, make sure they have the mental wiring that allows them to "see" a problem and possible solutions. It's difficult to solve a problem if we can't "see" the alternatives. See the discussion of visualizing and verbalizing in Chapter 7.

WHAT DOES PROBLEM SOLVING LOOK LIKE IN THE REAL WORLD?

We

- Look for misplaced and lost belongings

- Call a plumber to fix leaky pipes; phone 911 in an emergency

- Find the doctor best for us

- Save money until there's enough to buy what we want without going into debt

- Apply for a mortgage before buying a house

- Develop a sales strategy to sell our old house

- Open the "Help" section on the computer program when something isn't working right

- Brainstorm solutions with family, friends, and coworkers

- Ask advice from someone who has had a similar problem

WHAT DOES PROBLEM SOLVING LOOK LIKE IN SCHOOL?

Staff

- Evaluate the budget and decide what to cut in order to stay within the team's budget

- Invite parents/guardians to confer about student's lack of motivation/progress

- Negotiate with another teacher to trade special class times (music, art, P.E.) so your students won't miss their time with the specialist because of a study trip experience

- Exchange duties with another staff member so they can attend a special meeting

- Use a variety of teaching strategies during lessons

- State curriculum content as concepts and "big" questions to solve

- Team with another staff member to share curriculum writing

- Brainstorm ways to create a more flexible schedule

Students

- Employ peer mediation strategies to resolve differences

- Ask for advice from a friend, teacher, or counselor

- Move their desks so they can fully see the teacher, video, guest expert, etc.

- Brainstorm ways to establish connection to the Internet

- Find a substitute for a broken shoelace such as a piece of string

INQUIRIES TO DEVELOP PROBLEM SOLVING

Whole Class Inquiries

- Listen to your teacher read *The Story of the Five Chinese Brothers*. Divide a piece of paper into six equal sections. In the first section, draw an elephant. In each of the other sections, illustrate what each of the five brothers thought an elephant was like. Explain to a partner two or more reasons why the brothers' problem-solving strategies weren't working.

- Write your name and a problem that you need help solving on the front of a paper plate. When the teacher tells you to, flip the plate like a frisbee towards the other side of the classroom (or playground, if done outside). Pick up someone else's plate and read the problem. Brainstorm a solution for the problem based on your life experiences. Write one possible answer on the back of the plate. Listen for the teacher's directions to flip the plate again. Repeat the activity with another plate and problem. Your teacher will do this five times. Find your own plate and problem after the switching time has ended. Read the five solutions from your classmates. Reflect on them and determine which one(s) you will try. Illustrate your favorite response on the front of the plate.

- As a class, create conflict resolution procedures to prevent or solve angry confrontations, fights, and outbursts. Brainstorm with your learning club at least four ideas. Offer your suggestions when the teacher asks for them. Actively listen when other learning clubs share their ideas. Look for similar ideas or for suggestions that can be "clumped" together. As a class, vote to select the four or five steps to be part of the final procedures. Write the procedures on a piece of colored paper using markers and crayons. Add illustrations to help you remember the process and then put the sheet in your notebook. Read it when you need to solve a conflict.

Small Group/Individual Inquiries

- Listen to the story, *Gus and Buster Work Things Out*. Think about a time you and a friend have solved a problem. Draw a picture on cardboard showing what happened. Cut the picture apart into puzzle pieces and ask the same friend to put it back together.

- With a partner and one set of classroom blocks, build the tallest tower you can build. Explain to the teacher or another set of partners, one problem that you had to solve while building with the blocks. Explain how you both decided to solve the problem. Build the tower a second time to see if your problem-solving idea works again.

- Create a desk arrangement for your learning club that will help you to work together as a team but at the same time, does not interfere with any other group. Share your plan with the class.

- Read one of the books in the Arthur or D.W. series by Marc Brown. Divide a piece of drawing paper in half. On one half, describe the problem using illustrations and words. On the other half, draw the character's solution and include one or more sentences explaining what happened. Compare your understanding of the problem and solution with a partner.

- Choose a book with many opportunities for problem solving. Practice reading it five or more times and then arrange to read it to a group of younger students. Stop at strategic places where the main character has to solve a problem. Ask the students to predict what will happen. Gather at least four ideas from the group, then continue reading. Stop and ask the students to compare their prediction to what happened. Continue reading, pausing, and predicting throughout the story. Review the author's problem-solving strategies at the end.

- In your journal, record each problem-solving situation you experienced within the previous 24-hours. Classify the problems in categories that work for you, such as family, friends, schoolwork, and situations. Create a second list with the following columns: "Problem Not Solved" and "Problem Solved." Now place the same problems into these new categories. Share the list of Problems Not Solved with your learning club and ask them for additional solutions. After trying some of the suggested solutions, share the results with your learning club.

- Research all sides of a community social, ecological, or economic problem. Interview one or two key people who represent different sides of the issue. Then write a brief summary of the problem, presenting all of the information to your classmates and sharing the solution(s) that seems most practical to you.

- Brainstorm five typical problems that students your age face every day, such as lost homework, tardiness, fights, being offered drugs/alcohol, finding money, losing a pet. With a partner, choose three of the problems to dramatize. Create two different endings for each problem. Ask the class to vote for the best solution.

- Interview a scientist about the steps involved in using the scientific process. Create a large chart listing the steps. Use two different colored markers—one per sentence with alternating colors. Add drawings or graphics as additional reminders of each part of the process. Hang this poster where everyone in class can refer to it as needed.

- Create a self-evaluation feedback sheet. List all of the Lifelong Guidelines and LIFESKILLS at the top. Provide room to write the problem and the solution you tried. Create a "Reflection" section. For this part, choose two or more Lifelong Guidelines/LIFESKILLS that you used to determine the best solution. If your solution didn't work, identify two or more Lifelong Guidelines/LIFESKILLS that you should consider using the next time you need to solve a problem.

- Look for examples of "brain teasers" or logic puzzles. Choose one that looks challenging. Keep a log recording how long you work to solve this puzzle each day. Use the LIFESKILL of Perseverance. Take notes or make sketches showing solutions that haven't worked. When you solve the puzzle or teaser, write or draw the answer on a piece of paper. Then take the puzzle apart and try to solve it a second and third time. Compare how long it took each time. Share your results with another puzzle fan in your class.

- Research a referendum on the ballot of an upcoming local election. Identify the main issues and determine your position based on the information you have obtained. Decide which political candidates/officials agree with your choice. Write a letter, create a political cartoon, or design a newspaper ad supporting his/her stand. Offer your finished product to the teacher for possible publication in the class/school newsletter.

SIGNS OF SUCCESS

Congratulations! Students are showing signs of Problem Solving when they

- Think of many solutions for a problem, rate the choices, and then determine which is best

- Enjoy a puzzle or a challenge

- Persevere until they find answers

- Share their thinking and reasoning with classmates

- Ask another person's opinion

- Clearly understand the problem

- Accept advice from someone who has solved the same problem

- Discuss misunderstandings in a calm, reasonable manner

Keep Trying! Students need more practice when they

- Don't like to make decisions

- Whine or cry when they have to solve a problem

- Consistently make "bad" choices

- Refuse to listen to advice from people with more experience

- Ignore problems and hope they will disappear

- Brainstorm one answer and stop thinking

- Let others think for them

- Ignore their "gut feelings"

- Provide "off the wall" responses

LITERATURE LINK ~ PROBLEM SOLVING

Primary Grades

Bargain for Frances, A	Hoban, Russell
Bitter Bananas	Olaleye, Issac
Doctor DeSoto	Steig, William
Five Chinese Brothers	Bishop, Claire Huchet
Gus and Buster Work Things Out	Bronin, Andrew
Hunterman and the Crocodile: A West-African Folktale, The	Diakite, Bab Wague
Jamaica Tag-Along	Havill, Juanita
Little Rabbit's Loose Tooth	Bates, Lucy
Sopa de Piedras	Brown, Marcia
Spoon for Every Bite, A	Hayes, Joe
Too Many Tamales	Soto, Gary

Intermediate Grades

Abel's Island	Steig, William
Baby Grand, the Moon in July, and Me, The	Barnes, Joyce Annette
Chevrolet Saturdays	Boyd, Candy D.
Cricket In Times Square	Seldon, George
Eighteenth Emergency, The	Byers, Betsy
Journey To Jo'burg	Naidoo, Beverly
Julie of the Wolves	George, Jean Craighead
Lupita Mañana	Beatty, Patricia
Mrs. Frisby and the Rats of NIHM	O'Brien, Robert
Sign of the Beaver, The	Speare, Elizabeth George

Middle School and High School

Endurance, The: Shackleton's Legendary Antarctic Expedition   Alexander, Caroline

Kids' Guide to Social Action, The: How to Solve Problems You Choose and Turn Creative Thinking Into Positive Action   Lewis, Barbara A., Pamela Espeland, and Caryn Pernu

Stones in Water   Napoli, Donna Jo

Teacher's Resource

Reducing School Violence Through Conflict Resolution   Johnson, David W. and R. Johnson

Date _____

Dear Family,

All of us spend the better part of every day solving problems of one kind or another. For example, our child is ill and we have to go to work, the usual route to work is closed for construction and we need to find an alternative path, it's time for dinner and what to cook, the money machine isn't working and we need cash for the grocery store, and the car breaks down, just to name a few examples. The LIFESKILL we need each and every day is

~ PROBLEM SOLVING ~

As a class family, we will be exploring problem solving in some of the following ways:

- Exploring jigsaw, crossword, logic, and word search puzzles

- Role playing many different kinds of situations and identifying the best solutions

- Keeping a journal about common problems and solutions

- Researching problem solving in many different occupations and sports

- Listing strategies for solving problems

Here are some ways to teach problem solving at home:

- Think out loud as you go through the problem-solving process. This will provide your child with many new ideas about ways to solve problems. Explain problems you face on the job and how you go about solving them

- Share stories of your own childhood, especially when you had to solve a problem; explain the results and your feelings during and after solving the problem

- Allow, within limits, your child to make mistakes. This will make him/her stronger from the learning experience and more ready to face real life

Remember, too, that problem-solving strategies are a very marketable quality in the working world.

Sincerely,

_____

Your child's teacher

Chapter 25

Resourcefulness

"THERE IS A WAY!"

> **resourceful** *adj* able to meet situations: capable of devising ways and means
> **ways and means** *n pl* **1:** methods and resources for accomplishing something and especially for defraying expenses

Resourcefulness: To respond to challenges and opportunities in innovative and creative ways

WHAT IS RESOURCEFULNESS?

Remember Apollo 13, stuck in space with dwindling oxygen and no heat? The ground crew was urgently assembled in a room with the exact items contained in the space capsule. Their assignment: Solve the oxygen problem before the astronauts die. Their solution, relying heavily on duct tape, is the epitome of resourcefulness in action. They applied innovative thinking skills to devise unusually imaginative and creative solutions through the ingenious use of ideas and materials. In a billion dollar space exploration program, they saved the mission and the lives of three astronauts with a $3.00 role of duct tape!

We all know family members, co-workers, and friends who are known for recognizing and taking on uncommon opportunities, applying unusual strategies, and landing on their feet! They are the people we go to when we have an unusual problem to solve or when all the tried and true answers aren't working. Resourcefulness is highly valued in any society.

Resourceful people stand out from the crowd. They tend to be multi-talented, multi-track thinkers with optimistic, "can do" attitudes. They are masters at making do with limited resources; in fact, they excel at going beyond "making do." When the going gets tough, they thrive.

Multi-Talented. As author Leslie Hart points out, creativity is the result of flexible use of known patterns and mental programs.* Resourcefulness isn't the result of wishful thinking; you have to know a lot about many things in order to be resourceful. MacGyver, the non-gun packing TV character

---

* See *Human Brain and Human Learning* by Leslie Hart (Kent, Washington: Books For Educators, Inc., 1999), pp. 166-167.

of the 1970s, couldn't pull off his escape and capture schemes without a formidable knowledge of science, especially chemistry. Similarly, it should come as no surprise that most of the early astronauts were mid-Western farm boys who had grown up on farms where resourcefulness was practiced daily and spelled the difference between economic success or failure. They grew up as Jack-of-all-trades and masters of many. Whether on the ground or in space, they were well-equipped to be resourceful.

Multi-Track Thinking. Resourceful people have multi-track minds. While exploring what seems to be the most feasible solution, they continue to mull over additional alternatives. At the same time, they keep testing whether the question is really worth asking and if their analysis of the problem is accurate. Often a different perspective is all that's needed.

Optimism. Resourceful people are visionaries who exercise perception and imagination. They are optimists with a "can-do" attitude; they are certain they will find a workable solution. They trust that there is no simple or right answer and that there is more than one workable solution. They expect to use a wide variety of techniques to accomplish their task. They know they may well be surprised by the options that become available as they proceed.

For the resourceful person, no idea is considered too foolish or unworkable to consider. The solution may emerge out of logical, deductive reasoning or pure happenstance. Resourceful people are not afraid of failure arising from trial and error experimentation. They enjoy exploring the possibilities as they reach into their bag of tricks, find a previous idea or solution, twist it, turn it, sometimes even totally reinvent it, or abandon it completely. They are pragmatists and they keep moving forward.

WHY PRACTICE RESOURCEFULNESS?

In the real world, few problems come with instructions about how to solve them. If we aren't resourceful, our problem-solving capabilities will be anemic and underpowered. In our fast-paced, ever-changing world, what worked before may not work now or ever again. Resourcefulness is a necessity, not a luxury.

Resourcefulness Is Needed for Everyday Living

From the number of problems we encounter each day, we might think that humans are problem magnets. No money for supplies? Tooth just cracked but the checkbook is empty? Nothing in the refrigerator for dinner? Two meetings scheduled at the same time? The forward on the basketball team has the chickenpox and no one else on the team has had them? All of these circumstances call for innovative problem solving and creative thinking. The more serious the problem, the greater the need for resourcefulness.

Resourcefulness Is Respected Everywhere. Resourceful people are often called upon to deal with problems and situations that have been mishandled or ignored, where problems have remained unsolved. People who can find solutions within the current circumstances and resources—without requiring an influx of money—are highly respected and carefully listened to.

Resourcefulness and Citizenship

Effective citizenship in a democratic society requires high levels of resourcefulness. We must be resourceful to ferret out information needed to identify and analyze problems. For example, today's expensive Superfund sites could have been avoided early on at minimal expense but we didn't see the potential problems at the time. Rachel Carson used the LIFESKILL of Resourcefulness to create environmental theories and criteria to help us recognize environment problems much earlier than ever before. Her book, *Silent Spring,* is a landmark contribution to environmental research and activist citizenship.*

Solving problems once identified requires even more resourcefulness. From my perspective, the challenges we face far outstrip available resources to solve them using conventional solutions. More of the same, reinvoking solutions that worked before but are ineffective now, ignoring a problem in hopes that it will resolve itself, are dead ends. If we are to thrive as a society, we must be resourceful enough to come up with new solutions.

To grow such a citizenry, we must give students lots of practice solving problems that require resourcefulness. In the ITI model, this is done through various social/political action projects. Here's an example.

A True Story. It wasn't too long after my first ITI training that I realized my children's desks (old, big, slant-top lecture type with chair attached and an opening for books on the left side) were not conducive to learning clubs or grouping of any kind. If I tried to group them in rectangles, half of the students couldn't get into their desk storage areas. When I tried circles, they bumped their heads on others' desks while bending over to get materials. In addition, everything left on top of the desks, such as baskets of materials to be shared or plants, slid right off.

My school couldn't afford new furniture and wouldn't for years. A few of us went to the principal and shared our dream of having flat-top desks with separate chairs and storage access from the top.

Shortly afterward, our principal found an offer of 700 desks, free for the asking, on the Internet. We suggested she take them sight unseen. A few months later we received a local address where the desks were being stored. On the third floor of a dusty old warehouse, our dreams were answered—enough "new" desks to outfit about seven classrooms.

The resourcefulness of our parent group was immediate and overwhelming. They borrowed trucks and recruited people to help move the desks to our school. Our resourceful students arrived at school wearing bathing suits beneath their clothes. The fourth graders hosed down the desks and chairs, the fifth graders scrubbed them clean and the sixth graders buffed them dry and carried them up to our classrooms. Our old desks were sold as "homework stations" for a few dollars each.

Not only did we get the desks free, but we made money in the process. A wonderful example of the LIFESKILL of Resourcefulness in action.

---

* See *Silent Spring* by Rachel Carlson (New York: Houghton Mifflin Company, 1962).

HOW DO YOU PRACTICE IT?

There is no patented formula or set of directions for becoming more resourceful. But, there are some tips. Some of the suggestions below are for you as a teacher; others are for students.

Be Open to Challenges

We can't sit home and play it safe if we want to practice resourcefulness. This doesn't mean that we should endanger ourselves but be willing to court uncertainty. By accepting more challenges, by opening our souls to new adventures, by taking chances, our brains develop new capabilities. We learn more and become increasingly resourceful—more of the person we want to be.

Volunteer for Projects

To stretch your "resourcefulness index," volunteer for a new committee or accept a new position. Start a new club or organization. Share a hobby or skill. Offer suggestions at staff meetings and don't give up if at first your ideas aren't embraced with enthusiasm. Think of Benjamin Franklin, Thomas Edison, Marie Curie, George Washington Carver, George Pullman, Steve Wozniak, and Bill Gates. Resourcefulness has to start somewhere. Why not with you?

Lessons from a Jedi Warrior

Resourcefulness is an attitude—one well illustrated by the Jedi warriors*: Stay in the present, use a new point of view to overcome obstacles, go back to the source, and don't accept failure as an option—try, try, and try again.

Stay in the Present. One of the key skills of a Jedi warrior is his mental capacity to stay in the present and ignore negative thoughts and anger. Stay focused on the task at hand. Ignore negative feedback from family, friends, peers, and co-workers who offer comments such as: "We tried that already. Been there, done that. It won't work!" "That's a crazy idea. Where'd you get that one?" "Don't tell that one to the boss."

Such negative responses turn off creative juices and stifle independent, innovative thinking. They also make us feel insignificant, unintelligent, and incapable of performing tasks. Worse, they focus our attention on ourselves instead of on the problem to be solved or the product to be created. They erect barriers where none existed before. They create restrictions and restraints in thinking that once flowed freely.

Overcome Obstacles by Changing Point of View. Resourceful people often surmount obstacles in their path merely by changing their point of view. What we may identify as a mountain, they see as a molehill. What we see as permanent, they see as temporary. What we see as a dead-end barrier, they see as a hurdle to be jumped, a delightful challenge to enliven the day.

---

* The Jedi warriors are the "good guys" of George Lucas' movie, *Star Wars*. Their ability to focus their thoughts, stay in the present, and control their emotions gave them access to the Force. Good lessons for us earthlings as well.

Go Back to the Source (And May the Force Be with You). When stumped, go back to the source of the problem. Retry an idea that may have first seemed unrelated or unworkable. Rework an alternative solution, or replay a solution. If it doesn't work, why doesn't it? Is it the concept that's unworkable or its execution? Can you adjust something? Try a different material? Use another source? Find a less expensive way to do it? If still stumped, go to someone you trust, someone who will listen to your ideas and dream with you. Then, go back to the source.

Don't Accept Failure As an Option—Try, Try, and Try Again. To be resourceful, we must persevere. Remember, if the problem we face were an easy one, it would already have been solved. Persistence opens doors. Don't accept failure as an option. Keep trying.

WHAT DOES RESOURCEFULNESS LOOK LIKE IN THE REAL WORLD?

We

- Recycle aluminum cans, plastic bottles, and cardboard

- Find new ways to use technology in medicine, education, government, and business

- Pass on wearable clothing and usable items to charitable organizations for redistribution

- Invent a tool, machine, or product to meet a need

- Create new, innovative ways to accomplish tasks

- Think "outside the box" and sometimes even build a new box

WHAT DOES RESOURCEFULNESS LOOK LIKE IN SCHOOL?

Staff

- Stay open to new and different ways to share information

- Brainstorm a variety of ways to solve a problem

- Find innovative resources to improve programs

- Create materials and approaches to match teaching styles with students' learning styles

- Create materials that support active and participatory learning

- Support curriculum development beyond textbooks

- Provide being-there experiences and information from experts that can build foundations for essential knowledge

- Allocate money in ways that support bodybrain-compatible learning

- Find time in the school day to plan with other teachers as a team

Students

- Use materials in new and creative ways

- Search for information outside of textbooks

- Appreciate different ideas and new ways of thinking

- Delve for the unknown and are innovative and imaginative when creating projects

- Show creativity in thinking, brainstorming original ideas, and conceiving unusual projects

INQUIRIES TO DEVELOP RESOURCEFULNESS

Whole Class Inquiries

- Listen as your teacher reads the book, *The Super Camper Caper.* List two or more ways the family tried to be resourceful and their results. Then write one idea of your own to solve the problem.

- Brainstorm three emergency situations that might happen to someone your age. For each situation, identify two plans of action to help resolve it. Add your ideas to the class list and be prepared to explain your choices to two other students.

- Discuss ways to share class resources (paper, markers, scissors, crayons, glue sticks, etc.) in fair and orderly ways. Identify the most practical and efficient. Write "Using Materials Procedures" of five steps or less that are easy to understand, positively phrased in sentences, and include a graphic for easy reference. Write the steps in alternating colors. Share one of your ideas during the group sharing time. Be prepared to vote on those steps that are most helpful for the whole class to follow as procedures. Copy the newly adopted procedures into your notebook.

- Analyze "boredom." Identify five ways you could use the LIFESKILL of Resourcefulness to overcome it. Discuss them with the class.

Small Group/Individual Inquiries

- Use three materials found in the classroom to create a new toy. Give your toy a name, show how to use it and explain why you think other children will enjoy playing with it.

- Find some objects or resources (books, videos, magazines) at home that add more to a topic you are learning about in school. Ask your parents for some information to explain the objects or materials. Share the information with your classmates.

- Using safe materials, design a toy for the classroom pet. Present it to the teacher for a safety check before putting it in the pet's cage or container. Observe the pet's reaction to the toy. Decide whether or not to make any changes in the toy's design.

- Choose a toy that you no longer care about. Imagine another life for this toy. Create a new use for it. Illustrate the toy and its new purpose. Share this with a partner.

- Identify a place in your community that needs some tender, loving care. Consider an empty lot or yard with trash scattered around that needs cleaning or a local statue or monument that needs repairs. Write a plan that includes the goal, obtaining the owner's permission, a list of free or inexpensive materials that will be needed, a time schedule, the skills needed, a sign-up sheet, and an evaluation sheet to determine the effectiveness of your plans.

- Create a game that uses three different items from our class (or your home) recycle bin. Write down the objective(s) of the game. Choose a name for your game; establish at least three rules and a simple scoring system. Invite your learning-club members to play the game with you. Ask for feedback and make any changes that will help other students to understand the goals, the rules, and how to score it. Invite some other students to play the final version of the game.

- Think of some object (perhaps a toy, item of clothing, computer equipment, or sports equipment) that you would like to own. Choose something that costs more than $30. Research legal ways that you could acquire it for less than $10. Narrow your search to three ways. On a chart illustrate the object you want, the three ways in which you could obtain it for less than $10, and which choice you feel is most creative and workable.

- Design a disaster kit for your region of the country. Decide which disaster is most likely—tornado, earthquake, blizzard, flood, or hurricane. Discuss with your family six or more items that will help sustain life for you and your family for three days. Choose a sturdy, easy-to-carry container that would hold up during a disaster and place all of the chosen items inside. In addition, choose one personal item that you would like to include. Label the container and share it with your family. Place it in a safe, easy-to-reach location. Check the supplies monthly and replace those that aren't good anymore.

- Plan a food garden for a family of four that would provide enough food for at least three nights a week. Choose three or more different-colored vegetables/plants from the following groups—yellow, green, purple, and orange/red. Determine the size of the garden, the kinds and numbers of plants you will need, a planting schedule, maintenance tasks, and a recipe for each of the vegetables. Share this information with your learning club. Ask your family if you can use your plans to create a real garden in your yard.

- Take care of your own clothes for one week. This includes spot removal, washing, drying, and ironing. Learn to do two or more simple repairs, such as sewing on a button, or mending a seam. Choose one outfit and redesign a part of it to make it look fashionable and new. Ask for permission before you make any permanent changes. Show the outfit to your family and record any reactions. Take a photo of the completed project and share it with a classmate who has similar interests.

- Search for a source of pollution (water, ground, air) in our community. Interview a local government official to determine what, if any, procedures are in place to clean up any current pollution and to prevent any further contamination. Create a news story video (three to six minutes long) telling the who, what, why, when, where, and how of the incident. Show this video to your classmates. Follow up with the politician every few weeks to make sure he/she is carefully monitoring the incident.

- Read local newspaper advertisements and visit a favorite supermarket. Plan a shopping list for a family of four for one week. Include food items for three healthy, nutritious meals (including one brown bag lunch) a day per person, paper products, and cleaning supplies. Create one list that keeps within a weekly budget of $70 or less. Then create a second list with items that cost more than $70 but less than $100.

- Invite someone from a local charity, such as Salvation Army, Rescue Mission, Goodwill. Ask him/her to explain to your classmates how they obtain their goods, the kinds of products they accept, how they prepare the goods for sale, and what they do with the profits. Organize a "Collection Connection" within your classroom. Create posters and flyers about the kinds of goods that may be donated. Set a date and time for the collection. Inspect the items to make sure that each one is acceptable. Record the donations on a chart and keep a running total. Share the progress during a class meeting.

SIGNS OF SUCCESS

Congratulations! Students are showing signs of Resourcefulness when they

- Think of new plans for old materials

- Brainstorm many ideas before choosing one

- Use skills and techniques in a new way

- Offer creative and innovative ideas that are out of the ordinary

- Share materials with other students

- Overcome obstacles that stand in the way of solutions

- Create a new product

- Determine the least expensive way to accomplish a goal

- Observe problems in their neighborhoods and search for answers

- Strive to protect the natural environment

Keep trying! Students need more practice when they

- Waste materials and money

- Don't show concern for the classroom and natural environment

- Repeat the same solution even though it hasn't worked the first few times

- Laugh and make fun of other students' imaginative and creative answers

- Try the first solution that comes to mind

- Are impulsive

- Have a limited choice of skills and techniques to use for problem solving

- Give up on a project

LITERATURE LINK ~ RESOURCEFULNESS

Primary Grades

Ben's Trumpet	Isadora, Rachel
Brave Irene	Steig, William
Brother Eagle, Sister Sky	Jeffers, Susan
Dominic	Steig, William
Gettin' Through Thursday	Cooper, Melrose
Hundred Dresses, The	Estes, Eleanor
Stone Soup	Brown, Marcia
Super Camper Caper, The	Himmelman, John
Sweet Clara and the Freedom Quilt	Hopkinson, Deborah
Thomas Jefferson: A Picture Book Biography	Giblin, James Cross

Intermediate Grades

Abel's Island	Steig, William
African-American Inventors	Sullivan, Otha Richard
Alexander Graham Bell: Making Connections	Pasachoff, Naomi
Black Inventors From Africa to America: Two Million Years of Invention and Innovation	Gibbs, C. R.
Family Under the Bridge, The	Carlson, Natalie Savage
Five Notable Inventors	Hudson, Wade
Great Women in the Struggle: Book of Black Heroes, Vol. 2	Igus, Toyomi, Editor
Lyddie	Patterson, Katherine
My Side of the Mountain	George, Jean Craighead
Sign of the Beaver, The	Speare, Elizabeth

Middle School and High School

Burning Up	Cooney, Caroline B.
But I'll Be Back Again	Rylant, Cynthia
Girls and Young Women Leeding the Way: 20 True Stories About Leadership	Karnes, Frances A., Suzanne M. Bean, and Rosemary Wellner

Teacher's Resources

Awakening Your Child's Natural Genius	Armstrong, Thomas
How to Think Like Leonardo da Vinci: Seven Steps to Genius Every Day	Gelb, Michael

Date _____

Dear Family,

Every day, in many ways, you overcome obstacles in life by using a wide variety of skills and techniques to support a family and carry a vision for the person you want your child to become (until he/she is old enough to have a vision of his/her own). All these tasks can be overwhelming at times. However, our current LIFESKILL is the one that supports you during these sometimes overwhelming days. It is the LIFESKILL of

~ RESOURCEFULNESS ~

During our class exploration of this LIFESKILL, we use some of the following strategies to further our understanding of how to be resourceful:

- Use literature to identify resourcefulness in story characters and real-life biographies

- Create plans for emergency situations

- Brainstorm ways to use classroom materials efficiently and wisely in a cooperative way

Some of our small group and individual inquiries will involve projects that need to be completed at home with your assistance while others are meant to be done solely by the child. All of the inquiries are designed to help your child think in an innovative and creative way.

You can help at home by . . .

- Teaching your child local recycling and resource preservation guidelines

- Encouraging creative answers and solutions to problems

- Sharing personal experiences in which you have had to be resourceful

By learning to identify and use the techniques of the LIFESKILL of Resourcefulness, your child will learn to make inventive and ingenious decisions in both family and employment situations.

Sincerely,

_____

Your child's teacher

Chapter 26

Responsibility

"PRIVILEGE DEMANDS RESPONSIBILITY."

responsibility *n* **1**: the quality or state of being responsible: as in
a: moral, legal, or mental accountability   **b:** reliability, trustworthiness
2: something for which one is responsible;   able to answer for one's conduct and obligations

Responsibility: To respond when appropriate, to be accountable for your actions

WHAT IS RESPONSIBILITY?

The root of the word responsibility is "to respond"—to respond to people, animals, things, and circumstances, moment by moment, with integrity and caring—with a sense of what's right. Being responsible means speaking up and/or taking action when the moment calls for it even if it's inconvenient, an unpopular cause, or there's no reward for doing so.

We hear much about irresponsibility these days. Most irresponsibility results not from doing the wrong thing but from doing nothing—failing to act when circumstances warrant a response from us. For example:

- Failing to speak up when someone has been put down or treated unfairly or when someone has broken the law, such as stealing time, services, or materials at work or school

- Withholding information or expertise that is important to successfully complete a team assignment

- Failing to pay child support or bills as agreed

- Failing to arrive on time for appointments

- Leaving tools, equipment, toys, and such out in the weather without adequate protection

- Ignoring a leak rather than fixing it immediately

Do any of these sound familiar?

We demonstrate the LIFESKILL of Responsibility when we say and do the right thing at the right time; we also demonstrate the LIFESKILL of Responsibility when, after the fact, we own up to our words, actions, and deeds or to our failure to respond.

Acting Responsibly Is a Choice

It's the rare individual who is responsible at all times in all areas. Even as adults, our performance is like a roller coaster ride with noble highs and ignoble lows. Some of us excel with responsibilities at work but at home are irresponsible as spouse, parent, and/or family member. Conversely, if we possess a strong sense of familial responsibility, it may clash with what's expected of us at work. And then come our responsibilities to our community and country.

Being responsible is not for the faint-hearted. It demands strength, endurance, competence, a well-integrated sense of values, and an accurate sense of what our time, energy, and available resources can accomplish. Above all, the desire and commitment to be a responsible person must be lit and nurtured from within. Consequently, teaching about responsibility needs to be clear, pervasive, noncoercive, and supportive of the long term rather than an issue of classroom control at the moment. Adults must model and expect it, but can't force or coerce it.

Being responsible can sometimes exact a terrible personal price. Consider the consequences, for example, the travails of corporate whistle blowers or the anguish we feel when we must tell a loved friend hurtful news. But being responsible is also a source of deep personal satisfaction.

WHY PRACTICE RESPONSIBILITY?

What would life be like without responsibility? Drivers would neglect to observe traffic laws. Lawyers would overlook material supporting their client's legal problems. Doctors would disregard current research. Teachers would refuse to plan lessons. Store managers would forget to reorder popular products. Mothers and fathers would ignore babies' cries. Bosses wouldn't have sufficient cash flow to pay their workers at the end of the month. The staff at your favorite fast food restaurant would abandon their posts. Sound a bit chaotic and unpredictable? Yes.

Having things work—be it within the family or between citizens and their federal government or anything in between—can only occur if both sides keep their agreements with each other. When we're responsible, others can count on us and we can count on them. Without agreement to be responsible, there can be no social structures or sense of family. Schools could not exist. Even government cannot exist without agreement to adhere to societal agreements which, in our system, are called laws.

Responsibility is the glue that holds our lives together. Without it, our lives would spin apart and sink into chaos.

HOW DO YOU PRACTICE IT?

How do we practice being responsible? How do we teach it? Typically, we admonish students to be responsible but offer little guidance about how to do so. The core of our messages is often "Just go out and do what's right"—somewhat like telling students to "Just say no to drugs" without helping them discover what to say yes to.

Although good advice, it is freighted with assumptions. It assumes that each student, especially younger ones, is well equipped with essential prerequisites such as:

- A well-developed sense of what is right and what is wrong, a "moral compass" to help them analyze what's going on at the moment and make a choice

- A belief that they can make a difference, that they know enough to speak out and act, that they can positively impact what is going on (rather than merely exposing themselves to ridicule and abuse)

- A belief that they are resilient and resourceful and that, no matter what happens, they will land on their feet and can move on

- A deep and abiding commitment to live "above the line"—living their lives in ways that contribute to society rather than becoming burdensome, giving back to the community because it's the right thing to do, being the kind of person others like to be around, doing their share

With such prerequisites in hand, one can tune into one's intuition—that inner voice or conscience—and then act accordingly.

Tips from Brain Research

As with all the Lifelong Guidelines and LIFESKILLS, the attributes of responsibility are many and rich. Students need numerous examples of responsibility and lack of responsibility and ample opportunity to discuss the fallout from each. As author Leslie Hart points out, we can't know what something is until we also understands what it isn't.* For good discussion prompts, use literature (see the titles on page 26.10), key turning points in history, or favorite quotes. Historical examples include the horror wrought by Nazis soldiers who were "only following orders" and the brutality of Columbus when dealing with the natives. Attention-grabbing quotes include:

- "Never doubt that a small group can change the world. Indeed that is the only way it happens." Margaret Mead

- "All that is necessary for the forces of evil to win in the world is for enough good men to do nothing." Edmund Burke (1729-1997), Irish-born British politician and author

---

* See Leslie Hart's discussion of making meaning through pattern detection and identification in *Human Brain and Human Learning* (Kent, Washington: Books For Educators, Inc., 1998), Chapter 7, pp. 115-132.

- "When Hitler attacked the Jews, I was not a Jew; therefore, I was not concerned. When Hitler attacked the Catholics, I was not a Catholic; therefore, I was not concerned. When Hitler attacked the unions and the industrialists, I was not a member of the unions and I was not concerned. Then, Hitler attacked me and the Protestant church—and there was nobody left to be concerned."*

Practical Applications. Set aside at least two weeks to introduce and focus on the LIFESKILL of Responsibility. Begin each morning discussing the "Quote of the Day" about responsibility. Apply it to current issues in the classroom (behavior and events as well as curriculum content), school, community, nation, and world. Ask how the situation would have been different if the LIFESKILL of Responsibility had or had not been used. Be sure to include examples of failure to act or speak up and stress that omission is as serious as commission. Also, read at least two books/passages a day from the literature list or from books of your choice. Allow ample time to discuss the issues and how they affect the characters.

Practice Makes Perfect. To be responsible in all areas of our life requires great focus and lots of practice. Be patient with yourself as a model. Although, in hindsight you'll realize that you weren't always perfect, each of us is a work in progress when it comes to the LIFESKILLS and Lifelong Guidelines. Being responsible is a bodybrain effort. More than "knowing" what's right, students must often juggle intense emotions as they consider the consequences of their actions or lack of actions. A classroom environment marked by absence of threat (real or perceived) and one in which reflective thinking is nurtured is an absolute must for students practicing the LIFESKILL of Responsibility.

WHAT DOES RESPONSIBILITY LOOK LIKE IN THE REAL WORLD?

We

- Pay bills in a timely fashion
- Complete a project to specifications
- Research issues and vote in local, state, and national elections
- Acknowledge when we have made a mistake or been wrong at work or at home
- Care for elderly family members as needed
- Abide by traffic laws
- Ignore gossip and search for the truth instead
- Provide for our own care by holding down a job, maintaining a healthy lifestyle, and contributing to society

---

* Martin Niemoller, quoted in the *Congressional Record,* 14 October 1968.

WHAT DOES RESPONSIBILITY LOOK LIKE IN SCHOOL?

Staff

- Model the Lifelong Guidelines and LIFESKILLS

- Create a bodybrain-compatible environment and curriculum

- Participate in workshops, courses, and conferences that support the concept of teacher as a lifelong learner

- Write and plan lessons with a focus

- Turn in completed paperwork before or when it is due

- Arrive on time for meetings, the start of school, and all events

- Attend all required functions

- Keep accurate notes and records for all students

Students

- Practice the Lifelong Guidelines and the LIFESKILLS

- Ask questions to expand their understanding of ideas and concepts

- Seek lifelong interests and hobbies by participating in class and school activities

- Commit to improving their skill, knowledge, and behavior

- Bring necessary supplies for projects

- Hand in signed permission slips for "being there" (field trips) experiences

- Return borrowed items to people or to their agreed upon places

- Be in charge of their educational progress

- Replace torn or lost library books

- Accept responsibility for their negative actions and stand up for others who have been rudely or unfairly treated

INQUIRIES TO DEVELOP RESPONSIBILITY

Whole Group Inquiries

- Develop T-Charts with your classmates for each of the Lifelong Guidelines and LIFE-SKILLS. Include three or more items for each of the following categories: Looks Like, Sounds Like, and Feels Like and Does Not Look Like, Does Not Sound Like, and Does Not Feel Like. Add additional notes throughout the year to continue developing understanding of each area.

- Research the minimum requirements for citizens to be eligible to vote in local, state, and national elections. Contact a representative from your local Board of Elections and arrange a "being there" study trip for the class on Election Day at a polling place near the school. Brainstorm three or more questions about responsibility and the right to vote. Obtain permission to ask some voters to share their feelings about being responsible citizens. With your class, determine if there are some common ideas among the responses.

- Plan a class celebration to honor learning. Decide what information you will share, with whom you will share it, and how and when. Assign committees the following responsibilities: reserving a place, sending invitations, preparing presentations, organizing practice times, providing refreshments, and arranging for clean-up.

Small Group/Individual Inquiries

- Look at the inside of your desk before you leave at the end of the day. Throw out any trash, sharpen your pencil for the next morning, place books in a neat pile, and put loose papers into a binder or folder where they belong. Leave nothing on the top of your desk. Fold a piece of 8"x12" paper in half. Open it up and fold it in half the other way. Open it up. In each box, draw a picture that will remind you of one of your end-of-the-day desk procedures.

- Bring in a story from your daily newspaper that demonstrates someone from your town/city using the LIFESKILL of Responsibility to help other people. Share the story during community circle time.

- Watch the video or listen to the story of Charlotte's Web. Create a card for Wilbur sharing one way he showed responsibility in the story. Ask the school librarian if she would display your card for a few days.

- Invite local politicians to your classroom to talk about their responsibilities. Ask if there are any unwritten responsibilities, too. Write a job description for his/her position specifying the duties that you feel are important.

- Volunteer to adopt a classroom responsibility (such as water plants, deliver messages, coordinate play equipment). Note the procedures that you use and write them up for other students to follow. Use only four or five steps. Print them on the computer and add graphics. Place the finished procedures in a plastic sleeve to protect them. Teach the procedures to the person who is to take on those responsibilities.

- Brainstorm a "real-life" name for each classroom job/responsibility. Some examples might be botanist (plant care specialist), maintenance engineer (sweeper), and "gopher" (messenger and details person). Create enough meaningful jobs so that there is one for each student. Develop procedures for each task, print them up, place in plastic sleeves, and put them into a procedure binder so that each worker will understand his/her responsibilities.

- Read the school handbook with an adult in your family. Ask questions about any parts that you don't understand. Then in your own words, explain the responsibilities that you feel students are expected to follow.

- Design an emergency first aid kit for use in your house. Use a watertight container; include a source of light, important phone numbers, and coins to make a call from a pay phone. Put in five or more other items that you feel are important in times of trouble. Share this kit with your learning club and explain why you chose the items you did.

- Create an EDITH (Emergency Drill In The House) plan for your family to use in case of fire or other emergencies. Post a sign in each room that lists emergency evacuation procedures, alternate routes, a specified place away from the house where everyone will come together for a safety check, and a phone number outside the area to be used as a message center. Ask your family to practice the drill at least twice. Make any adjustments necessary for safety reasons. Share the plan with an adult at school.

- Learn how to manage a checking account and be responsible for your own money. Design ten or more checks for your use (look at a real check as a model).

    ~ Include your name and address in the upper left-hand corner.
    ~ Create a name for your bank. Print that in the lower left-hand corner.
    ~ Number your checks starting with 1000. Write the number in the upper right-hand corner.
    ~ Include lines for the date and the person/company to whom you are writing the check.
    ~ Create a place for the amount of money in numerals and another for the amount written out in words.
    ~ Place a line in the lower right-hand corner for your signature.

  Decide how much money will be in your account, then pretend to make some purchases by check. Ask an adult to demonstrate how to write a check. Balance your account as you spend money so that you don't run out!

- Create a personal plan to use the family computer responsibly. Include how much time you will spend on the computer each day (one hour or less) and the programs you'll use. Keep a computer log noting when you sign on and off, how much time you spent using each program and any products you created. Share this plan and journal with your family and your teacher.

- Create a yearlong celebration calendar for your family. Design one sheet for each month. Illustrate with appropriate drawings. Mark each important day (birthdays, anniversaries, holidays, and special family events such as weddings and reunions) with a special symbol and words. Share the completed calendar with your teacher. Give it to your family to hang in a prominent spot so that no one person is responsible for remembering family events.

- Practice three or more ways to receive and send messages (such as telephone, voice mail, e-mail, pager, snail mail). Research the proper manners expected for each method of communication. Ask an adult to check all messages for accuracy. Learn how to make a "911" call (but do *not* practice on a real phone). Also compose a "safety" message that you can use if there is no adult in the house. Print it out and place it near each phone in your home.

- Research a Native American tribe in your state or region. Discover why Native Americans are considered the "original conservationists" of our country. List three or more responsibilities they followed to conserve the "gifts from Mother Earth." Create a three-sided presentation board and illustrate one responsibility on each section. Display this in your classroom or media center.

- Research the origins of Citizenship Day, September 17, created by Congress in 1952. Organize a celebration of that day in your classroom. Invite students from another class to be your audience.

SIGNS OF SUCCESS

Congratulations! Students are showing signs of Responsibility when they

- Consistently use the Lifelong Guidelines and LIFESKILLS
- Offer to help a friend understand something new
- Locate the rightful owner of a "found" object
- Return borrowed materials on time and in good condition
- Do something that needs to be done without being told to do it
- Perform their classroom jobs as described
- Practice a musical instrument until they are fully prepared for an upcoming lesson or concert
- Enter the classroom, follow the procedures, and copy the agenda every morning

Keep trying! Students need more practice when they

- Are frequently late for school without a legitimate excuse

- "Forget" to do and turn in assignments

- Cheat on work and tests

- Neglect their duties

- Misuse free time or room passes

- Ignore requests for assistance

- Use put-downs

- Are unorganized

LITERATURE LINK ~ RESPONSIBILITY

Primary Grades

Amazon Boy	Lewin, Ted
Berenstain Bears and the Messy Room	Berenstain, Jan and Stan
Berlioz, the Bear	Brett, Jan
Courage of Sarah Noble, The	Dalgliesh, Alice
Did You Carry the Flag Today, Charlie?	Caudill, Rebecca
Down the Road	Schertle, Alice
Ollie Forgot	Arnold, Ted
Why Mosquitoes Buzz in People's Ears	Aardema, Vera
Wilfred Gordon McDonald Partridge	Fox, Mem

Intermediate Grades

Christmas in the Big House, Christmas in the Quarter	McKissack, Patricia and F. McKissack
Circuit: Stories from the Life of a Migrant Child, The	Jiminez, Francisco
Day No Pigs Would Die, A	Peck, Robert Newton
Indian in the Cupboard, The	Banks, Lynne Reid
Life Around the Lake: Embroideries by the Women of Lake Patzcuaro	Prisilla, Marciel, and G. Cotto
Runner, The	Voight, Cynthia
Sing Down the Moon	O'Dell, Scott
Strider	Cleary, Beverly
Summer of the Swans, The	Byars, Betsy

Middle School and High School

Armageddon Summer	Yolen, Jane
Kid's Guide to Service Projects, The: Over 500 Service Ideas for Young People Who Want to Make a Difference	Lewis, Barbara A., and Pamela Espeland
Man Who Was Poe, The	Avi
Pigman, The	Zindel, Paul

Teacher's Resource

Parenting with Love and Logic: Teaching Children Responsibilities	Fay, Jim and Foster Cline

Date _____

Dear Family,

Our next LIFESKILL is one that is constantly in demand both inside and outside of family life. We will focus on being accountable for words, actions, and deeds. We'll examine which skills develop a greater sense of

~ RESPONSIBILITY ~

Every day, in many ways, we expect children to be responsible for chores, schoolwork, manners, and attitudes. Responsibility is a true LIFESKILL, one that strengthens family relationships, reinforces employment capabilities, and empowers friendships. Some of the classroom experiences that encourage accountability include:

- Learning to take charge of their own learning projects, e.g., gathering needed materials, seeking resources, raising relevant questions

- Making good choices about use of time

- Taking leadership roles in their learning club

- Returning library books by the due date

- Speaking up when others have been treated unfairly or received a put-down

- Acknowledging one's actions and words

Some examples of a child using the LIFESKILL of Responsibility at home include:

- Waking and getting up when the alarm clock rings

- Choosing clothes suitable for the occasion and dressing with little or no assistance

- Packing his/her own book bag

- Arriving at school on time

- Doing chores in a timely fashion

- Learning to manage money

Sometimes children's attempts to be responsible fail but that doesn't mean that we should give up. As Abraham Lincoln once said, "You cannot escape the responsibility of tomorrow by evading it today."

Sincerely,

_____

Your child's teacher

Chapter 27

Sense of Humor

"Laughter feels good."

sense *n* **1: a:** meaning conveyed or intended **b:** discerning awareness and appreciation
humor *n* **1:** a quality which appeals to the sense of the ludicrous or absurdly incongruous
2: something that is designed to be comical or amusing

Sense of Humor: To laugh and be playful without harming others

WHAT IS SENSE OF HUMOR?

A sense of humor enables us to experience joy and laughter even when faced with misfortune. It is a state of mind and a spirit that we carry through life. It flows through our lives and relationships, enhancing them daily.

A sense of humor allows us to find and experience joy and delight. It removes feelings of stress and tension. And, it just happens to be my all-time favorite LIFESKILL! How could anyone survive without it? Especially a teacher! Humor is one of the healthiest and most powerful methods of maintaining perspective about life's difficult experiences.

Two Kinds of Humor

There are various kinds or genre of humor. One is teller based. We tell stories about ourselves and our mishaps or we tell stories reflecting our perspective of life's situations (a funny thing happened on the way to the forum). This kind of humor is usually not perceived to be threatening; it is safe and is enjoyed by the widest audiences. Comedian Jack Benny was famous for this kind of humor. A hallmark of his career was that he never generated humor at the expense of other people. This is the model for the LIFESKILL of Sense of Humor.

Another kind of humor, however, is aimed at other individuals (mother-in-law and spouse jokes) or groups (racial, ethnic, blondes, and liberals). This humor may be, and often is, harmful and mean-spirited. It is often used to build up the teller at the expense of others. Sitcoms specialize in this brand of humor. It is the realm of put-downs and should be eliminated from classrooms and schools. See Chapter 7 for a discussion of the Lifelong Guideline of No Put-Downs.

WHY PRACTICE A SENSE OF HUMOR?

A sense of humor generates laughter. Laughter, in turn, is very beneficial for everything from your imagination to your physical health to your relationships with others. By cultivating laughter, you not only make life more enjoyable, you make it longer, healthier, and happier.*

The Many Benefits of Humor

Laughter makes us feel better. Our problems and worries are temporarily suspended. We experience a flood of "feel good" molecules of emotion** after which the day looks brighter and our hurdles less formidable. A sense of humor allows us to discern and value the incongruities in life and provides moments of joy and pleasure. Very importantly, such natural chemicals jump-start emotions that promote more active learning and a healthy level of self-esteem.

There is a social benefit as well. Our sense of humor helps people see us as fun to be with, likeable, and interesting, making us feel confident, self-assured, and relaxed. In addition, when we make others laugh, we help them to feel better, too.

Physical Benefits. Laughter benefits us physically, from reducing tension to boosting the immune system to curing life-threatening illnesses.*** It releases natural substances (such as endorphins) which help relieve pain, block substances which suppress the immune system (such as epinephrine and cortisol), and speed up the production of immune enhancers (such as beta-endorphins).

Since the diaphragm is being used when we laugh, our respiration increases and so does the amount of oxygen in the blood. This movement of the diaphragm also provides an "internal massage" to other organs including the stomach, kidneys, and liver. Studies also show a direct correlation between blood pressure and laughter; high blood pressure decreases as laughter increases.

In summary, recent research emphasizes the importance of the bodybrain connection in relation to good health. Certainly, in the classroom, humor is a well-known antidote to stress and can be a strong force in building community.

---

* Two classic works in this area are *Molecules of Emotion: Why We Feel the Way We Feel* by Candace Pert and the popular press books of Norman Cousins, *Anatomy of an Illness As Perceived by the Patient: Reflections on Healing and Regeneration* (New York: W. W. Norton & Company, 1995).
** *Molecules of Emotion: Why We Feel the Way We Feel* by Candace Pert is a "must read" book for teachers and administrators.
*** See *Love, Medicine, and Miracles: Lessons Learned About Self-Healing from a Surgeon's Experiences with Exceptional Patients* and *Peace, Love, and Healing: Bodymind Communication and the Path of Self-Healing* both by Bernie Siegel, M.D. (New York: HarperCollins, Publishing, 1990).

Sense of Humor Is a Choice

We all know people who have a great sense of humor. They are fun to be with and make time pass more quickly with less energy expended, even for difficult tasks. They brighten up the room.

We also know people who never seem to crack a smile or offer so much as a twinkle in the eye over a funny comment. For whatever reason, a sense of humor isn't a priority for them. It's too bad because their brains and bodies—and the brains and bodies of those around them—are losing out on healthy jolts of natural chemicals that enhance well-being.

Responding to others' sense of humor and developing our own is a choice. Through our modeling of the LIFESKILL of Sense of Humor, students can see the choice clearly and make a life-enhancing decision.

Humor and Leadership

Make no mistake: Displaying a sense of humor is a critical quality of those who lead and gain the support of others.* From George Rogers Clark** to John F. Kennedy to the beloved neighbor down the street, humor and laughter are a powerful attractor, spirit lifter, and relationship glue. Commit yourself to developing a sense of humor. It is a professional and personal imperative.

HOW DO YOU PRACTICE IT?

How do we go about laughing if it's not easy for us? How can we develop that humorous perspective which can influence our spirit, body, and mind so positively? One of the best ways is to stay in touch with our "inner child" or "playful clown." We all have it but many times we conceal it due to the seriousness of work and life. We must allow ourselves to be playful and childlike (which is very different from being child*ish*). Watch babies play peek-a-boo. They laugh and giggle with glee. Glee is definitely something adults need more of in their lives.

Begin to enjoy life more and note the humorous situations that occur daily. Learn to relax and to see the "funny" side of predicaments. Study how other people, known for their sense of humor, react to circumstances. Watch their signals and body language; listen to the words they use. Then use these as models for improving your own ability to recognize, appreciate, and use humor.

Humor is infectious if you allow it to be. Join in the fun!

---

* See "Theory and Implications Regarding the utilization of Strategic Humor by Leaders" by C. B. Crawford, Department of Communication, Fort Hays State University. http://www.fhsu.edu/htmlpages/faculty/cocc/lead03.htm

** George Rogers Clark, older brother of William Clark of Lewis and Clark fame, taught William his formula for leadership—give your followers jokes, songs, and a vision of glory. Not bad advice for the classroom. See *From Sea to Shining Sea* by James Alexander Thom (New York: Ballantine Books, December 1986). It is also a thoroughly researched and beautifully written historical novel, terrific for classroom use.

Humor Is Developmental

Our sense of humor goes through stages.* Babies laugh and coo at our funny faces and sounds. Young children adore nonsense jokes that may have no meaning to anyone except themselves. The primary age child likes simple jokes and riddles, and often finds "bathroom" humor hilarious (much to the embarrassment of his/her parents). Students in intermediate grades begin to understand word plays and puns, often trying some of their own, although they may have to explain the punch line to you.**

Understanding verbal humor also depends heavily on one's ability to turn words into images, a mental wiring that can be developed (see Chapter 6, Active Listening).

Experience Is the Best Teacher

Experiment with humor. Come up with your own jokes, puns, riddles, and situations. When doing so, always be mindful of your audience. Are they laughing out of genuine enjoyment or out of embarrassment and nervousness? If the latter, re-read Chapter 7 about the Lifelong Guideline of No Put-Downs.

The Best Humor Is Spontaneous and Circumstantial

Some people seem to dedicate their lives to collecting and telling jokes. Consider the staff meeting that can't begin without the latest joke from the informal master of ceremonies on staff. Often, however, such canned jokes can have a put-down edge to them; at a minimum they often derail the conversation at hand. In contrast, the most beneficial humor is spontaneous and circumstantial— teller-based humor arising from the moment, the task at hand, the circumstances.

As you hone the LIFESKILL of Sense of Humor, focus on developing teller-based humor whose content is of the moment—spontaneous, circumstantial, welcoming, and inclusive.

WHAT DOES SENSE OF HUMOR LOOK LIKE IN THE REAL WORLD?

We

- Laugh at jokes, riddles, limericks, puns, and skits

- Enjoy comedians

- Read comic books, humorous stories, and watch funny movies

---

* See *Thinking and Learning: Matching Developmental Stages with Curriculum and Instruction* by Lawrence Lowery. (Kent, WA: Books For Educators, Inc., 1989.)

** My personal favorite came from a second grade boy, David, who said that his mom was coming home from the hospital. When I inquired about her health, David replied, "Oh, she's okay. We just had her spayed." Talk about humor being circumstantial!

- Laugh at ourselves in funny situations

- Use humor to alleviate stress and tension

- Play games that make us laugh ("Twister," "Trivial Pursuit")

- See the bright side of difficult experiences

- Laugh when a baby does something cute

- Enjoy listening to funny experiences shared by friends and relatives

- Chuckle when toddlers try to make sense of language (such as calling every man "daddy" or every four-legged creature "doggy")

WHAT DOES SENSE OF HUMOR LOOK LIKE IN SCHOOL?

Staff

- Enjoy each others' company at school parties and get-togethers

- Laugh at jokes and riddles

- "Play" with words to create puns

- Use humor to alleviate a student's fears and make him/her feel more comfortable

- Inject humorous comments during lessons

- Wear funny costumes for special lessons to make the material memorable

- Delight in unusual comments that come "out of the mouths of babes"

Students

- Share jokes and riddles from books they are reading

- Write jokes, riddles, and puns that are age-appropriate

- Laugh at themselves when they do or say something funny

- Laugh at themselves when they make a mistake

- Understand what is appropriate humor for class and school

- Chuckle, when appropriate, as they work with a partner, learning club, or small group

INQUIRIES TO DEVELOP SENSE OF HUMOR

Whole Class Inquiries

- Compile a class joke and riddle book by asking each person to select a personal favorite or one from class/library books. Check your choice with a friend to make sure it will not offend anyone. Copy it onto a 4"x 6" index card. Decide the categories for organization (e.g., people, animals, aliens). As a group, decide the order of appearance of the jokes. Create a *Big Book of Jokes* by grouping white 12"x 18" drawing paper, one page per person. Add pieces of colored paper for the front and back covers. Reserve one page for each index card. Have each person copy his/her own selection onto the assigned page and illustrate it. When the book is completed, volunteer to read it to another group of students.

- Watch a segment of a Charlie Brown video together. Analyze the humor and divide it into two kinds: "Humor That Hurts People" and "Humor That Doesn't Hurt People." As you watch the video segment, make a tally mark in the appropriate column. Total the columns. Compare your analysis with your learning-club members. Which kind of humor was used more in the video? Discuss how hurtful humor relates to the Lifelong Guideline of No Put-downs. In your journal, describe your feelings about the humor used in the Charlie Brown segment you watched.

Small Group/Individual Inquiries

- Listen to the story *The Day Jimmy's Boa Ate the Wash*. Retell the story using a different critter. Decide if the story seems funnier or less funny with the new critter.

- Learn two or more silly songs (e.g., "On Top of Spaghetti," "Shake Your Brain," "Froggy Went-a-Courtin'") that are fun to sing. Add some dance steps or motions that go with the words and music. Perform the song in music class or in a school talent show.

- Read three or more funny poems by Shel Silverstein, Kalli Dakos, or Daniel Prelutsky. Decide which one you think is funniest of the three. Recite that one from memory for your classmates. Write a funny poem of your own that contains four lines or more. Read this poem to a class partner.

- Design a humorous birthday card for a friend or relative. Use humor that doesn't hurt or offend. Illustrate your card and make an envelope for it. Sign the card and present it on his/her special day.

- Read some one-frame cartoons (such as "All in the Family") and study the words and illustrations for examples of humor. Create a one-frame cartoon based on something funny you did or said as a young child (ask your family for help if you can't remember any). Using marker or watercolors, fill in the drawing with bright colors. Sign your name in the lower right-hand corner. Show it to your family.

- Study some longer cartoon strips or collections (e.g., "Calvin and Hobbes"). Observe how the story develops and how the cartoonist uses art to expand the reader's understanding. Experiment with a joke or riddle and turn it into a three- or four-frame cartoon. Design your own drawings and use special print for the words. Show it to three or more people.

- Read a fairy tale. Rewrite it through the eyes of a different character (such as *Cinderella* as seen through her step-sister's eyes or *The Emperor's New Clothes* through his wife's eyes). Read the new story to a friend and ask for his/her opinion.

- Research the history of clowns and create a poster with some of the following information: clowns through the ages, various clown faces, clothes that clowns wear, and clown actions. Organize a "Clown School" and practice making audiences laugh through the use of mime, pantomime, and funny skits. Invite a local clown to your classroom to share tips about performing and make-up. Volunteer to perform at a local children's hospital or for a younger group of students in your school.

- Watch a video/movie of a famous pantomime artist such as Marcel Marceau, Charlie Chaplin, or the Cirque de Soleil performers. Observe how they use humor and movement. Create a routine for you to perform. Practice until you feel comfortable then perform it for a friend and observe any reactions to your act.

- Study a book such as *CDC* or *CDB!* (see "Literature Link" on page 27.9). Notice how puns and alphabet letters are used to convey fun and humor. Write four or more alphabet puns of your own. Illustrate each one and staple them together in book form. Design a cover with a title and your name and put it in the classroom library for others to enjoy.

- Research humor in another culture and the part that humor plays in that culture. Determine two or more ways that humor is the same and two or more ways it is different. Chart the information on a Venn diagram. Explain what you learned to the class.

- Dramatize three or more different ways you can show concern or displeasure when someone tells offensive jokes attacking a person's looks, race, religion, or culture. Practice your skit until you can remember your part without any prompting. Share your ideas with the class.

SIGNS OF SUCCESS

Congratulations! Students are showing signs of a Sense of Humor when they

- Laugh with classmates over a funny incident

- Use humor that doesn't hurt or offend individuals or put-down ethnic, racial, and religious groups; ask others *not* to tell such jokes

- Share comments that are optimistic and upbeat

- Understand political cartoons

- Write, direct, or act in a skit that pokes fun at a situation

- Laugh spontaneously because they feel great and life is wonderful

- Giggle with a friend over something silly

- Create their own jokes, riddles, and puns that other people understand and enjoy

- Laugh at humorous songs

Keep trying! Students need more practice when they

- Offend people with racial, ethnic, or religious jokes and other put-downs

- Don't realize that no one else appreciates their attempts at humor

- Often have to ask others to explain the meaning of a joke or humorous play on words

- Are the only one not laughing during a humorous incident

- Haven't laughed once in an hour or two

- Forget to "play" for part of each day

- Can't write simple jokes and riddles

LITERATURE LINK ~ SENSE OF HUMOR

Primary Grades

Aldo Applesauce	Hurwitz, Johanna
Beware of the Dragons	Wilson, Sarah
Book of Humor for Children	Random House
CDC!/CDB!	Steig, William
Class Clown	Hurwitz, Johanna
Day Jimmy's Boa Ate the Wash, The	Nobel, Trinka H.
Ming Lo Moves the Mountain	Lobel, Arnold
Mucky Mouse	Allen, Jonathon
Old Man and His Door, The	Soto, Gary
Rose for Pinkerton, A	Kellogg, Steven
Stories Julius Tells, The	Cameron, Ann
Why Mosquitoes Buzz in People's Ears	Aardema, Verna

Intermediate Grades

Anastasia Krupnik	Lowry, Lois
Be a Perfect Person In Just Three Days	Manes, Stephen
Best Christmas Pageant Ever, The	Robinson, Barbara Parks
Charlotte's Web	White, E.B.
Fortune Tellers, The	Alexander, Lloyd
Pistachio Prescription, The	Danziger, Paula
Ramona the Brave	Cleary, Beverly
Secret of Gumbo Grove, The	Tate, Eleanora E.
Tales from Wayside School	Sachar, Louis
Tales of a Fourth Grade Nothing	Blume, Judy

Middle School and High School

Dinky Hocker Shoots Smack	Kerr, M. E.
Drawing on the Funny Side of the Brain: How to Come up with Jokes for Cartoons and Comic Strips	Hart, Christopher
Rules of the Road	Bauer, Joan

Teacher's Resources

Are You As Happy As Your Dog?	Cohen, Alan
Laughing Classroom, The	Loomans, D. & K. Kolberg
Serious Laughter	Conte, Yvonne F.

Date _____

Dear Family,

Question: Why did the chicken cross the road? Answer: To get to the other side! Remember when you were so proud that you could tell jokes and how you would repeat them over and over again to anyone who was willing to listen? Well, we have reached our study of the LIFESKILL of

~ SENSE OF HUMOR ~

In class, we will have fun in a variety of ways including:

- Reading humorous stories, plays, and/or poetry

- Learning songs with funny lyrics or surprise endings

- Drawing cartoons in a series of frames

- Writing our own jokes, riddles, and puns

- Learning the difference between "hurtful" and "helpful" humor

This "humor" fest will probably spill over into your home, especially at dinnertime. If you could share some jokes, riddles, and puns with your child, this will strengthen his/her ability to recognize humor in the "real world." Also, you and your child can

- Enjoy comedies (plays, movies, videos) together

- Laugh at silly things that happen when you are together

- Read humorous stories together

- Sing funny commercials to replace those between programs on TV

- Explore cartoons as a form of communication.

Look for humor in each day—laughter helps to release helpful, natural chemicals into the brain that make us feel better and, surprisingly, increase the likelihood that we will commit more information to long-term memory. Try some of your favorite childhood jokes and riddles on your family, read the funnies with your child, and enjoy life.

Sincerely,

_____

Your child's teacher

Chapter 28

LIFESKILLS in Real Life

Once launched in the classroom, the Lifelong Guidelines and LIFESKILLS have a way of taking on a life of their own. Teachers and parents begin to see applications beyond the contexts in which they are taught. They appear in surprising—and wonderful—ways. The two stories included in this chapter illustrate such uses of the Lifelong Guidelines and LIFESKILLS in real-life situations. The first story, "Acorns in Our Hands" by Mary Miller, describes how the Lifelong Guidelines and LIFESKILLS lead a third grade class to invite a classmate's mother to join the class to learn to read. As one third grader sagely stated, "Everyone has the right to read." The students believed they could help her do so.

The second intersection with real life, "LIFESKILLS Are Test-Taking Skills" by Joanne H. Robblee, shows how the Lifelong Guideline of Personal Best and its LIFESKILLS can be used to improve test-taking skills.

ACORNS IN OUR HANDS BY MARY MILLER*

"What is a caring classroom community? What are we hoping to teach our children beyond mere academics? Day in and day out, we seek to instruct and exemplify character building and life skills, hoping it will make a difference in how our children grow and learn. There are days when it seems nothing is getting through and then there are those moments in a classroom when time seems to stand still, when our children inspire us with their words, and we are reminded that our efforts are not in vain. I was privileged to witness just such a moment recently.

For weeks, Ginger Weincek, the third grade teacher with whom I work at Creekside Elementary, had been faithfully and systematically introducing her students to the LIFESKILLS, part of a curriculum for building character and community in the classroom used in the Kovalik ITI model. She had taught the children the meanings of LIFESKILLS such as Initiative, Integrity, Flexibility, Perseverance, Responsibility, Caring, and Courage. Each week, without fail, she would introduce a new LIFESKILL, discussing it, thinking through examples, role playing, and trying to identify it in students' interactions throughout the week. There were times when it seemed that the students understood the concepts clearly, times when it was difficult to tell if they were comprehending beyond mere use of the word. However, an eight-year-old boy in our class, William Martin**, and his mother led us into an opportunity that showed us again that our efforts to teach character are not without return.

In the course of talking with Will about his reading challenges, he shared that his mother also had trouble reading. Will's mom reads at about an early second grade level. Mrs. Weincek began working with Will's

---

* Adapted with permission of Mary Miller, from Creekside Elementary, Elgin, Illinois, © December, 1999.
** All the children's names used in this story are fictitious.

mom after school, trying to tutor her in her spare time. It became apparent, however, that more consistent instruction was needed. As Mrs. Martin's reading level was actually not too far from many of the children in her class, Mrs. Weincek began to consider the possibility of Will's mom joining the class every afternoon for reading instruction. There were all kinds of concerns. What would Mrs. Martin think? What would the class think? What would Will think? If the obstacles could be overcome, Mrs. Martin's participation in class would provide a unique chance to grow, particularly in their understanding and acceptance of adult illiteracy and in their tolerance and compassion for others' struggles in general.

Mrs. Weincek recognized the need to address each of the concerns before proceeding. First, she approached Mrs. Martin with her plan. Mrs. Martin was immediately interested but wanted to be sure that her son would feel comfortable with the idea. Will was tentative at first, expressing concern that the kids might make fun of his mom. Mrs. Weincek assured him that they would not proceed with anything until he felt comfortable.

Will's apprehension made it clear that adult illiteracy is a concern that had not been adequately addressed in our society. Mrs. Weincek began reading some wonderful books to the children— books that explored the issues of adult illiteracy and its impact on people and families. As she read stories like, *My Mom Can't Read, Papa's Storks, Jeremiah Learns to Read,* and *Read to Me, Mama,* the children began to discuss and consider the trials and obstacles faced by those adults who cannot read. Mrs. Weincek often had them write their personal responses to the books which caused them to think even further.

One day during a class discussion, Rosa, and then Juanita, revealed to the class that their Hispanic fathers could read and write only minimally in English. As they shared their stories, it seemed that there was a sense of relief for them, that someone was aware of their situation. The class listened quietly to them, and responded with acceptance. Some important seeds were sown in those discussions.

Rosa and Juanita's willingness to share was not only a relief to them. As time went on, Will indicated to his mother that he would now feel comfortable having her in the classroom. With this in mind, Mrs. Weincek arranged for a class meeting. What unfolded was remarkable. She began by asking the children what kinds of ideas they might have to help adults they know learn how to read better. By now, the children were familiar with the scope of the problem and the wonderful possibilities for those who confront and overcome it. Their suggestions, ranging from using phonics to finding "just right" books, included the possibility of adults coming to school with children to learn how to read. It was so encouraging to hear their thoughtful, creative ideas. More importantly, however, they were beginning to think through what their own personal response to this might be. Many were thinking from the perspective of their own struggles to learn to read. Concern and desire to help was genuine even during this generic discussion.

At this point, Mrs. Weincek asked Will if he would like to ask the class a question. Will came and sat in front of them. He began to speak in a soft, halting voice, "I wondered if you would help my mama read better." I watched as every one of his classmate's faces filled with compassion and every set of eyes became intently fixed on his. Silence settled over the room. Mrs. Weincek quietly asked the class how many would like to help Will's mom learn to read better. Immediately every hand In the room shot up. Brian looked earnestly at Will and responded soberly, "We're with you, man." Following his lead, others began to express similar sentiments.

"You can count on us."

"Yeah, we want to help."

Nodding and caring came from every direction. Then Mrs. Weincek asked Will what he and his mom would like to do.

"We was [sic] wondering if my mama could come to school with us and do reading with our groups."

Before Mrs. Weincek could even ask for reactions, the children were responding enthusiastically, hands already raised, ideas surging forth. She began explaining to them what Mrs. Martin's participation would actually involve and asked for their suggestions. The discussion began with some sensitive, yet practical, ideas.

Ellen said, "I think it will be kind of a cool experience to be able to help someone that way!"

"I think we should find some 'just right' books for her," said another.

"Yeah, but they might not be the kind she'd be interested in."

"Maybe Will could find out what kind of books his mom likes."

The comments and suggestions kept pouring out. Then the flood gates opened when someone said, "Hey, this is like the LIFESKILL of Flexibility, for us to change things to help make Will's mom feel at home."

"It will take the LIFESKILL of Effort, too, for Will's mom to work at this."

"And Perseverance!"

"I think our class will need the LIFESKILLS of Friendship and Caring to help Will's mom."

" And what about the LIFESKILL of Courage. Will's mom had a lot of courage to want to try and read."

The class was silent again as someone offered, "I think Will also had to have the LIFESKILL of Courage to tell everyone that his mom needed help."

At this point, my eyes were brimming with tears as I listened to the outpouring of caring and strength of character the students were displaying. As Mrs.Weincek began to speak, her voice betrayed tears as well. This was one of those transcendent moments when teachers are amazed and touched by the hearts of their students, when the seeds that have been planted blossom and grow right before their eyes.

"You have all amazed and encouraged me by your response. I am so proud of each one of you! I know this will mean a lot to Will and his mom."

With childlike innocence and incredulity, Mandie responded, "I think grownups should be able to read."

With wisdom beyond his years, Adam said, "I think everyone has a right to read."

Armed with those attitudes, our class is embarking on an adventure in the LIFESKILL of Caring that will probably change and challenge all of us. We feel excited and privileged; we wonder what impact it will have on each of us. The impact in Mrs. Weincek's and my life cannot be denied. We want to nurture the seeds of character that bloom and begin to grow in these students.

Ralph Waldo Emerson has said, "The creation of a thousand forests is in one acorn." How fortunate we are to be a part of the planting.

LIFESKILLS ARE TEST-TAKING SKILLS by Joanne H. Robblee*

Over the years, I have been involved with different aspects of test taking. I have developed test preparation activities and given lessons to students on test taking. I have administered tests. I have analyzed test results for my school. I have explained test results to teachers, parents, and students. As an observer of people, I believe that test taking involves more than book knowledge. A major factor in how a person performs on tests is individual character. It is an immeasurable variable that influences much in life, including how a student performs during testing.

More and more we read about "emotional intelligence." As a former school counselor, I have observed the powerful influence that attitude and feelings can play in an individual's life. In the past, we have focused almost solely on the intellectual side of education—basically book learning. My belief is that we need to expand our focus and include character building into every aspect of our curriculum, even testing.

All too often across America, there is a flurry of pre-test activities held in most classrooms the month prior to standardized testing. Unfortunately, in most cases, this is a day late and a dollar short. Preparing students for testing begins the first day they are in your class, when you begin to talk about what good character is. Good character is comprised of learned skills which take months, even years, to develop.

One of the few educators I know who has incorporated character education into daily instruction is Susan Kovalik. Her approach makes the development of character an explicit teaching process. She incorporates her Lifelong Guidelines and LIFESKILLS into every aspect of the classroom. I propose that these same character traits be viewed as effective test-taking skills.

In this essay I discuss how each of the LIFESKILLS developed by Susan Kovalik can play a role in test taking.

CARING—To feel concern for others

The quality of caring is important because of the atmosphere it creates in the classroom during testing. If a student has only experienced put-downs day after day, he/she already feels at risk doing even the simplest task. Adding pressure to excel during standardized testing to a classroom environment already permeated with unease and insecurity negatively affects student performance.

Another aspect of the LIFESKILL of Caring is the reality that students are aware of each other's ability. No matter what we label reading groups (blue birds or vultures) or how flexible our math grouping may be, the kids know.** As adults it is important that we foster a sense of caring for everyone in the classroom. A mutual support system should be created which will bolster any child through difficulties and challenges. Differences among children are a reality and it is up to the teacher to foster a climate of acceptance that permeates the classroom The pay off for this kind of pervasive caring is that every child will feel safe enough and secure enough to attempt the risk of test taking with minimal anxiety.

Another vital element to the LIFESKILL of Caring is that the teacher model this quality for all children. One of the awesome responsibilities of being an educator is that we are constantly being observed by 20+ pair of curious eyes. Children overhear comments, watch reactions, and observe our actions throughout the day. An educator is always on display, not just during formal lessons. It is not enough to talk about good character or caring. We must consistently model these traits ourselves—towards our students and our colleagues.

---

* Adapted with permission of Joanne H. Robblee, ©2000.
** In *Designing Groupwork: Strategies for the Heterogeneous Classroom*, Elizabeth Cohen states that students as young as first grade can accurately rank the entire class, including themselves, on ability to read. Their ranking is shockingly accurate, a mirror of the teacher's.

COMMON SENSE—To use good judgment

This LIFESKILL is a vital one to develop throughout the school year. Basically, we are trying to build within each child a sense of what is reasonable and possible and what is not. This character trait can play two roles during testing.

The first role is that of staying objective as the student reads a question and considers possible choices. Now this might seem a somewhat mundane test-taking skill but it comes in handy repeatedly during testing. Most questions on standardized tests are multiple choice. Not all of the choices are reasonable. It is the ability to determine what is reasonable that helps to eliminate incorrect choices. However, most students believe that all four choices are equally close to being right and don't have the ability to differentiate among them. National testing companies admit that only two answers are either close or correct and that the other two choices aren't even rational. It is this sense of what is reasonable, based on good common sense, that helps the student make the right choice.

As simple as that sounds, if the teacher has not taken the time to model this "common sense" approach to test taking, the students will not trust themselves enough to use it. Students' belief in their common sense is something that must be built up over the months and affirmed during class activities.

There is another role for common sense during test taking. More and more testing is shifting to short essay questions. From all reports, even standardized testing will have this type of question in the future. The LIFESKILL of Common Sense will have to come to the forefront here because the student will have to make sure that he/she actually responded to the question asked. Now that may seem ludicrous in some ways but, if you have ever corrected an essay question, you will have often noticed answers that aren't even related to the question. Thus, there is a need to build the LIFESKILL of Common Sense into test taking strategies. Just having the sense to check to see if we actually answered the question is a true indicator of common sense.

COOPERATION—to work together towards a common goal or purpose

This LIFESKILL is one that can make a difference during testing. It is easy during testing for a student to think that his/her test scores don't really count, that they will get lost in the process. It is important that he/she remembers that the test scores are used to assess how a teacher or a school is performing. The student needs to realize that his/her effort makes a difference to others.

Teachers should emphasize daily that behavior, effort, and decisions make a difference in the classroom and to the school. By providing different cooperative activities and lessons, students learn to share responsibilities and carry their individual loads. Whole class projects that focus on service and community involvement help the students realize that they truly can make a difference. When testing comes around, there is no doubt in the students' minds that their scores count for themselves and for the class as a whole. Each has become a citizen of the classroom and school, a contributing member of the educational community.

COURAGE—To act according to one's belief

Courage is not an inbred quality. It is one of those LIFESKILLS that comes forth when a person is challenged or threatened. Test taking is one of those challenging, often threatening, annual experiences; we need to recognize it as such. It takes courage to work through a standardized test. No one likes to be judged and everyone likes to do well. When students take a test, they know that they are going to be judged and that there is the possibility that they might not do well. Not only that but also other people, including their parents, will know exactly how they did. How do you prepare a student to annually face that kind of challenge? The teacher can build the LIFESKILL of Courage by having the student experience risk-taking challenges throughout the year.

Teachers nurture the LIFESKILL of Courage in the classroom by modeling it, reading about it, and identifying it in students when it is exhibited. We are not talking about the confronting-the-universal-enemy kind of courage but rather courage to make the right choice, an act of courage demanded of us daily. It is easy for us as educators, for the sake of time and simplicity, to make the decisions for our students. However, doing so is not helping them practice the LIFESKILL of Courage but rather protecting them from encountering any challenges whatsoever.

In test taking, the LIFESKILL of Courage means being brave enough to try your personal best. It means admitting you care enough to work on the test the whole time, even when other people are finished. It also means having the courage to recognize what you need to work on and to really focus on mastering that skill.

CURIOSITY—A desire to learn and know about one's world

This LIFESKILL comes in handy throughout testing because it keeps the student looking for the answers. All too often a student mentally quits attending to the test but keeps filling in the circles. Building a sense of curiosity—an appetite for learning—helps sustain the student as he reads the all-too-lengthy passages or examines the all-to-complicated graphs. Maintaining alertness makes a huge difference in test scores.

The ability to sustain one's curiosity—interest in the test questions and what they are asking—is a LIFESKILL that needs to be taught in the classroom daily. Frequently, teaching becomes so teacher-focused that the student sits passively and watches the teacher work her/himself to death while trying to get a concept across. In this instance, the student's LIFESKILL of Curiosity is stifled.

By planning lessons that excite the LIFESKILL of Curiosity and expecting students to actively do the learning, teachers can build focus and interest that will carry over to test taking. We need to foster in the children an ability to sustain curiosity until they find the answers.

EFFORT—To try your hardest

There is no other LIFESKILL that pays off more than effort during testing. It amazes me that every year teachers expect students to perform well during standardized testing, yet they have never expected the students to put forth that much sustained effort during the school year. I am not saying that teachers across America should submit students to test after test. What I am saying is that the teacher should facilitate activities where the students need to stay on task until an assignment is completed and completed well.

No wonder students get frustrated and quit halfway through a standardized test. They never have had to work that long and hard before. They haven't developed within themselves a belief that they can sustain focus for a long period of time. This internal effort level needs to be built and expanded gradually over the months prior to testing.

Another aspect of the LIFESKILL of Effort is the need to try hard on every question of the test. This ability is developed in the classroom when the teacher sustains high expectations every day on every assignment. If the student knows the teacher doesn't really care about the quality of work, then the student will naturally cut back on the effort put forth. It doesn't take long for a student, even a very young one, to determine which teachers expect more and to adjust accordingly. It is the teachers who maintain high expectations for effort who get the payback in higher test scores.

FLEXIBILITY—To alter plans when necessary

To this LIFESKILL I would also add resilience—the ability to deal with feelings of dread, inadequacy, and sometimes hopelessness and still have the ability to bounce back. Our society today has not fostered this quality of coping, yet it is one of the most invaluable. The LIFESKILL of Flexibility is vital to keep a student going during the test. Remember, every student initially believes that he/she will know every answer on the test and do well. So the first time the students run into difficulty, they need to be flexible or resilient in order to handle the test situation internally. Test taking requires the ability to take another approach to a question, to search for experiences that might relate to it and to trust that we will be able to figure it out.

If you try to get into a student's head while he/she is taking a test, imagine the self-talk that occurs as the student moves from one question to the next. "Gee, that one was easy. So I must be doing all right." "Uh-oh I don't get this one. What do they want me to do? I'm not going to get it right. I probably won't get any of them right." "There's no way I will do well on this test. I might as well give up." This self-defeating thought pattern occurs too often in students who encounter adversity and lack LIFESKILLS. They just give up.

To counter this downward spiral in attitude, it is vital that the teacher daily model how to handle difficulties. For the most part children have not been expected to handle problems in our quick-fix society. Students need opportunities on a daily basis to solve meaningful problems so that they can build the confidence that they can handle situations.

With the LIFESKILL of Flexibility, the inner conversation is something like this. "Gee, that question was easy. I guess I'm doing all right. Uh-oh, this one is tough. Let me read it again and see if I can understand it a little better. Let me look at the answer choices to see if they give me any clues. Hmmm, now don't get excited. Just sit back and take a deep breath and then let's try it one more time. I'm not really sure about this but I'm going to take the best guess I can and move on to the next one. I'm not going to let this one question drag me down. I know there are questions up ahead I do know or that I'll be able to figure out if I try hard enough." Those are the thoughts of a student who has learned the LIFESKILL of Flexibility.

FRIENDSHIP—To make and keep a friend through mutual trust and caring

This LIFESKILL is important before taking a test. The of LIFESKILL of Friendship crosses all contexts and situations in our lives and in the classroom. If students can go to each other for help, then everyone will learn more and be more prepared to succeed on tests. If students are not fighting and arguing throughout the day, then instructional time is not wasted by refereeing our way through petty differences. So, the LIFESKILL of Friendship needs to be fostered all year long. The academic payoff is monumental. This kind of mutual support can make the whole class more emotionally comfortable during testing and the scores will be more likely to reflect achievement accurately.

INITIATIVE—To do something because it needs to be done

The important thing about the LIFESKILL of Initiative is that it overcomes "learned helplessness." Instead of letting young children try things, there is an overwhelming need to do it for them. We, as teachers, need to show them how they can take care of themselves and their learning every day.

It is important to remember that the LIFESKILL of Initiative should be taught explicitly; don't assume it will burst forth spontaneously. If a test requires problem solving, the teacher must model this in the classroom. When a problem is taught or discussed, take the time to ask what the student could do to help solve the problem. Don't accept or provide one answer or one solution to problems/questions. Given the different learning styles, you will be amazed at the different strategies students generate.

The LIFESKILL of Initiative is important for another aspect of testing. The student has to make the repeated decision that he will move on to the next question and try just as hard on this question and every question on the test. The LIFESKILL of Initiative overlaps with the LIFESKILL of Effort but initiative adds to the formula a willingness to self-start without being told. During testing, because the teacher must maintain the distant role of test administrator, it is important that the student has internalized the ability to initiate work on every problem.

INTEGRITY—To conduct oneself according to a sense of what's right and wrong

It would be easy to minimize this LIFESKILL during standardized testing because the formal testing environment reduces the opportunity for cheating. However, I have seen even the youngest child not trust him/herself and look on someone else's paper. Integrity is a character trait that should be defined and focused on daily in class. Even the smallest act of honesty should be recognized and discussed. Our society's role models have not been paragons of the LIFESKILL of Integrity and I can assure you that the children are watching.

Another aspect of integrity, which I don't believe is addressed enough, deals with students' honesty about themselves and their ability to judge their own performance, particularly on a standardized test, or any test or measurement for that matter. As the focus on testing has increased, there is a greater need to involve students in their own assessment process. Rather than merely test and file the results away, I would recommend conferencing individually with the student about test results, practices, and ways to improve. This process would develop within the student a sense of honest understanding as to exactly where he/she stands and hopefully on ways to improve. Without meaning to, we have left the most important component of the assessment process out of the loop—the student. By including the student in this results analysis, he/she can develop a greater awareness of his learning as well as a sense of INTEGRITY about judging himself and his work product.

Another way to emphasize the LIFESKILL of Integrity is to stress that when a student doesn't rely on his/her own abilities to take a test, then the test score is not really a reflection of him/her but of the person he copied. To put it more simply, if you cheat, the grade you earn really isn't yours. I sincerely think that this needs to be stated explicitly and repeatedly before students will believe it.

To make a painful digression here, I have heard teachers on numerous occasions say that if the "powers that be" keep emphasizing test scores, then they, the teachers, will just have to start teaching the test. Teachers have to realize that the very integrity we say we expect from the students should be expected of us. As professionals we need to know the difference between right and wrong. If we don't, and if we deliberately compromise the testing process, then we have devalued education and ourselves. Bottom line, we need to trust ourselves to do a good job and model the LIFESKILL of Integrity throughout the entire process.

ORGANIZATION—To plan, arrange, and implement in an orderly way; to keep things in an orderly, readily-usable way

To me this LIFESKILL pays off when you talk about a student pacing himself during testing. This is a skill that the teacher needs to develop daily in the classroom. The student needs to be able to determine how long an assignment will take and ensure that he organizes tasks to make the best use of the time available. Even the best student will get low scores if he gets stuck on one problem and doesn't complete the last half of the test. Again, the daily expectation of organizing tasks and time effectively is key in developing this LIFESKILL.

Another aspect of the LIFESKILL of Organization involves developing the ability to work math problems neatly and correctly. On many of the math tests, scratch paper is allowed. Yet, time and again, the students feel that they can solve the problems in their heads or their work is so sloppy that they make careless mistakes. Students should always be prepared to show their work and to make it neat enough that you and they can read it.

PATIENCE—To wait calmly for someone or something

As I said earlier, this is a quick-fix world. Students aren't used to having to wait for results. They aren't trained to stay calm and deal with stressful situations. So when it comes to testing time, they are already having difficulty with the testing situation before it even starts—just from the stress of waiting for it to begin. This is where an educator can make a real difference. By discussing feelings openly, the student will understand better what everyone is feeling. By addressing self-doubts, the teacher can help the students be more patient with their own feelings and anxieties. In my experience, students are more impatient with themselves than you can possibly imagine. The teacher can help create calmness and self-confidence about testing that can make a difference in student performance.

The LIFESKILL of Patience is one that teaches the student to slow down during test taking. I like to refer to this student as "Speedy Spike." He doesn't like testing. He doesn't like focusing for long periods of time. And he is in a race to get the test finished first, no matter how poorly he does. To counter this tendency, the teacher needs to address the LIFESKILL of Patience from the very beginning of the school year. The "Speedy Spikes" show up in a classroom almost immediately. The teacher needs to make explicit that the expectation is not to get the work completed first but to have it done well.

One last note, most test preparation programs point out that many answers are missed towards the end of the test. This could be attributed to students hurriedly finishing the test as time runs out. However, often I find that it is because students speed up at the end merely because they want to get the test over with, no matter how much time is left. So, providing lessons about the importance of keeping an even pace throughout the testing, or during any assignment, could make a significant difference in test results.

PERSEVERANCE—To continue in spite of difficulties

This LIFESKILL is the quality that will sustain a student during the isolation of test taking. There is nothing you can say or do to support a student during testing. He must have the perseverance to make it all the way through. That is why giving multi-step assignments can make a difference. All too often a student might do well on one assignment and do minimal work on another. As far as he/she is concerned, the goal is just to hand it in, not to produce the best quality. Or there is the student who starts off being very careful and doing quality work only to degenerate into a morass of carelessness later in the task. It is important to have the student experience long-term involvement in a task and sustain the quality of work throughout. This doesn't have to be a complicated assignment but merely one where the parts are connected and different tasks need to be completed to successfully accomplish the job. All too often our assignments are short, brief, and don't teach the LIFESKILL of Perserverance.

In young children especially, the LIFESKILL of Perserverance can be a difficult concept to understand and to teach. The first attempts might seem humble to an adult, yet recognition of those first efforts can inspire greater perserverance the next time. The students have to be able to see it before they can begin to practice it. Recognizing perserverance when it occurs is the most powerful reinforcer of this character trait.

PRIDE—Satisfaction from doing your personal best

Susan Kovalik added pride to the LIFESKILLS list because she noticed that students were practicing many LIFESKILLS but the quality of work was careless and sloppy. Basically this character trait provides the motivation to do our best on anything we do. Sadly, we have gotten away from the feeling that showing pride can be positive. Pride has somehow gotten confused with arrogance about being "the best"—an external measure. Pride arises from an internal sense of doing one's best. Instead, students simply say they don't care, so why should they try. This attitude is hard to overcome when testing time arrives so it is imperative to build the LIFESKILL of Pride from the first day of school.

The LIFESKILL of Pride simply means we expect the students' best work every day and we don't accept less. This is easier said than done. However, we need to keep in mind that it would be better for the student to produce less work of the best quality rather than produce a mountain of mediocre work. We need to re-think what our assignments are supposed to accomplish. Is it really a question of merely covering the materials and accepting a pile of slipshod work? Or, should students truly learn how to gather information, analyze it, and produce quality work that reflects their learning. We need to assess what our goal should be. Have we really given the students time to take pride in their work or have we just rushed through the materials leaving a trail of sloppy work in our wake?

Another aspect of the LIFESKILL of Pride is that students might not feel that they are good enough to really be proud of what they do. I have worked with middle school students who are actually scared to put forth effort on a test. They are scared because they might do poorly. In their minds, if they haven't really tried, then they haven't run the risk of failure. This convoluted way of thinking discourages their taking pride in anything they do. They don't want to show they care because if they don't do well then they have somehow lost face. To counteract this faulty thinking, the teacher needs to create an atmosphere of accomplishment in the classroom. Celebrate real successes (not artificial ones). Recognize effort and small improvements so that the students begin to see that they can learn and improve. Show them what they did right while still pointing out areas to improve. Let them find in themselves that sense of pride.

PROBLEM SOLVING—To seek solutions in difficult situations and everyday problems

Standardized tests appear to be moving away from "trivial pursuit" questions. If you analyze recent test questions, they are more inferential and seek relationships. So, being a problem solver is more important than ever. If we hand out worksheet after mindless worksheet then we foster the "trivial pursuit" approach to learning. Students need to time to identify problems, come up with solutions, and see if those solutions actually work. We cannot be the one with all the answers, doling them out to save classroom time. Students quickly realize that if they just wait long enough, we will provide the answer. Students then stop thinking for themselves, if they ever start. Again, the key is to provide learning situations where students come up with the answers and try out the solutions.

RESOURCEFULNESS—To respond to challenges in creative ways

As a student sits at his desk pondering the answer to a difficult test question, the LIFESKILL of Resourcefulness might make the difference in finding the correct answer. Think of the many times we have observed a student who is stuck on a question. We watch as he/she reads the question, studies the answer choices, and then sits there not able to make a choice. We feel his/her frustration level build as he/she tries several times to solve the problem. Then the student lights up as he/she figures out another way to determine the answer. Without making a noise, that student has practiced the LIFESKILL of Resourcefulness. When one method didn't work, the student looked inside and found another way that did. That is a LIFESKILL that we all need and that we, as educators, should focus on every day in class.

The LIFESKILL of Resourcefulness is often neglected because teachers don't feel that there is time for it. Instead of finding the time to discuss alternative solutions, the focus has been on getting the concept taught, practiced, and graded. We need to make sure that we are not overlooking this LIFESKILL because it expands students' ability to see alternatives, find solutions, and invent new concepts. Just as resourcefulness will help a student's performance on a standardized test, it also prepares him for the job market of the future.

RESPONSIBILITY—To respond when appropriate, to be accountable for your actions

Here is a LIFESKILL that we wish every student had the first day he/she walks into the classroom. Unfortunately, that is often not the case. Therefore, it falls on us to teach that character trait. The reason this carries over to test taking is that students need to realize that they are responsible for the scores that they get. It isn't the teacher. It isn't their parents. It isn't where they sat that day. They are the ones who create that test score. If they don't put forth the effort, that is their responsibility, not ours. However, we can teach the LIFESKILL of Responsibility in little ways in the classroom throughout the year. By expecting homework to be completed, notes returned, and materials to be taken care of, we let the student know he/she has responsibilities.

The implication for testing for the teacher is that throughout the year, time is taken to discuss test scores and to analyze student responses on prior tests. One teacher I knew spent the first weeks of school discussing what learning the student was responsible for during the year. She even took out a copy of a student test results sheet (with the name removed) and went through the different concepts on the test. She shared that she would be teaching those concepts but it was up to the student to learn them. Throughout the year she repeated this phrase over and over again and the students gradually came to realize that the responsibility for learning was theirs, not the teacher's.

During testing, taking responsibility for working hard, staying focused, getting a good night's rest, eating breakfast, drinking water, and doing one's best can make a difference on a student's test scores. I think that sometimes we give these standardized tests and we don't let the students know enough about them. The tests take on a mystical aura—an "other worldliness." The students begin to believe that they really have no control over the situation and that is where problems start. By explicitly talking about the tests, you remove the mystery from them. The students will realize that they have the responsibility for how they do because they know more about what is expected of them.

SENSE OF HUMOR—To laugh and be playful without hurting others

Now how can the LIFESKILL of Sense of Humor help with test taking? My goodness, it keeps us sane! Remember the negative thoughts that a student was having during testing? Remember how self-defeating they became? This kind of thinking can cause test scores to plummet. A sense of humor can turn those thoughts around and allow the student to move on to the next questions relaxed and ready to try. The worst thing that can happen to students is that they get so down that they can't do their best work. That is where the LIFESKILL of a Sense of Humor comes in. We must model the ability to laugh and to learn from mistakes. The lesson of laughter can help anyone handle stress and problems.

One of the most powerful things I ever learned about the LIFESKILL of Sense of Humor and testing was when I chatted with some fourth graders following a testing session. They were pretty down and discouraged until suddenly one of them piped up, "Well, that sure was a whole lot of no fun. I just love not knowing all the answers." Everyone in the room laughed and you could see the tension fall from their shoulders. Fortunately, one student had realized that the LIFESKILL of Sense of Humor could make a difference. He didn't attack anyone or make fun of anyone. He just allowed himself and others to see that they were taking things a little too seriously and it was not helping anyone.

How can you foster the LIFESKILL of Sense of Humor prior to testing day? As students work on projects and get frustrated, model humor for them and help them relax. Perfection is a goal. If students fall short, they can't get so down on themselves that they quickly write themselves off as failures.

CONCLUSION

I've listed the LIFESKILLS and discussed each one in relationship to test-taking skills. I'm sure that if you sat back and reflected, you could expand on how the LIFESKILLS could positively impact test scores, if they were truly integrated into your daily instruction. The one thing that we need to remember is that test scores are not the person. We need to focus on the student and his/her emotional and intellectual development. I truly believe that if we instill constructive character traits into our students that the result will be rising test scores. The students will be better prepared to demonstrate what they know. But more importantly, we will have instilled in our students the LIFESKILLS they need to succeed in life.

Bibliography

Bell, Nanci. *Visualizing and Verbalizing for Improved Language Comprehension*. Palo Alto, CA: Gander Publishing, Inc., 1991.

Belvel, Pat. See training manuals by Pat Belvel, Training and Consulting Institute, Inc., San Jose, California. http://www.trngedu.com/

Burke, Edmund. *Letter to Sheriffs of Bristol*, dated April 3, 1777.

Calvin Coolidge Memorial Foundation. http://www.calvin-coolidge.org/

Canfield, Jack and Mark Victor. *A 2nd Helping of Chicken Soup for the Soul: 101 More Stories to Open the Heart and Rekindle the Spirit*. Deerfield Beach, FL: Communications, Inc., 1995.

Carlson, Rachel. *Silent Spring*. New York: Houghton Mifflin Company, 1962.

Cohen, Elizabeth. *Designing Groupwork: Strategies for the Heterogeneous Classroom*, Second Edition. New York: Teachers College Press, 1994.

Cole, Robert W. (Editor) *Educating Everybody's Children*. Alexandria, VA: ASCD, 1995.

Coontz, Stephanie. March 1995. *Phi Delta Kappan*, p. 16.

Cousins, Norman. *Anatomy of an Illness As Perceived by the Patient: Reflections on Healing and Regeneration*. New York: W. W. Norton & Company, 1995.

Crawford, C. B. *Theory and Implications Regarding the Utilization of Strategic Humor by Leaders*. Department of Communication, Fort Hays State University. http://www.fhsu.edu/htmlpages/faculty/cocc/lead03.htm

Dietal, J. Edwin. *Exceptional Leadership: Leading Through Patience and Persistence*. Practice Development Website. http://www.abenet.org/lpm/newsletters/skills/w98Dietel.html

Donne, John, *Devotions Upon Emergent Occasions. Meditation XVII*, 1624. John Donne Society Home Page http://www.csus.edu/org/

Edison, Thomas Alva. Hope Page http://www.thomasediso n.com. Webmaster: Gerald Beals. October 1999. Online AOL. (Chapter 8.3)

Garbarino, James. *Raising Children in a Socially Toxic Environment*. San Francisco: Jossey-Bass Publishers, 1995.

Gardner, Howard. *Frames of Mind: Theory of Multiple Intelligences*. New York: Basic Books, Inc., 1985.

Gibbs, Jeanne. *TRIBES: A New Way of Learning and Being Together*. Sausalito, CA: CenterSource Systems, LLC, 1995.

Glasser, William. *Choice Theory: A New Psychology of Personal Freedom*. New York: HarperPerrenial, 1998.

Glickman, Carl. *Renewing America's Schools: A Guide to School-Based Action*. San Francisco: Jossey-Bass Publishers, 1993.

Gurian, Michael. *The Wonder of Boys*. New York: G. P. Putnam's & Sons, 1996.

Hannaford, Carla. *Smart Moves: Why Learning Is Not All in Your Head*. Arlington, VA: Great Ocean Publishers, 1995.

Hart, Leslie A. *Human Brain and Human Learning*. Kent, WA: Books For Educators, Inc., 1999.

Healy, Jane. *Failure to Connect: How Computers Affect Our Children's Minds—For Better and Worse*. New York: Simon & Schuster, 1998.

"The Importance of Effective Communication," Northeastern University, College of Business Administration, October 1999. http://www.cba.neu.edu/~ewertheim/inter/commun.htm

Keirsey, David. *Please Understand Me II: Temperament, Character, and Intelligence*. Del Mar, CA: Prometheus Nemesis Book Company, 1998.

Kohn, Alfie. *Punished by Rewards: The Trouble with Gold Stars, Incentive Plans, A's, Praise, and Other Bribes*. New York: Houghton Mifflin, 1993.

Kouzes, James M. & Barry Z. Posner. *The Leadership Challenge*. San Francisco: Jossey-Bass, Inc., 1996.

Kovalik, Susan J. with Karen D. Olsen, *ITI: The Model*. Kent, WA: Susan Kovalik & Associates, 1997.

Kryger, Abraham. *Benefits of Telling the Truth*. http://www.wellnessmd.com/tellingtruth.html

Lindamood-Bell Learning Processes Center, 800/233-1819.

Lowery, Larry. *Thinking and Learning: Matching Developmental Stages with Curriculum and Instruction*. Kent, Washington: Books For Educators, Inc., 1989.

Mayer, Jeffrey J. *If You Haven't Got the Time to Do It Right, When Will You Find the Time to Do It Over?* New York: Simon & Schuster, 1990.

McGeehan, Jane et al. *Transformations: Leadership for Brain-Compatible Learning*. Kent, WA: Susan Kovalik & Associates, 1999.

Miller, Mary. *Acorns in Our Hands*. Creekside Elementary, Elgin, Illinois, 1999.

Olsen, Karen D. *Making Bodybrain-Compatible Education a Reality: Coaching for the ITI Model*. Kent, WA: Books For Educators, Inc., 1999.

Olsen, Karen D. *Synergy: Transforming America's High Schools Through Integrated Thematic Instruction*. Kent, WA: Books For Educators, Inc., 1995.

Olsen, Karen D. & Susan J. Kovalik. *ITI Classroom Stages of Implementation*. Kent, WA: Susan Kovalik & Associates, 1999.

Olsen, Karen D. & Susan J. Kovalik. *ITI Schoolwide Stages of Implementation*. Kent, WA: Susan Kovalik & Associates, 1998.

The Orman Health Letter, published monthly by TRO Productions, Inc., Baltimore, MD, and http://www.wellnessmd.com/tellingtruth.html

Pert, Candace. *Molecules of Emotion: Why You Feel the Way You Feel*. New York: Scribner, 1997.

Rich, Dorothy. *MegaSkills: How Families Can Help Children Succeed in School and Beyond*. Boston: Houghton-Mifflin, 1992.

Robblee, Joanne H. 2000.

Roosevelt, Eleanor. *You Learn by Living*. New York: Harper & Brothers, 1960.

Ross, Ann & Karen D. Olsen. *The Way We Were...The Way We CAN Be: A Vision for the Middle School*. Kent, WA: Susan Kovalik & Associates, 1995.

Ross, W. D. *Nicomachean Ethics by Aristotle*, 350 BC, translated by W.D. Ross. *The Internet Classics Archives/Works by Aristotle*, http://classics.mit.edu/Browse/browse-Aristotle.html

Siegel, Bernie. *Love, Medicine, and Miracles: Lessons Learned About Self-Healing from a Surgeon's Experiences with Exceptional Patients*. New York: HarperCollins, 1990.

Siegel, Bernie. *Peace, Love, and Healing: Bodymind Communication and the Path of Self-Healing*. New York: HarperCollins, 1990.

Smith, Charles A. *The Peaceful Classroom: 162 Activities to Teach Preschoolers Compassion and Cooperation*. Beltsville, MD: Gryphon House, 1993.

Thomas, James Alexander. *Sea to Shining Sea*. New York: Ballantine Books, 1986.

Twain, Mark, *Notebook*, 1984.

Book List

Index

Lifelong Guidelines & LIFESKILLS Resources

Lifelong Guidelines and LIFESKILLS

A wall poster set $39.95

The ITI Lifelong Guidelines call for trustworthiness, truthfulness, active listening, no put-downs, and personal best. What is personal best? The LIFESKILLS poster set provides colorful definitions and examples. Set includes a Lifelong Guidelines poster, a Personal Best Clubhouse poster (18" x 22 1/2"), and posters for each of the 17 LIFESKILLS (8 1/2" x 11"). LIFESKILLS include such traits as cooperation, caring, responsibility, initiative, and problem-solving. Artwork is whimsical, action-oriented, and multi-ethnic. Ideal for incorporating character education.

Example of 3 of the 18 small posters included

Spread Your Wings: The Lifelong Guidelines

(audio tape) $11.95

Original lyrics, music, and vocals weave a vivid tapestry of images as Jeff Pedersen strolls with us on a walk through a zoo while highlighting each of the Lifelong Guidelines. Each song is introduced with heartfelt comments about what it means to apply the Guidelines in every aspect of one's life. The Lifelong Guidelines are based upon respect for others and self.

Spread Your Wings: The Lifelong Guidelines

(19 min. video) $24.95

With original lyrics, music, and vocals, Jeff Pedersen illustrates the Lifelong Guidelines as he takes us on a walk with students through a zoo. He introduces each song with heartfelt comments about what it means to apply the Guidelines in every aspect of one's life. The Lifelong Guidelines are the cornerstone of interpersonal skills, and are based upon respect for others and self.

LIFESKILLS (audio tape) $12.50
LIFESKILLS (compact disc) $16.50
LIFESKILLS (songbook) $5.95

Music is a wonderful way to introduce the LIFESKILLS, which can become a partner in creating a trusting environment that enhances learning. These original tunes and lyrics are whimsical and memorable. Cassette and CD contains 17 songs. Lyrics booklet includes all 17 songs and has large print ideal for making sing-along copies or overhead transparencies. Created by R&J Productions. Each sold separately.

Lifelong Guidelines Mugs

Susan Kovalik & Associates. $6.00

Like the popular posters you have in your classroom, these mugs offer a daily reminder of the Lifelong Guidelines, with an added bonus—you can fill them up with sixteen ounces of your favorite beverage! They're insulated, and come in an oatmeal shade.

Lifelong Guidelines & LIFESKILLS T-Shirts & Sweatshirts

T-Shirts $17.00
Sweatshirts $26.00

Send the message that you care about how we treat each other—wear a LIFESKILLS T-Shirt! The Lifelong Guidelines are printed over the heart, and the LIFESKILLS, which help you do your personal best, are on the back. The garden design displays the Lifelong Guidelines on the front and LIFESKILLS on the back. The LIFESKILLS LIVE IT! design appears only on the front.

T-Shirt (LIFESKILLS LIVE IT!): white with multi-color design (50/50 Cotton & Poly.)
T-Shirts (Garden Design): yellow haze, mint green & ash gray (Preshrunk 100% Cotton)
Sweatshirts Colors: ash gray only (50/50, crew neck)
Sizes: L, XL, XXL

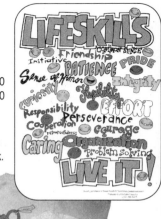